Dillināmā

The Cities of Delhi

A.K. Jain

SYNERGY

Synergy Books India

(An Imprint of M/s Bookwell Publications)

New Delhi

ISBN: 978-93-82059-14-1 (Hb)

Published by:
Synergy Books India
(An Imprint of M/s Bookwell Publications)
24/4800 Ansari Road, Darya Ganj
New Delhi-110002
Phone: 011-23268786, 23257264
Fax: 011-23281315
Email: Synergybooksindia@gmail.com
bookwell@vsnl.net

Printed at
Mudrak, 30A, Patparganj, Delhi-110091

Contents

Preface

Delhi is a unique place where one inhales history with every breath. With its multiple cultures, antiquity and ancient monuments, Delhi is a cosmopolis which is parallel to cities of Rome, Athens, Damascus and Cairo. From Indraprastha of Mahabharat to the present New Delhi, it has grown into a major metropolis. It always had been a fascinating place to live in for everyone from beggars to emperors. The explanation for its charm is not just its strategic location, nor its proximity to the perennial Yamuna. It is its complexity, multidimensional and multilayered character, which make it attractive. It is the warmth of the various cultures, vibrance of its markets, solace of its gardens and the dignity and elegance of the monuments which create image of Delhi.

From the Dilli of Raja Dillu to the New Delhi, it has always commanded power. It was born to war and glory. It lives by ambition, rivalry and opportunism. It is a city of contradictions and contrasts.

Discovering Delhi can be an exciting experience. Its historical-political-cultural evolution is more difficult to perceive than its rich architectural heritage. As Dr. Michael Brett-Crowther in his Foreword succinctly states—"Delhi is more than convenience, decoration and logic. It is power, authority and beauty, an intellectual statement of India's reality as many nations and traditions united. This is a valid reason to conserve Delhi's rich heritage and redefine planning, urban renewal and development which have a uterine relationship and reference with historical and cultural heritage."

This book is the continuation of the efforts of many researchers, scholars, and other colleagues who have been passionately involved with Delhi's heritage. This book would have not seen the day without the enthusiasm of S.S. Khurana, and his team at the Synergy Books India, who worked with dedication in giving a presentable shape to the manuscript.

A.K. Jain

Foreword

The Significance of Delhi

Every nation (and India is a collection of nation states) sees its tradition as unique, but admits to the possibility of parallels. In regards to the plans of capital cities, this subordinate element—the parallels, their origins etc. can be analysed with more ease wherever the archives are ample. Thus in the case of New Delhi, the garden city image was a motive force; and the plan of Walter Burley Griffin for Canberra affected the planning by Edwin Lutyens for New Delhi. Girouard says that "The New Delhi plan show the influence of that of Canberra, and those of both Wren's London and L'Enfant's Washington. But their long vistas, diagonal avenues and star-shaped constellation of roads were accompanied by very low densities and so much open space that almost all resemblance to a conventional great city was lost. The influence of the garden cities was clear, but so was that of what was known as the City Beautiful movement in America.[1]

The star-shaped constellation of Paris and Berlin to focus traffic movement and provide for saluting bases in those cities; the avenues for parade and for ease of troop movements to control apprehended uprisings; these features may be seen in New Delhi. If Girouard is right about Canberra, Wren's London, and L'Enfant's Washington, is he also right about the City Beautiful movement? Girouard cites the fact of F.L. Olmstead's re-planning of Washington and his proposals for other American cities, and finds that 'Lutyens' gigantic open spaces at New Delhi are in the same tradition; the King's Avenue leads to the War Memorial Arch up through the two blocks of the secretariats to the Viceroy's Palace, and space not all that much smaller than the entire City of London is allotted to about fifteen buildings. At Canberra another great central vista runs from the Capitol across the lake to war memorial.[2]'

What Girouard calls'the Capitol' is actually Capital Hill; and rising out of it is the new parliament House, an amazing success of (again) American planning done with Australian textures, colours and ideas, so as to epitomize (a) the Australian Aborliginal meeting place at a pool; (b) the impact of the land on the invading White man's consciousness; (c) the development of an independent spirit among the British settlers; and (d) the emerging New Australian identity, of which the British and Aboriginal traditions will be merged with those of other European immigrant and even Asian immigrants.

When Lutyens planned New Delhi, the several components of the Indian tradition were still help in a relationship of which the British Crown was the apogee; but a British Crown made an Imperial *Indian* Crown, by the relations with the Princely States, by the customs of the Delhi Durbars, and by a whole set of image of Briton and Indian as the events of 1857 and since had transformed them. Furthermore, New Delhi was intended to be the final statement of a series of such statements; for all the major cities were created through the effects of British trade and government since 1757[3]. New Delhi evoked earlier empires and dynasties of India, to which the Raj looked for some considerable part of its authorization; but these evocations were related to those British and imperial values which originated outside of India.

The endeavours of Lutyens and Baker were meant to convey *all these* realities; not the realities of a consumer-oriented, aggressively capitalist society claiming to be *rus in urbe*—which is what the American City Beautiful Movement manifested.

New Delhi was intended to honour the enormous sacrifices of the Indian Army in the wars where it had loyally bought for the Crown, and to remind the native population that the tragedy of 1857 was also a human development, in relationship and understanding between cultures and nations. In other words, New Delhi was *not meant to convey* the revivalism of any form of Indian tradition, but *the development* of the traditions.

There are, strangely, profound reasons for this fact. The British period of Indian history (1757–1947) wrought serious change. A revolution occurred throughout sub-continent; just as the French Revolution changed French thought and possibilities. In Britain, the Industrial Revolution merely re-distributed a low level of power and resources to the masses, while strengthening an unreal system of power relations. Nothing really new entered the mentality. In France, the revolution changed everything. In India, the new cities, the railways, the trade patterns, the ideas of law and order all did the same. Gandhian ideas remain attractive partly for this reason: Gandhi *developed* Indian ideas *in relationship* with Western ideas. And whatever some political commentators may think, the relations between Briton (or Anglo-Indian, in the Old sense) and Indian carried a quality which was frequently much more brotherly than the idea of failed relationship which pervades both E.M. Forster and Paul Scott.

No one looking at contemporary Australia can really believe that the conflicts between European immigrants (e.g., Serbs and Croats) or the Whites (in general) and the Aborigines are abolished by the mere fact of the new Parliament House. No one aware of the murder rate in Washington D.C. can think that the City Beautiful there—or in its other version at Chicago, Cleveland and San Francisco—has produced a satisfying balance between town and country.

Thus, if the Great American Dream has not become a waking reality through the City Beautiful in major American cities—if they are not as beautiful and contended as they were meant to be—has the success of Canberra or of Delhi been better? Both Canberra and Washington are rich in landscape, and Canberra has allowed much more of the bush (the countryside) of remain;

despite its appalling quantity of big roads. But Canberra has nothing like the treasures of the Smithsonian Institution; there is no equivalent of Washington's National (Episcopalian) Cathedral—a successful replica of Canterbury Cathedral. Canberra has an abundance of poor quality architecture and banal design, indicating a failure to co-ordinate the features of the axes and the principal views on those axes with *the traditions as such.* True, the new Parliament House has an almost cathedral—like significance, like the War Memorial; but there is no cathedral or church in Canberra of equivalent structural authority, and the Australian national University has lost its assets of space and relationship of buildings of the landscape with the overdevelopment of its site by uninteresting structures. The huge resource of Lake Burley Griffin and the hills around it have so far been wasted opportunities.

Canberra has not been an imperial capital—as New Delhi has been, as Washington has attempted to be. Canberra is, however, a very remarkable opportunity in terms of landscape and climate; as if Shimla were transported to flatter terrain with more space to move. Like Shimla, Canberra is a more British than Australian environmental experience in many respect; just as Washington is much more like the civilized country estates of the Founding Fathers of the American Constitution, than, say, Portland or Salem in Oregon.

Some comparison of Indian town planing ideas with those of Europe is justified. The pattern of segregation of classes corresponds to the planning principles of the *Arthasastra* and to the plan of New Delhi. But what city does not segregate classes? It is also arguable that Hyderabad resembles in the Old City the Moorish cities which influenced the Muslim invaders, and which were themselves results of the Roman grid plan[4]. It is also almost certain that the model for Adelaide was Valletta, and that is, pre-eminently, a Roman grid plan using the resources and constraints of landscape to full, profitable effect[5]. But the distinctive use in Adelaid of surrounding parklands, like the waters of Grand Harbour and Marsamxett Harbour, and the open space cleared to the west of City Gate; the far-sighted policy of wide roadways; and the continued spread of the city on a logical rectilinear plan, show the utilitarian, equalitarian approach to life of a nineteenth century city state for free settlers. These featurs are uniquely convenient, as well as decorous. But Delhi is more than convenience, decoration, and logic. It is power authority, and beauty: an intellectual statement of India's reality as many nations and traditions united.

If New Delhi is the capital of modern India, a system of relationships still being analysed and re-defined, if perhaps, one day it will be a focus for the entire sub-continent (if that is, there were ever a friendly merging of sovereignties between India and its neighbours in the sub-continent), then no representative Hindu, Muslim, Christian, Buddhist or Sikh; no representative Marwari, Rajput, Madrasi, Gujarati or Bengali could fail to find *something of his tradition* within this collection of experiences.

The complex development of the Council House, its eventual form and ornamentation, its political and constitutional history, past and present: these are capable of being understood in a way which unites meanings and allows for the enrichment of meanings. In an obvious sense, the plan of New Delhi is a *mandala*; but every *mandala* is also the things which are not obvious, the things of the spirit.

The British who would recall New Delhi before 1947 would see in its landscaping the patterns of the English country house. It is important to realize that Lutyens developed a great deal of his idea of built and natural environment within the framework of English landed estates[6]. If Miss Gertrude Jekyll did not devise the actual details of New Delhi's gardens, her influence is undoubtedly to be seen in many such features. Equally, no-one should forget that the Order of the Star of India is represented to some degree by the Jaipur column; but that what is *really* represented is the things to which that Order pointed—the big realities of noble and proper conduct, justice, true service with 'Heaven's Light our Guide'. If Lutyens' own design for the Anglican Cathedral for New Delhi had been built, it would indeed have a catholic and evangelical British and Indian statement of ultimate reality[7]; and the actual Cathedral of the Redemption, by Lutyens' disciple, H.A.N. Medd, is a successful attempt to make a big religious statement of that kind[8].

But when the elements of the Cathedral of the Redemption, or the (Roman Catholic) Cathedral of the Sacred Heart, of the Central Vista, and the civilian and military components of the New Delhi are all considered, it is the questions of *the years since 1947* which arise in their perplexing variety. Is Delhi—the New and the Old—really capable of sustaining immigration on the scale which it continues to attract? Is the economic life of North India really capable of being sustained from this conurbation? It has been said that 'cities need to be built more to human scale, and with particular reference to the needs of the elderly, such as good public transport, higher density—but not high-rise—urban layouts to allow greater mobility and readier contact with others, and readily accessible local parks, promenades and informal meeting places.[9] These are questions which the struggler on his motor scooter or in a bus going from Mori Gate knows in a different ways from the average London commuter, the rich motorist of Washington, or even the civil servants of Canberra.

New Delhi is probably more 'on the human scale' than Washington, or Canberra because of the intellectual endeavour to create it. The realities of India *had to be expressed.* They did include the smallest village and the weakest economic groups. There was meant to be protection of all citizens and justice for all citizens. These are still legal and political objectives in India; and the development by Mr. Ashok Jain of Dwarka sub-city (Papankala) is, indeed, a new city continuous with Lutyens' dream, as adapted to Mahatma Gandhi's people[10]. There are many ways of making this continuity. The sculptures of Devalankunda Vadiraj are one[11]; the political sagacity of Field–Marshal K.M. Cariappa represented other such capacity[12].

Although every tradition may be unique, and may have its parallels, its failures and its evils are boringly similar. No Westerner can ignore his own society's injustices, the moral wrongs of his people, the many evidences of human ineptitude and sin. It ill becomes a British observer to criticies New Delhi because the poor are always evident in its ceremonious forms, or because unauthorized structures have had to become authorized, on political and humane grounds. London (like

Gloucester) has its white beggars and drug addicts, its homeless and disenchanted; the poor are in Paris, Amsterdam and St Petersburg. But New Delhi was intended to offer a political, urban statement of the ultimate values of its time and place, which were—like those values of the Upanisads—capable of being believed because they were true, because they worked, and because they were able to be replicated. Gandhi's *samadhi* is a special place for this reflexion; and those who are concerned with urban living must make their reflexions effective in action.

It is very telling that Malaysia, so much a development under the influence of the Indian Empire, uses its Indo–Saracenic railway terminus in Kuala Lumpur to advertise its attractions as a society. Those Indo–Saracenic forms, those domed towers of Baker's may looks like imperial *topees*; but they echo Mughal forms, the authentic style of the Red Fort. Thus, the New Delhi of Baker and Lutyens conveys an Indian reality which includes genuine national elements, without the dangers of a revision of history which all revivalists undertake in an illusion: the illusion that relationship is not normal, that tradition is pure. It is simple egotism. The architect and the planner know that reality is more complex.

So may this book of Mr. Ashok Jain convey to Indians the essential facts that their inheritance is merged with that of many people, those people love India for many reasons, and those who make its future have many duties, with 'Heaven's Light our Guide.'

© M.R. Brett–Crowther
MSc, PhD, DIC, Dip Law, STh. GCOH
Editor, International Journal of Environmental Studies, England

References

1. Girouard, M., *Cities & People*, Yale University Press, New Haven, 1985, p 353.
2. op cit, p 354.
3. Alam, M. 'The national settlement system of India', In Bourne, L.S., Sinclair, R., and Dziewonski, K., Eds., *Urbanization and Settlement Systems* : International Perspectives, Oxford University Press, Oxford, 1984, pp. 453–472, at pp. 455–457 especially.

4. Brett-Crowther, M.R., 'The Renewal and Conservation of Hyderabad: Historical and Cultural Perspectives' in Ravindra Prasad, D., Ed., *Urban Renewal*: The Indian Experience, Sterling Publishers Pvt Ltd, New Delhi, 1989, pp. 211–218, at p. 212.
5. This is evident from the fact that Col William Light had special opportunity to study Valletta in 1831, 1832 and again 1835, before becoming Surveyor–General of South Australia, 1836. Cf Dutton, G., *Founder of a City*: The life of Colonel William Light, Melbourne, F.W. Cheshire, 1960, pp. 124–5, 129–30, 157.
6. Cf Jekyll, G. and Weaver, L., *Gardens for Small Country Houses*, Country Life London, 1922, 4th ed (1st ed, 1912). This deals extensively with Lutyens' designs of houses and gardens with grounds comparable in size to those which comprise elements in sectors of New Delhi. Lutyens and Miss Jekyll worked on over 80 garden designs, which combined formal design and natural planting.
7. Irving, R.G., *Indian Summer*: Lutyens, Baker and Imperial Delhi, Yale University Press, 1981, p. 272 misunderstands the liturgical realities intended to be served by the unexecuted design. The sub-conscious envy of an American escapes from time to time, but apart from the Anglican religious items, the general interpretation of symbols is sound.
8. Op cit, pp. 322–327. Some of the comments are a little confused. Irving's book is, however, a beautiful homage on the whole.
9. Remarks of Dr. Lincoln Day, lecture, 'The future of low-birthrate-populations', reported, *ANU Reporter*, 25 November 1992, p. 2.
10. Brett-Crowther, M.R., Foreword, In Jain, A.K., *The Making of a Metropolis*: Planning and Growth of Delhi, National Book Organisation, New Delhi, 1990, pp. vii-x, at p. viii.
11. Obituary, *The Times*, March 16, 1993.
12. Obituary, *The Times*, May 28, 1993.

1. Introduction

Here we stand in Delhi City—symbol of old India and the new. It is not the narrow lanes and houses of old Delhi or the side spaces and rather pretentious buildings of New Delhi that count, but the spirit of this ancient City. For Delhi has been an epitome of India's history with its succession of glory and disaster and with its great capacity to absorb many cultures and yet remain itself. It is a gem with many facets, some bright and some darkened by age, presenting the course of India's life and thought during ages. Even the stones here whisper to our ears of the ages of long ago and the air we breathe is full of the dust and fragrance of the past, as also of the fresh and piercing winds of the present. We face the good and bad of India in Delhi City which has been the grave of many empires and the nursery of a Republic. What a tremendous story is here; the tradition of millennia of our history surrounds us at every step, and the procession of innumerable generations passes by before our eyes..."

Jawaharlal Nehru

Delhi, a megacity of 16.75 million is a symbol of India's growth story. It manifests the co-existance of heritage and modernity, ecology and bio-diversity, success and failures, conflicts and contradictions, and richness and poverty. The footprints of its growth are apparent in its heritage, morphology and ecology.

Delhi is unimaginably antique. It is a legend that lives. The scattered tombs of emperors, forgotten fortresses and lost dynasties are hidden behind the dust of the vernacular. Steeped in history, Delhi is like no other place in the world. Its past reveals the present. Like the many layers on what it is built, Delhi unveils itself to reveal its different facets.

Delhi, is not a single city, but has many cities within it. Its fabric is imprinted by many cultures of innumerable kingdoms. Its tapestry is embellished with the annals of glorious cities that have risen and fallen here. It is a city of contrasts and contradictions, of triumph and tragedy and chaos and order. All this adds up in a unique character—a vibrant, throbbing, inimitable charm. Time and again through history, the great builders of yore fell in love with Delhi and contributed in its evolution.

According to the tradition Delhi has been the capital of no less than seven different empires. Through antiquity, its cities provide a glimpse of the intertwined socio-cultural-political process and forces. These provide a tour de force of historical Delhis, remains of which conceal and reveal the splendour of many cities built, abandoned, razed and rebuilt by the successive waves of time. The layers of various cities are the grandiloquent testimony of its past.

For centuries the river Yamuna has witnessed the rise and fall of several Delhis and transported the sediments of its culture, its banks have been the abode of the prehistoric man. The legend of Mahabharata, the great epic, mentions of Indraprastha, the capital of Pandavs. The archaeological explorations confirm its location at the site of the Old Fort. The excavations at the Old Fort (Purana Qila) have revealed painted grey ware (100BC), Black polishware (c. 300 B.C.), human and terracota figurines, punch mark coins, copper coins, pottery, glassware and jewellery of great antiquity. The remains of the cities of Rajput dynasty are still discernible at Lalkot and Raipithora, near Mehrauli. Besides the city walls, its remains were recycled in the successive cities. The rustless and ageless iron pillar, installed by the Tomar Rajputs and the remains of numerous temples which were employed in building of the Qutab Minar Complex, tell their own story.

The various cities of Delhi are the stamps of its several invaders and conquerors. Khilji's Siri, Tughlaq's Tughlaqabad,

Jahanpanah and Ferozabad, are the reminders of Delhi's embattled past. These are the tales of terror and valour, bloodshed and violence. The reconstruction of cities at the site of Purana Qila—Dinpanah by Emperor Humayun and Dilli by Shershah Suri are the expressions of thrift and nimbleness of the rulers.

Shahjahan's Shahjahanabad is a reminiscent of the past and expressive of the present. It is a climax of the glory of the Mughals and their art of city building. Immensely rich in cultural heritage, Shahjahanabad with its palaces, mosques, bazaars, gilded domes, havelis, katras and a maze of lanes and bye-lanes had been one of the most beautiful cities of the Orient.

Emperor Shahjahan expressed his love for Delhi by inscribing the following in the Diwan-i-khas at Red Fort.

"If there be paradise on the earth,
it is here,
it is here,
it is here".

The celebrated poet Mirza Galib, maintained the same fervour and wrote: "if the world is the body, Delhi is its soul"

The Colonial British rule gave altogether a new turn to the physical form of Delhi. From development of 'colonies' by the East India Company, and subsequently by the British Raj, Delhi was resurrected as the capital of India. This was the beginning of a new chapter in the history of Delhi. It culminated in the building of the Imperial Delhi, which continues to be national focus of power and politics. Lutyens' Imperial Delhi was conceived as an "Anglo-Indian Rome". It is a subtle bend of the India and the West.

The New Delhi founded in 1911, was planned as a showpiece of the glory and magnificence of the British. It was built as the new capital for India and its architect Edwin Lutyens called it the Rome of Hindoostan. With the coming up of Imperial Delhi, the new capital of India. Shahjahanabad became 'old' and was rejected as a big slum. It was relegated as a potential area of danger, insanitation and crimes. Once termed as a most glorious and beautiful city in the Orient, Shahjahanabad was referred and devalued as a slum, congested, dark, dirty and overcrowded. This perception started with the hostilities of the war of 1857 and became more pronounced with the comparisons between the grand Imperial Delhi and the indigenous Old City.

To improve the Old City the government in 1937 constituted the Delhi Improvement Trust (DIT). The DIT took up various schemes for decongestion of Shahjahanabad together with slum clearance, industrial and commercial schemes. The DIT Schemes covered about 10,000 acres of area, as compared to 1,500 acres by Shahjahanabad and 8,200 acres by New Delhi.

After the independence of the country, the government resolved to make a new beginning, build a new India and a new Capital. It replaced the DIT by Delhi Development Authority. For Old Delhi it adopted the policy of Urban Renewal, land use zoning, decongestion and slum clearance. A phased program for shifting non-conforming land uses, wholesale markets and slums redevelopment was undertaken. The major schemes implemented were Jama-Masjid redevelopment, Turkman Gate and Dujana House slum clearance and redevelopment, which faced violent resistance of the public. The replacement of traditional, organic and indigenous urban form of the traditional city by modern apartment blocks is a mute edifice which reminds that the concept of urban renewal, pigeonholed under the physical manifestations, like slums, overcrowding and blight had been inadequate to deal with the human rights and the conservation of the unique culture heritage. The priorities, such as decongestion, open space, land use zoning, building byelaws and physical accessibility do not coincide with those of the local community. This is a clear expression of separation of planning programs from cultural, heritage and social needs. A review of the top-down, government-centric urban renewal of Shahjahanabad points out towards a need to evolve alternative strategies based on a deeper understand of historical, social and cultural aspects of Delhi's heritage, and a participatory and community based approach.

Delhi is a unique repository of traditional urbanism. The variety of its built environment—settlements, villages, heritage structures, artifacts, streets, parks, water bodies and precincts of historic, aesthetic, cultural and religious significance is amazing. Various cities that came up comprise the built heritage of Delhi. As an irreplaceable and non-renewable cultural resource, these cities need to be protected, nourished and nurtured and passed on to the coming generations. These settlements enhance Delhi's environment, giving it identity and a unique character. The imperial Delhi covering 3300 Ha is the only surviving garden city in India, with a central vista, capital complex, historic villages, buildings and gardens, canals, bridges, water bodies, forts, palaces, places of worship, tombs, etc. The World Monuments Fund has designated Lutyens' Bungalow Zone (Imperial Delhi) covering 2612 Ha, as one of the world's 100 most endangered sites. New Delhi has been acknowledged as the 'most beautifully designed urban form in India'.

New Delhi celebrated its 100 years in December 2011 which highlighted its glorious heritage. It provokes to think what will be Delhi after 100 years, that is, in year 2112. Will the citizens of Delhi take pride in celebrating the legacy which we will pass on to them? The population of Delhi is moving through a phase of slowing down and stabilisation. Between 2001 (13.8 million) and 2011 (16.75 million) it increased by 2 per cent per year and it would be around 20.5 million in 2021,22.5 million in 2031 and around 25 million in 2051 when it will reach its zenith. Thereafter this may decline gradually. There is going to be an almost total shift toward service sector of employment, reduced bureaucracy and almost no manufacturing in the city. The city with lesser children and more elderly poses several challenges for its future.

Historically Delhi has grown between River Yamuna and the Ridge, the last traces of Aravalis. The built heritage of Delhi has a uterine relationship with the natural heritage. Delhi Ridge covering 7777 Ha of area is characterized by biotropical thorny secondary forest commonly known as rakes or an arid, open scubs and trees, capable of draught resistance. The topography of the ridge undulating with uniformally disturbed drainage network. The ridge has number of perennial tanks and pits which act as groundwater recharge points. Geomorphologically Delhi area has been classified into seven land forms. Each of these units have different geological characteristics which have attained through long span of geological time. Out of these seven units, Delhi Older Alluvial Plain was recognized as the most suitable site for the development of city on account of advantageous geomorphic setting. This north-south range forms triangular plain with the River Yamuna in the East Badarpur-Mehrauli Range of the Aravali as the base. It is this triangle that has been the cradle of so many ruling dynasties in the Indian sub-continent. Conservation of Delhi's biodiversity and natural features is of utmost importance for its eco-system.

However, the borrowed concepts of urban 'development' have overlooked the ecological, cultural and symbiotic heritage. Like a human being, a city is an organism with five senses (vision, hearing, smell, taste and touch). It is a city of intellect and learning, a multicultured city with a history. It has emotions — love and sorrow, happiness and tragedy, birth and death and celebrations and mourning. It is a city with a soul and energy, peace, enlightenment and bliss. It is a city of millions of living blood cells energized by the *prakrti* and *prana*. Akin to nerve system and veins, its infrastructure services and communication channels are its lifeline. Its multiple cultures are the facets of the gem called Delhi. It had been the cradle of the 64 varieties of fine arts—the manifestations of culture, cuisine, etiquettes, festivals, relationships, education, dance, drama, stories, poetry, architecture and so on. Several cities of Delhi evolved with place and time, interaction and education, explorations and adventures. Delhi represents the realm of the ethereal, exotic and cultural enrichment, variety and identity. Its syncretic culture that came to be known as Ganga-Jamuni *tehzeeb*, found expression in everything from language, poetry, food and dress to architecture, influenced the entire sub-continent. As Jawaharlal Nehru said, 'Delhi is a symbol of old India and new'. Its future lies in its past and conservation of its unique heritage, culture, bio-diversity, and ecology.

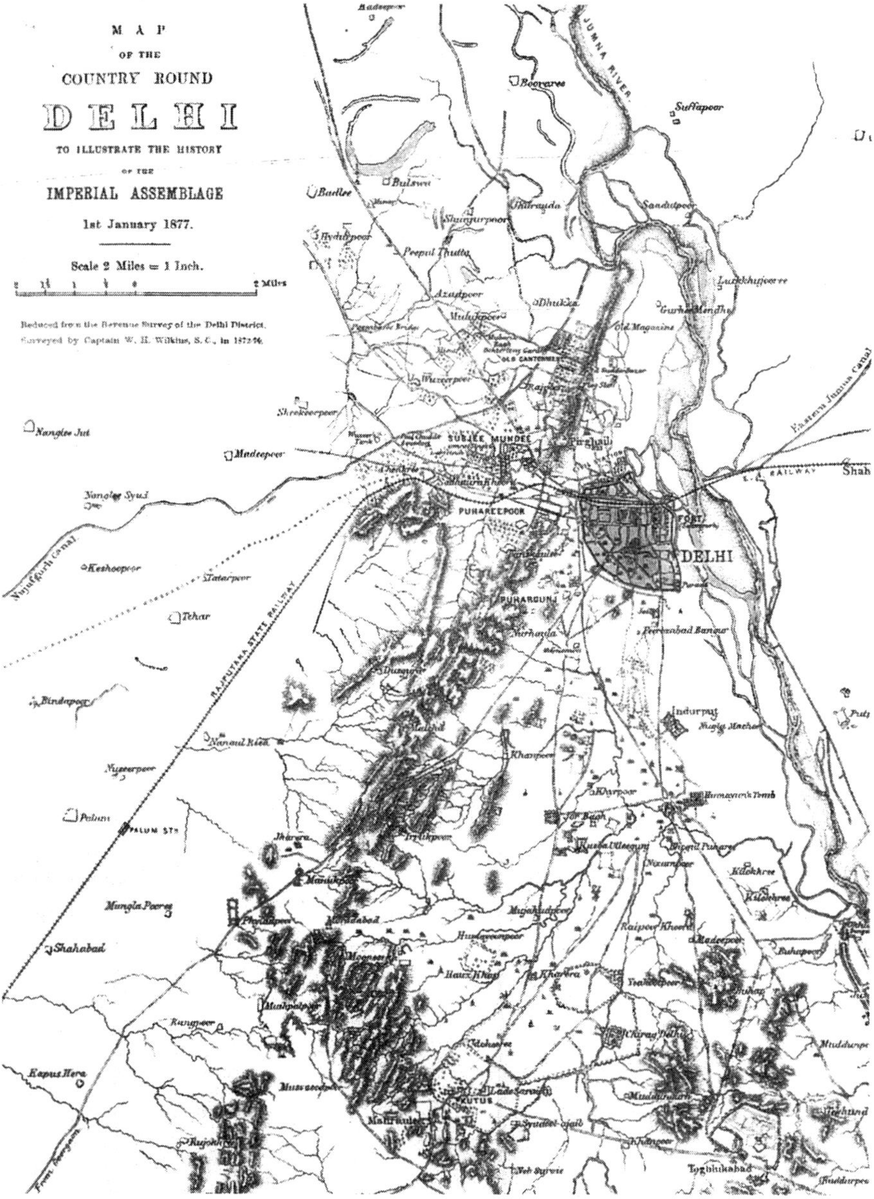

Map of Delhi in 1877 depicts the entire country south of Delhi, that was Shahjahanabad, virtually empty of habitation. The Ridge shows up prominently.
Source : Survey of India, 1877.

2. The Prehistoric Settlement

Once the celebrated poet Galib asked—What is Delhi? He himself replied: "If the world is the body, Delhi is its soul." There can be no better attribute for a city. With its charming surroundings, ethnic and cultural diversity and cosmopolitan characteristics, Delhi has fascinated the visitors and historians. Some have called it the Rome of Asia, while some believed it to be most beautiful and glorious empire in the Orient. Few citites in the world are parallel to the long historical status that Delhi enjoys. Delhi has witnessed repeated phases of destruction and construction. Its ramnants and monuments stand as a witness to its turbulent history of transitory existance. They stand in silent testimony of its majestic grandeur intercepted by phases of violence and destruction during last 3500 years.

But that is not all. Delhi even defies history. It is much more old. The archaeological excavations at Anangpur, near Suraj Kund, reveal that about, 1,00,000 years ago the area had been a nursery of human civilization. On 19th June 1991, the prehistoric branch of the Archaeological Survey of India made a stunning discovery which took antiquity of the Delhi Metropolitan area beyond one lakh years. Proto-historical man might have roamed on the same land on which stands New Delhi. The discovery of stone age tools made out of sandstone and quartzite proves that the area was once a cradle of civilization. The tools found at Suraj Kund are similar to those found which Govardhan hills in Mathura. Many varieties of stone axes, discords, scrappers, choppers and cleavers have been found in the Aravali ranges. Stone axes were used for hunting, while cleavers and choppers were used for skinning on dismembering various parts and scraping fat. Large number of flakes and cores prove that the tools were sharpened from the raw material available at the site. The early man used the bed rock making the tools.

It is believed the Aravali ranges are older than the Gondwana land, which is one of the oldest ranges. Aravali ranges have granite and sandstone rocks. The earlier geological and archaeological surveys done by Dr. Terra and Peterson had not indicated any prehistoric site in or around Delhi. It is now believed that Delhi might be the abode of the prehistoric man. In 1986, some tools were found in the sands of Suraj Kund and Badarpur area. Also in the Delhi university area, one or two prehistoric tools were found in 1991, while excavating the site of Anangpur area, the archaeologists again discovered the tools of prehistoric man. Excavations are continuing to discover more evidence of one of the earlist civilizations of the man. Indications are that this could be one of the biggest paleolithic site in the subcontinent. The prehistoric civilizations survived only where there was plenty of water, thick forests and the raw material for the tool-making. It is now established by the satellite pictures of the area that there were five Palaeo-channel of Yamuna. It is said that during the course of history this river changed its course five time due to silting and earthquakes. Anangpur falls in the fifth palaeo-channel of Yamuna, whereas the present Delhi falls in the sixth channel. Around the Aravali range there used to be thick forest. The fourth Palaeo-channel of Yamuna is 60 km west of Anangpur.

Extensive mining is going on the Aravali hills for red sandstone and Badarpur sand. Environmental degradation apart, a serious disadvantage of indiscriminate mining is that the valuable evidence of existence of ancestral civilization would be washed out. It is important that the entire hill tracts of Aravali ridges are declared reserved forest and the mining should be banned. If it is not done, only river Yamuna would remain a silent witness of the past glory, which would be lost in depth of time. The mother earth would not be able to tell the tales which were hidden under her for thousands of years.

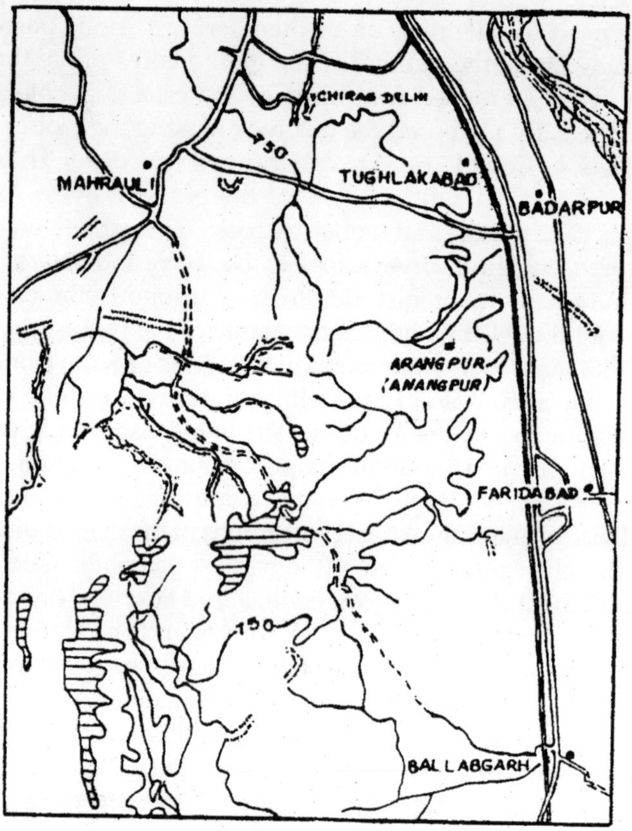

The Paleolithic site of Anangpur

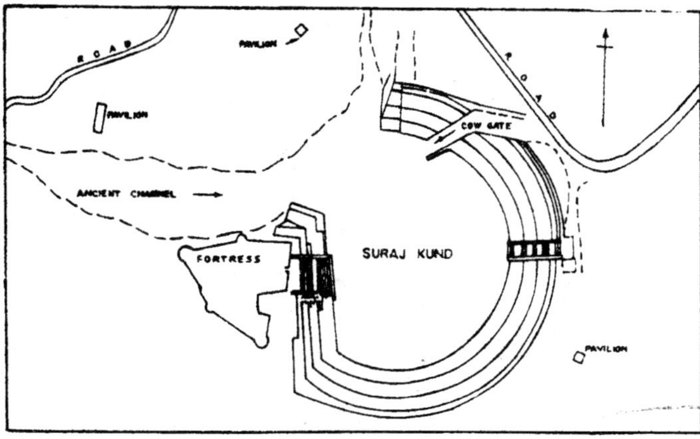

Suraj Kund

Source : *Archaeological Survey of India*

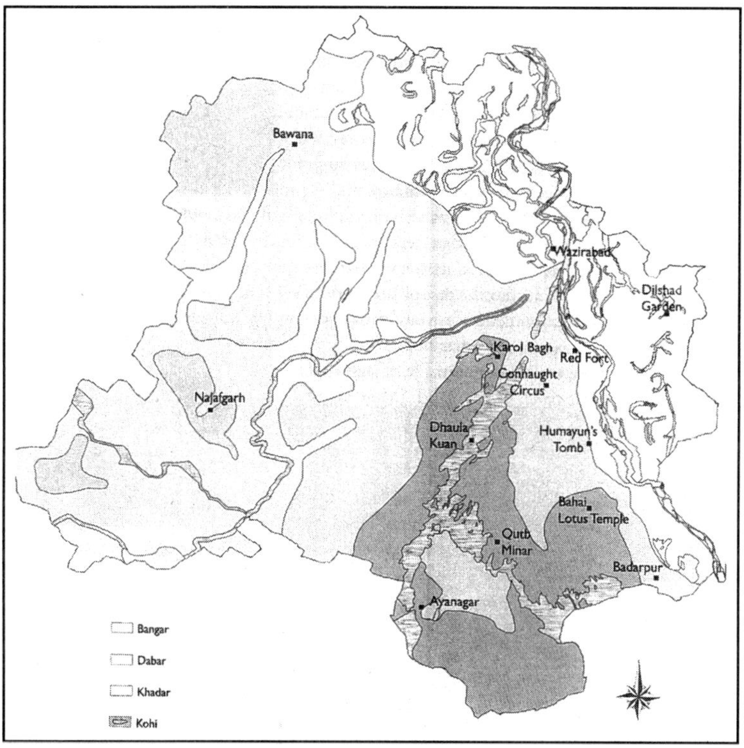

Delhi's Ecological subdivisions based on soil and geological maps

Source: Pradip Krishen, Trees of Delhi (2006)

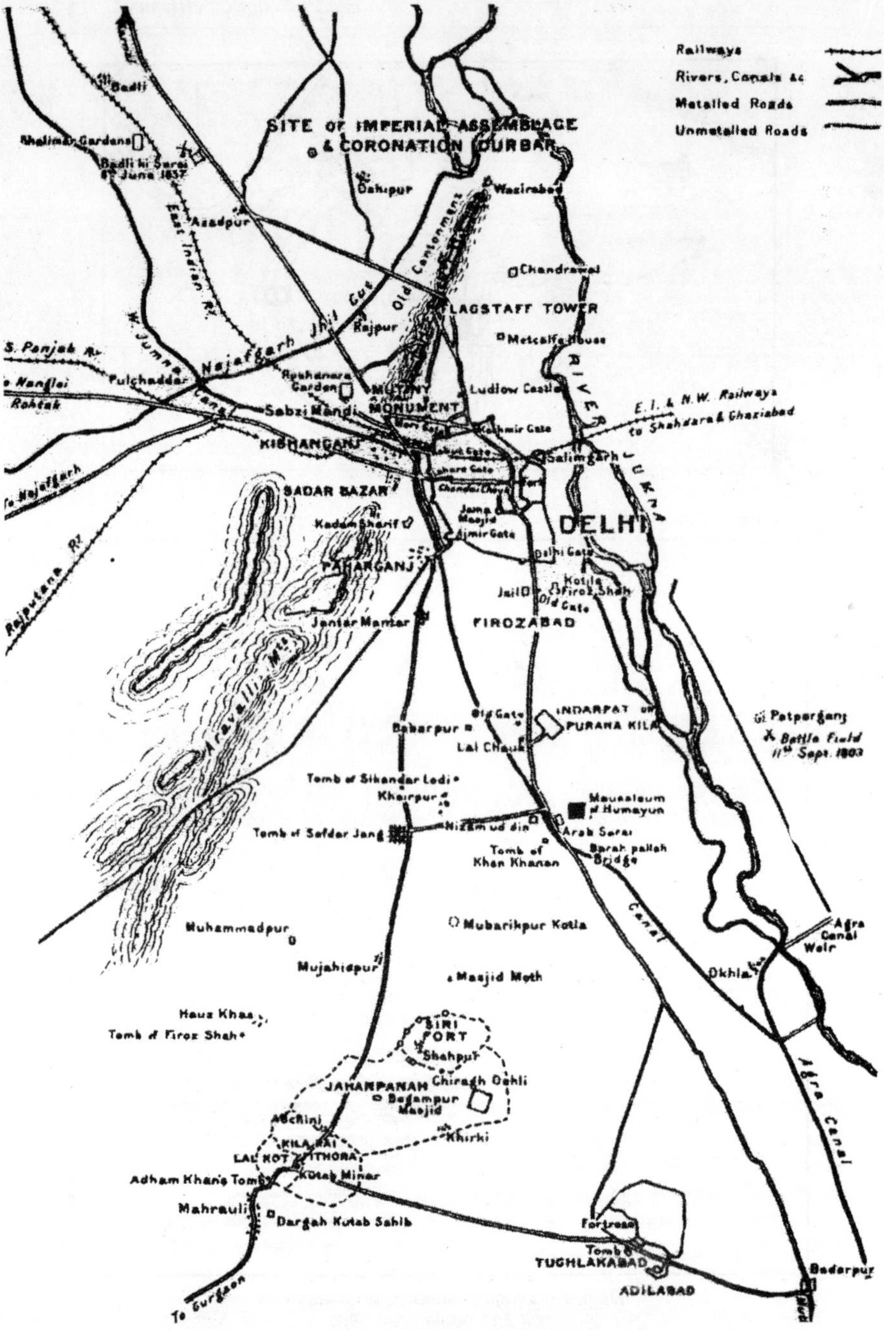

Map of Country around Delhi, 1877

Source: Survey of India, Revenue Survey of Delhi District.

भूरं भूमिरचलानन्ता रसा विश्रंभरा स्थिराधरा धरित्री धरणिः क्षोणिर ज्या काश्यपी क्षितिः– सर्वंसहा वसुमती वसुंधरा गोबा कुः पृथिवी क्ष्मावनिर् मेदिनी मही त्रिष्वथो जगती लोको विष्टपं भुवनं जगत आर्यावर्तः पंण्यभूमिर् मध्यं विन्ध्यहिमालयोः अयनं वर्त्म मार्गाध्वपन्योनः पदवी सृतिः सरणिः पद्धतिः पद्या वर्तन्येकपदीति च पूंः स्त्री पुरी–नंगयौं वा पत्तंन पुटभेदनम् आंपणस् तु निपद्याया, विपणिः पण्यवीथिंका गृहाः पुंसि च भूम्न्येव निकाय्य–निलयालयाः वातायंन गवपक्षो,ऽथ मण्डपोऽस्त्री जनाश्रयः

Where everything is ground, immovable, endless, fertile, sustainer of all, stable

One which supports, bears, sustain, can be dug, is vast, created by Kashapa, is deep

One which endures all, is laden with riches, contains vast wealth, holds treasures

The source, the womb, the global, which is accommodative, substantial, colossal

Container of three worlds, one which moves, can be seen, supports, it is habitat, which rotates

Aryan settlement, sacred land, middle region, between the Vindhyas and Himalayas

Road, course, route, which is worn out, track, for aimless wandering

Path, beaten track, footway, single lane along which a person moves

Settlement, town which is protected, town with natural surroundings for sports, market town, junction town

Whole market, established market, with a variety of goods, a general market

Container of everything, shelter made of bamboo and cloth, where one enters, feels at home

Where one rests in the context of life-style, a house for raising a family, where one enjoys

House, home where there is a sense of belonging, where belongs are housed, a place of rest

One which ventilates, round like cow's eyes, adorned by the presence of an onlooker, serves as a refuge.

–Amarkosha

Amarkosha (4-5th Cent. AD) has a section on architecture and town-planning which provides guidance for organisation of physical space and its inter-relationship with life.

3. Indraprastha—the Legendary City

Delhi is a legend that lives. Few cities in India could parallel the long and historical status that Delhi enjoys. It is an anthology of several cities presenting different layers of history with their own landmarks and legends. Delhi is popularly known as the site of seven cities, the earliest being built around 10th century B.C. However some archaeologists believe that the habitation of Delhi begun around 3500 years ago.

Indraprastha, the legendary city of Mahabharata was the first city which dates back between 1000 BC to 1800 BC. It was located on the western bank of River Yamuna, where now Purana Qila stands. The legend says that the capital of Pandavas, named after God Indra, was built by Maya Danav. According to Mahabharata when the relation between Pandavas and Kauravas became strained, Dhratarashtra, the father of the Kauravas, gave away the region of Khandavaprastha on the bank of the river Yamuna to the Pandavas. There they built the city surrounded by the ditches and provided a high defensive wall. Indraprastha was a part of the Khandavaprastha empire, where the Pandavas ruled. There is also a reference in Mahabharata about the five villages demanded by the Pandavas, which are Indrapat, Baghpat, Tilpat, Sonepat and Panipat. The

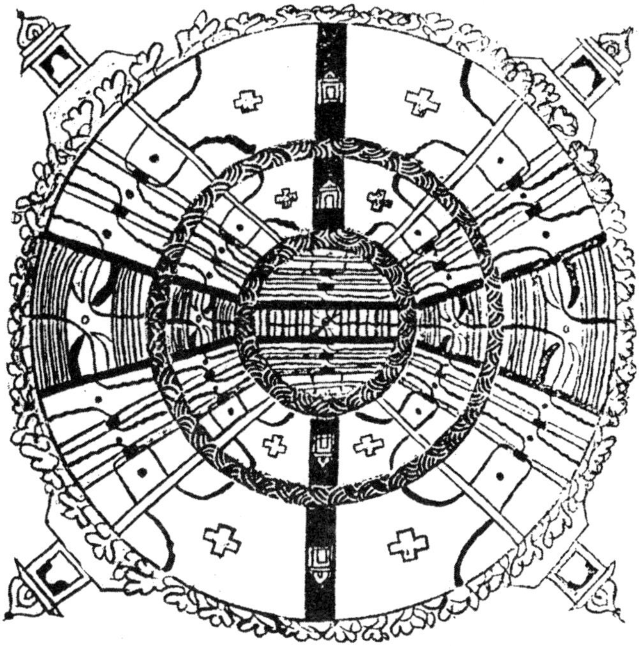

Mandala – a symbolic interpretation of the cosmic principles of city design

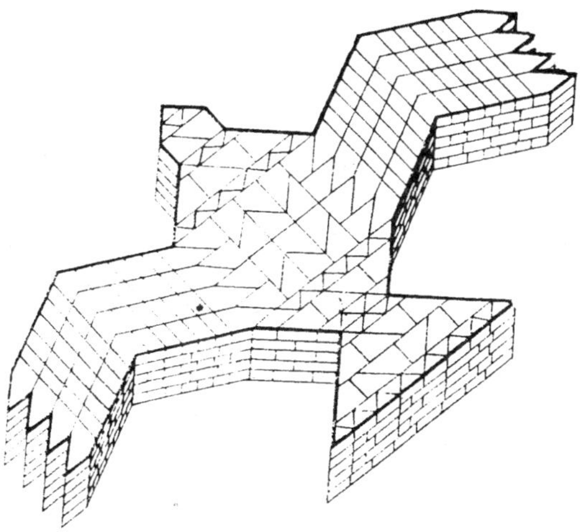

An altar (Vedi) for Yagna

excavations of these settlements have yielded painted grey earthenware which dates back to 1000 BC, and are similar to those found in the excavations at the Purana Qila. These are simple in design and black in colour. The village of Indrapat, which is derived from Indraprastha, did exist in the Purana Qila in the beginning of the 20th century. When New Delhi, the Imperial capital, was constructed, it was cleared alongwith other villages like, Raisina, Jaisinghpura, Narsimhpura, etc. Indraprastha was stated to be a district Pratigana as mentioned in a Sanskrit inscription dated 1328, which is preserved in the Red Fort museum. On the basis of the evidence, it can be said that the society that time was quite advanced and used iron and copper. Tools were made of stone, iron, bones, glass ect. Clay was used to make pots and precious stones were used for the ornaments. The houses were built of mud bricks, wattle and daub.

In the Mahabharata there is also a reference of the palace built by Pandava which was designed by Maya Danava. It was so beautiful that Duryodhan was envious. Its floor, and walls were made of crystal, which gave illusory effect. By this, it was a unique building and looked like a mirror. At the end of Mahabharata war, the Pandavas shifted to Hastinapur and handed over the Indraprastha to the Yadavas. Thereafter the city went into oblivion and became deserted as a mere village. However, the excavations have shown the remains of Maurya, Gupta, Sultanate, Tughlak and Mughal dynasties. The city fort was once again rebuilt by Shershah Suri in the middle of sixteenth century and the city was renamed as Shershah's City.

The Vedic Principles of City Design

In the Mahabharata, the description of the Indraprastha is as follows:

".......The fortress sported massive iron wheel and well laid plan of streets that avoided collision with fate; and it had beautiful building of many kind. Thus Indraprastha shone like the image of heaven, like a mass of packed clouds that are encircled by lightning...............Lovely gardens surrounded the city with mango trees, Amratakas, Nipas, Ashoka, Kadambs,

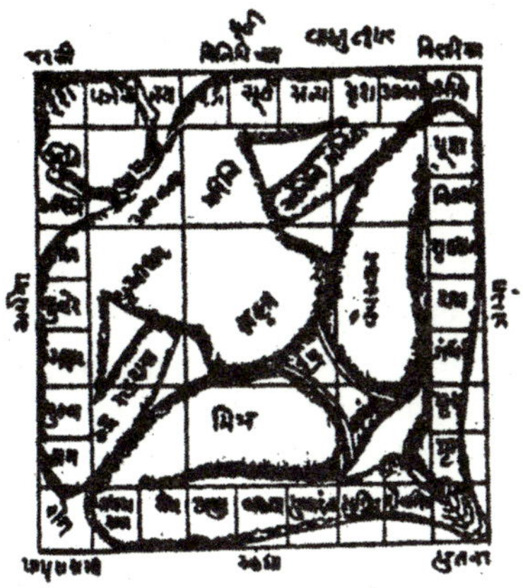

Vastupurush Mandal; Ancient Cosmic diagram as a basis of spatial composition and the celestial zoning of deities and men in a hierarchical system of intersquared modular grid. The innermost zone belongs to Brahma, the God, which is surrounded by the king and the Brahmins. The next zone houses the warriors and then businessmen. The peripheral area is for the workers.

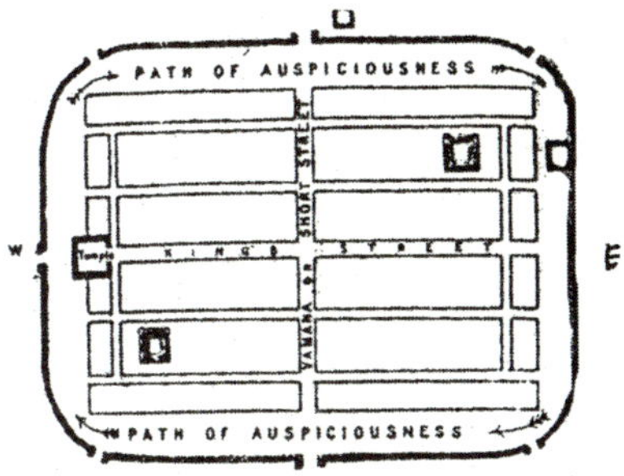

Dandika

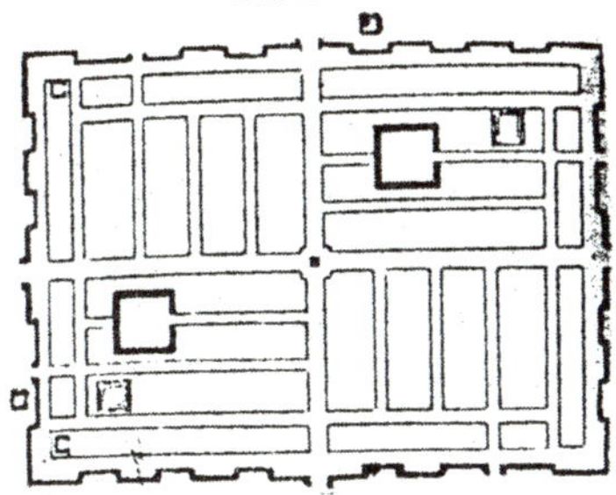

Swastika

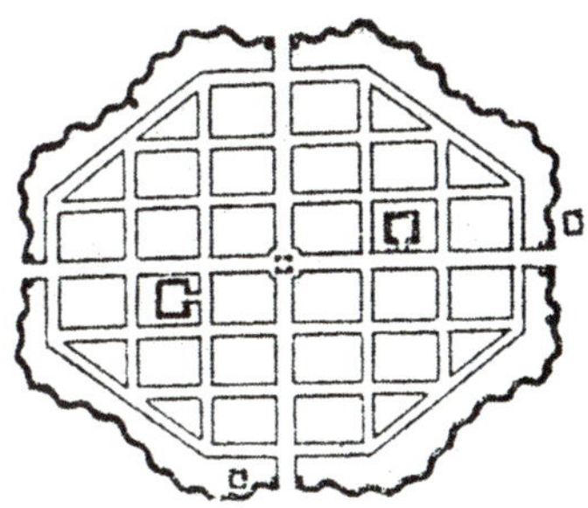

Padmaka

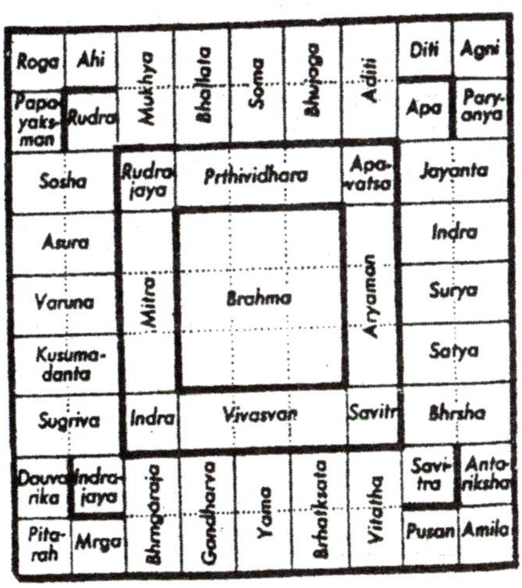

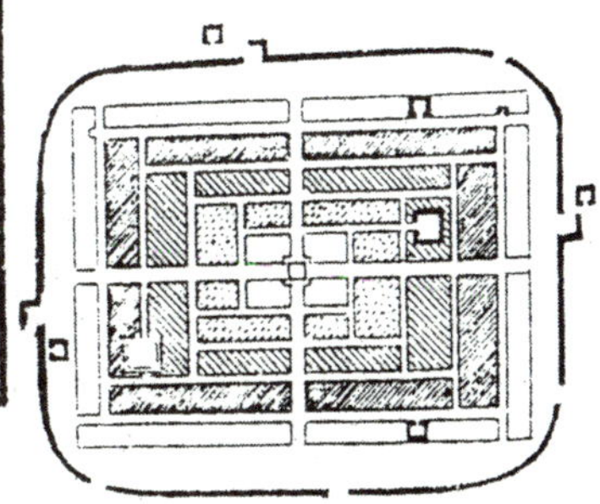

Nandyavarta

Modular Zoning grid of celestials in Vastupurush Mandala

Bakulas and Jasmine..............Swarming of the birds of all kinds, always joyous cuckoo. There are houses white like mirrors and all kinds of pavilions, lovely painted house and pleasure hillocks; and many ponds filled with pure water. And most charming lakes redolent with the fragrance of lotuses and water lilies, colourful with wild geese and ducks.........lotus ponds of all shapes and broad and big tanks of great beauty. As they dwelled in their great realm, which was peopled with honest folk, the joy of the Pandavas, great king grew externally, and thus the Pandavas, when Bhishma and the king had displayed the law, became inhabitants of Khandva tract........."

The city was planned according to the vedic knowledge and the canons of Mansara, the treatise on town planning and architecture. As a basic principle, a city would be planned within an integral system of broad cosmic cycle. It was inter-related with the surrounding cities, like the planets in the astrological chart. A system of ashtha (8), Navgrah (9 planets), 24 matrika pithas, etc. also signified the settlement system. The five elements symbolised the settlements. The five cities–Indraprastha, Bagpat, Panipat, Sonipat and Tilpat, signified the 5 elements of nature, namely air, vegetation, water, fire and earth.

The form of a city was derived on the principle of Vastupurush Mandal. It established an interrelationship of physical from of a settlement with the spiritual, cosmic and behavioural system. It determined the basic form, its location, orientation and various functions in a settlement.

The Mandala means 'circle', which includes the idea of centre and 'circumference'. In Indian rituals it signifies a complex design of concentric circles, in which a square is inscribed. The square is divided by its diagonals into four triangles. There are innumerable variations on this basic scheme, which express iconographic system of symbolic figures, plants and animals. It is the cosmography of universal order. It is a source of self identification and thus integrates oneself into the order of the universe.

The Mandala appears in various forms, constructions, rituals and arts. In its various menifestations, the Mandala form had three basic properties, viz., a centre, symmetry, and cardinal points. The centre is constant while the latter two vary according to the nature of the particular Mandala. Symmetry could be bilateral, dynamic, rigid or fluid. The number of cardinal points would depend upon the situation. These could be several, infinite or non-existant as in a circle.

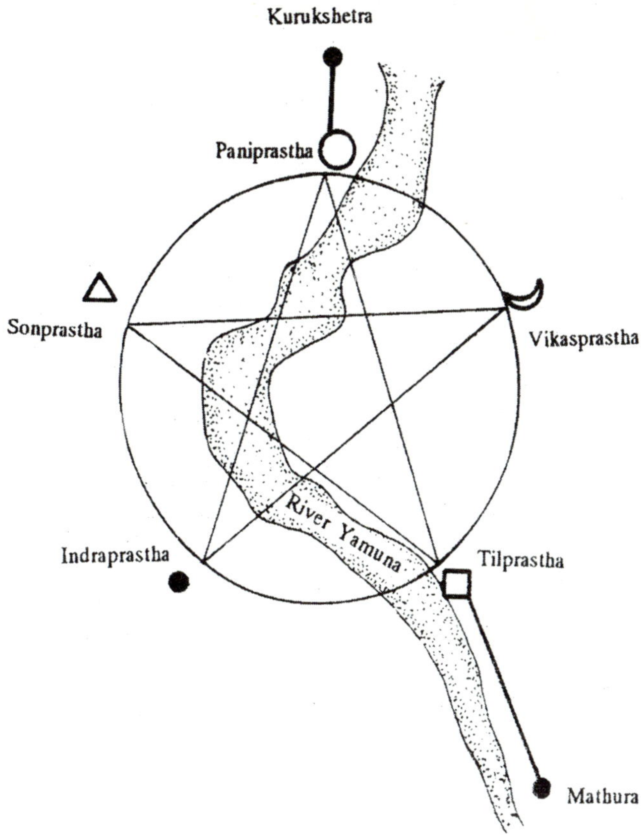

As a basic principle of Mansara, a city would be planned within an integral system of broad cosmic cycle. The five cities namely, Indraprastha, Vikasprastha (Bagpat), Paniprastha (Panipat), Sonprastha (Sonipat), & Tilprastha (Tilpat), signified the five elements of nature, namely, air, vegetation, water, fire and earth.

The Brahmasthan, the soul supreme, is identified with the centre of the mandala. The physical from of a city or a temple is determined by the geometry of the Vastupurusha Mandala. This is a square whose sides may be divided by any number from 1 to 32. Thus the square may be divided up to 1024 units. These are apportioned in various combinations to a number of deities. Vastu means the physical extent, or the site of the building, Purush refers to the cosmic man, the origin of existence. The word may also mean the spirit or man. Thus, the Vastupurush Mandala has been defined as a diagram of cosmic man, summing up the whole of ordered being and so manifesting what is beyond being. It is the spirit of the ground-plan, or of the site. This diagram is drawn with a religious ceremony on the ground and is offered flowers, light and incense. The square form connects the four cardinal points established by the pairs of opposites; north, south, east and west—sunset and sunrise, and the two ends of the world axis. The earth is therefore called chaturbasti, four cornered. The ceremonial square is constructed by drawing intersecting circles with cords fixed on poles.

The Vastupurush Mandala had been so universal that it could be applied to an altar, a temple, a house, a city or the entire cosmos. The symbol relates physical form with the outer from and the inner vision. The Mandala is not only a spatial axiom but a temporal process as well. It is a module encompassing the principles of organacity: inter-relationship of parts, inter-dependence of systems, resonance and synchronicity.

Radiating from the centre, which was the place of Brahma, the city would grow in various directions. The focus of the city, either a temple of a palace was built facing towards the east so that it may receive morning sun and cool breeze. Adjacent to it, along the four sides, the major communities, viz., Vivasvat, Aryaka, Mitra and Shudra were located. The city was further divided into sectors, which give it a form. For example, the Udaditha layout had 25 sectors, Chandita layout had 64, Param Sayika had 81 sectors. Its road layout was based on topographical and symbolic structures, such as, Swastika, Nandavrata, Prasara, Sarvatobhadra, Dandaka and Padamka.

The central square is consecrated to Brahma. The application of Vastupurush Mandala is all embracing; from a marriage altar or the Vedic fire-altar to a temple and a city. However, the focus of every mandala on any scale has been the Brahma. The mandala functions from the inside to outside. The buildings and growth thus function from the centre outwards. In case of a temple, it is from the 'garbha griha', 'the womb chamber'. This is where the temple's statue is consecrated. At this place, a brass vessel containing wealth from the earth; gems, metal, soil, roots, herbs was placed in the foundation. The position and time are decided on the basis of astrological calculations, so that the city or structure are auspicious.

Apart from Mansara, the Vedic principles and directions of city planning are contained in the form of Sanskrit verses. The Amarkosha or Nomalinganushasana and the Astadhyayi of Panini contain such verses. The Amarkosha is the most authoritative ancient dictionary, dealing with synonyms and antonyms in the Sanskrit language. It is believed to have been drawn up by Amara, an illustrious lexicographer. Despite his fame, little is known about Amara and the date of the Amarkosha. Some believe it to be between the first century B.C. and the fourth century A.D. The Kosha was considered one of the "nine jewels" of the court during the Gupta period.

The Amarkosha comprises of three volumes, each divided into chapters and then into sections. In the second part, the dictionary deals with the terms related to agriculture, trade, medicine, textiles and social aspects of the culture. In the section related to architecture and town planning, a classificatory structure has been followed. The terms follow a graduated sequence. From 'earth' (region, city, market, house) to window, all the associated terms are ordered and classified. The concepts and aspects of the physical world and their interrelationship are structured from parts to the whole.

Any attempt to draw the map of Indraprastha would rather be pure fantasy. As in music, the basic principles can create an infinite range of compositions, likewise the principles of Mansara can be applied to innumerable forms of a settlement. There is nothing such as an ideal city or an ideal music composition.

Today the Indraprastha, i.e., Purana Qila is surrounded by the zoo, Nizamuddin, Humayun Tomb, Exhibition ground, Sunder Nagar and Ring Road. It is a protected monument, being maintained by the Archaeological Survey of India. Purana Qila can be conserved depicting its mythological evolution.

The Purana Qila excavations establish existence of settlement from Late Harappan to Medieval period, covering about 2500 years of history.

Source: ASI / INTACH–Delhi a Living Heritage, 2010.

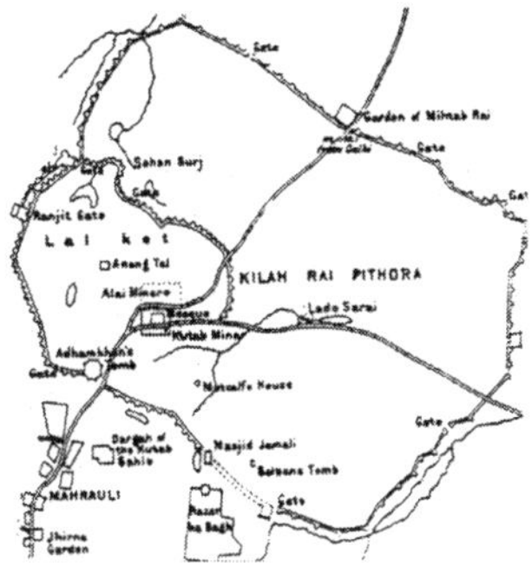

4. Dilli and Lal Kot

Delhi had been continuously in the limelight since the ancient times. The archaeological evidence indicates that ancient Delhi was not only an important city, but being situated on the trunk route, connecting prominent trade centres from Khyber pass to Mathura, it had been an international nerve centre of politics and commerce.

Some people believe that Delhi acquired its name from Raja Dhuloo, who built the capital of his empire around 100 B.C. This is said to have existed at the site of the ridge about 8 km. from the Qutab Minar. But there is little evidence of the city.

The evidences of earliest habitations around Delhi come mainly from the excavated sites of Purana Qila, Srinivaspuri, Lal Kot and Mehrauli area. At the excavated site of Purana Qila soakwells, bricks, streets, pottery, coins and many other remains of the Rajput, Gupta, Post–Gupta, Saka–Kushan, Sanga, Mauryan and Sultanate periods have been found. The evidence of Mauryan dynasty is provided by the existence of black polished ware, punch marked coins, terracotta seals, pottery and figurines. Terracotta rings and burnt brick have also been found. Most of the houses were made of mud brick or wattle, and daub, sometimes reinforced with wooden posts. The association of Emperor Ashoka, who reigned from 273 to

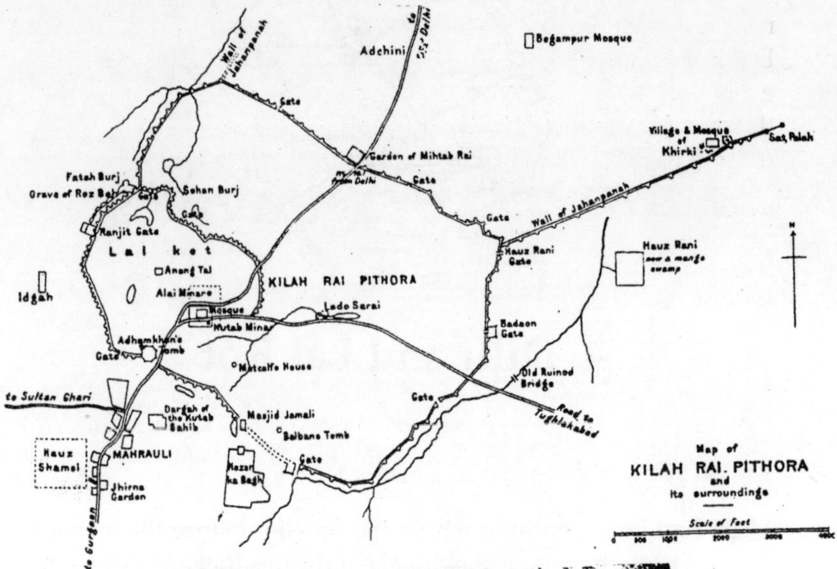

An Ashoka inscription on a rock at Srinivaspuri, near Kalkaji

236 BC, with Delhi came to light by discovering a rock edict near Srinivaspuri in 1966. It is situated near Kalkaji. Written in Brahmi script, the inscription states that as a result of his excursion for the cause of Dharma, he had been able to bring the people of Jambudvipa (India) closer to God. He appealed to the people of all castes to exert so that may attain heaven.

In the second layer of Purana Qila, the rule of the Sanga period from (200-100 BC) is evident. During this dynasty, the houses were built of local rubble or of mud brick over rubble foundation. The red plain pottery, inscribed cast coins, terracotta seals and terracotta semi divine models of Yakshis and Yakshas tell about the religious, social and economic life of Sanga's epoch. The third layer of Purana Qila's excavations reveal the existence of Saka-Kushan rule during 100 BC to 300 AD. The evidence is provided by red decorated earthenware with stamped marks and copper currency. Burnt bricks were used to make the houses, and the city had a more urban look during that era.

The Gupta dynasty (400 to 600 AD) marked a period of civilisation and prosperity. The houses were made of brick–bats. Gold plated coins, with the figure of archer have been found. On their reverse the figure of Srivikrama clearly tells their lineage to the Gupta rule. Inscribed seals, human figurine, red earthenware have been found in the excavations, which belong of the Gupta period.

In the 11th century AD, Anangpal, a Tomar Rajput king shifted the capital of his empire from Kannauj to Delhi. He and his successors during one century of their rule, built the walled city of Lal Kot (meaning Red Fort) which is still a living city—Mehrauli. It had been the site of the capital of many succeeding dynasties. The city had a regular system of water supply through dams and tanks. During the reign of famous Chauhan King, Prithvi Raj, the city was remodelled as Rai Pithora, with a defensive wall of 8 km circumference. The iron pillar, standing at Mehrauli in utter defiance of rust and ravages of time, tells the glory and prosperity of the Rajput dynasty. The remains of Rai Pithora can still be seen in the present Saket, Mehrauli, Kishangarh and Vasant Kunj areas.

The city of Qila Rai Pithora had 28 gates. Badhawan

Darwaza was the largest gate. Al–Mindawa gate was situated besides the grain market. The Darwaza of Jal opened into garden. The darwaza of Shah, darwaza of Palam, darwaza of Kamal and darwaza of Ghazna were called after the names of prominent men, village and routes. Outside the darwaza of al–Bajalisa were the cemeteries, with beautiful domed pavilions and mihrab.

The buildings were mainly of stone of brick. These were roofed with wood and floored with local stone. The floor was paved with marble only in the royal palace.

During the era of Rajput Pratiharas and Tomar Chauhans magnificient temples had been built in Delhi. It is believed that a large temple existed at the present site of the Sultan Ghori Tomb, 5 km. West of the Qutab Minar. The temple might have been erected by Pratiharas or Tomar Rajputs, whose seat of empire existed at Lal Kot and extended in the hills of south Delhi. Mehrauli itself is a Sanskrit name, meaning the garland of the stars. The remains of 27 Hindu and Jain temples are too evident in the Qutab Complex. The inscription on the famous Iron Pillar at Qutab Minar is a testimony of this period. It reads: "By the breeze of whose prowess the Southern ocean is still perfumed". The reference is made to Chandragupta II.

In the existing reservior of Suraj Kund which is nowadays a famous picnic spot and the venue for annual handicrafts fair, one can have a clear glimpse of the Rajput art and architecture. Richly carved ramparts, door jambs, lintols, carved, thought mutiliated, pillars and ceiling slabs of Hindu temples were reused by the early Muslim rulers in Quwwat-ul-Islam mosque and Sultan Ghori's tomb.

Anangtal and the White Palace

The historians believe that during the 10th and 12th century, a royal residence of the Rajput rulers and the early Sultans existed at Lal Kot in the Qutab area. It is said to be the site of the famous Kasre Safed or White Palace, an elaborate palace complex of the Slave Kings. The lost palace, mentioned in the writings of the traveller Ibn Batuta, is supposed to have been built by Qutubu'd–Din Aibak in the 1204. It is believed that the Rajput

Tomar King Anangpal built this first medieval fortress city of Dilli with living quarters and several temples during the early 10th century. Later expanded by the succeeding Chauhans, it was renamed Kila Rai Pithora. With the Muslim advent in the late 12th century, Lal Kot was sacked and a city with impressive palaces and fortifications was rebuilt in its very ruins. These Hindu and Muslim structures thereafter sunk underground with decay and the ravages of a thousand years. It is said that probably the 13th century White Palace, as the white lime–plastered floorings and walls suggest, must have been a grand structure with broad corridors mounted with several arches. Some of the pillar bases are of Rajput origin.

Excavation of the two top layers has revealed insignificant Thghluk structures, for this palace site was abandoned in the late 13th century and was consequently used as the State prison, while the Capital shifted to the banks of the Yamuna. The third and the fourth layers have revealed artefacts of the early Sultanate period, i,e,. glazed pottery, porceline and jade green 'celadon' pottery, imported form China or Japan. The fifth and the sixth layers have yielded typical Rajput knife-edged bowls and red-slipped pottery. The potshard with 4th century Gupta inscriptions and two potshards of the painted Greyware period (1000-800 BC), in the vicinity indicate some kind of habitation since proto-historic times. The palace was linked with an elaborate water harvesting and supply system. A Rajput tank Anangtal with hamam like water system have surfaced in the excavations. It is eight-petal, lotus-shaped and octagonal tanks were built inside the palace. These were probably for storing cool and scented water, which would be supplied from the Anangtal. Anangtal was a huge 48 meter x 45 meter water tank with a depth of about 10 to 12 meters. It was the lifeline of the region until the Khilji period. Constructed by king Anangpal Tomar, the tank had its sides neatly bound with a walls of stones fixed with iron clamps. The stone bear mason's marks—swastika, bow and arrow and trident. These indicate Hindu (Rajput) features of construction.

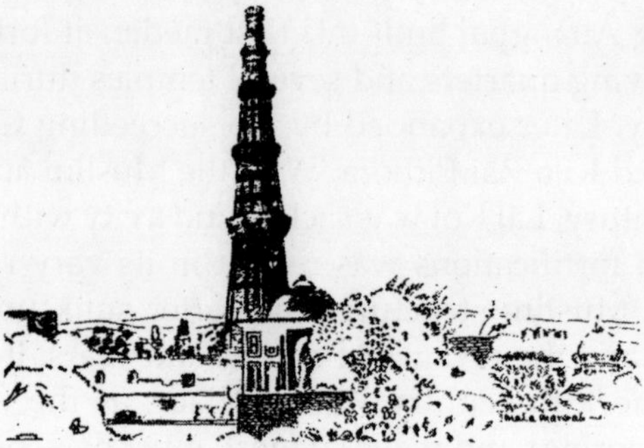

5. Mehrauli—the City of Qutab

Delhi is a destiny through the ages. Several cities were constructed, fortified, besieged, destroyed and again reconstructed in a strange cycle one after the other. After a dramatic defeat of Prithviraj Chauhan, the rule of the Hindu dynasty over Delhi came to an end in 1191 AD. It was captured by Qutabuddin Aibak, the slave commander of Mohammad Ghori, after numerous defeats. This was the beginning of Delhi Sultanate and for next 600 years Islamic dynasties prevailed. The seat of the rule of the invaders had been Mehrauli, which was the living capital of Hindu predecessors. In 1260 Qutabuddin Aibak became the first Sultan of Delhi and Quwwat-ul-Islam was laid on the site of Hindu fort as Delhi's first mosque. It is a symbol of the triumph of Islam. The mosque enclosed a spacious courtyard by cloisters built by scuplted pillars from 27 Hindu and Jain temples. Its facade was interwoven with Quranic calligrahy and delicately carved screens. The structure was extended by his successor Illtutmish. Loaded with abundance of Hindu motifs, an Indo-Saracenic style of architecture emerged. The construction of Qutab Minar, the celebrated victory tower, was started by Qutabuddin Aibak and was continued by Illtutmish and his successors. It is the most dominating symbol and a landmark of Delhi since last

Qutab Minar drawn by John Luard

7 centuries. Its fluted pietra-dura marble and red sandstone towers with bands of Quranic calligraphy and girdling balconies make it a beautiful structure. However, legend says that the Rajput King Prithvi Raj raised this minarate for astronomical

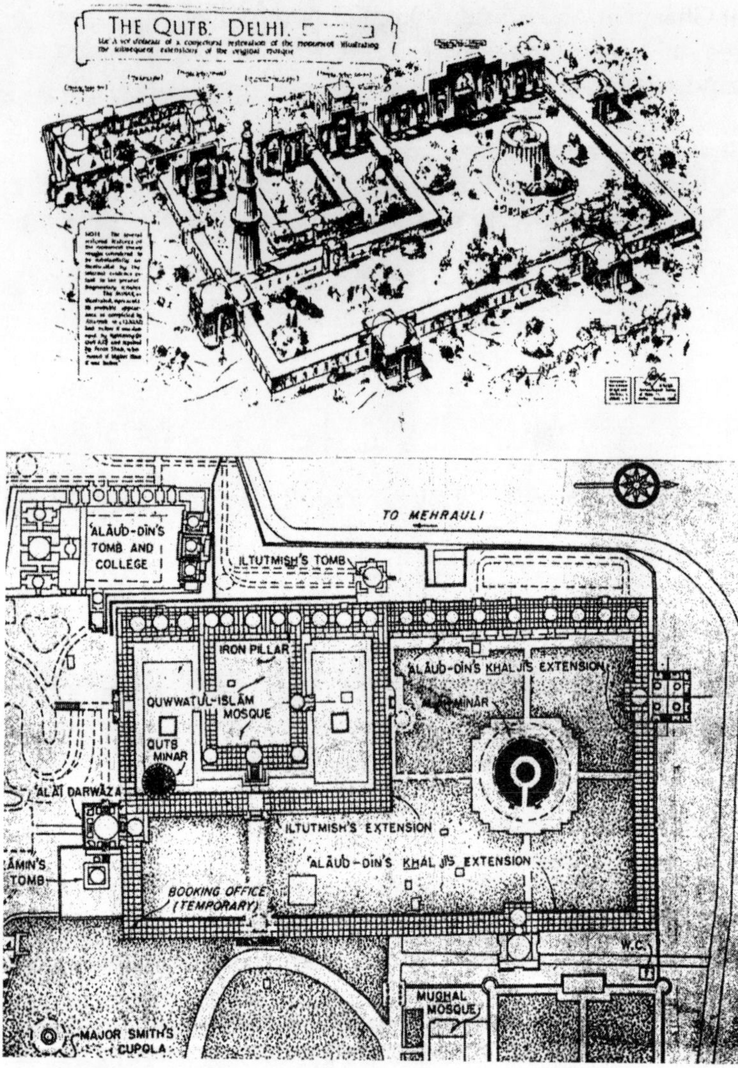

The Qutab Complex
Source: Archaeological Survey of India

observations. His daughter could see the holy Yamuna from its top. The Qutab Minar is 73 metres in height and has a base of 14.5 meters diameter, which tapers to 2.5 meters at the apex. The minarate appears to have been modelled on a similar tower at Ghazni in Afghanistan. Out of 5 stories, the first three are of red sandstone and top two stories are built in marble and and sandstone.

On the outskirts of Mehrauli a water reservoir known as Shamsi Talab and Jahaz Mahal were built over a faint footprint, said to be that of the Prophet. Jahaz Mahal, built in 1230 AD is a beautiful structure of grey and red sandstone. It is the venue of annual festival of Phool Walon Ki Sair. The citadel wall, observation towers, numerous tombs and other lofty structures of Mehrauli dominate its hilly landscape. These reflect that Mehrauli during the Sultanate era was one of the most magnificient and thriving capital city, with an urban and cosmopolitan look. Although attempts were made several times to shift the capital, Mehrauli had always remained a living city. Being the oldest among all the settlements, it had often been referred as Old Delhi till the construction of New Delhi in this century, after which Shahjahanabad was termed as the Old Delhi.

Illtutmish, in 1231 AD, also built a large tomb for his eldest son Nasiruddin, who died sometimes during 1228 or 1229. Known as Sultan Ghori's tomb, it exists in the present Vasant Kunj area on Mehrauli Masoodpur road. It is considered to be the first monumental tomb, apart from a pre-sultanate tomb which was built in Qutab Complex. It was built by assembling the architectural members removed from the Hindu temples. The ceiling of the chambers and corridors are built with the brackets, columns and beams. The arches and vaults are corbelled.

Five years later, i.e. during 1235–36 AD, Illtutmish built his own tomb, which is quite different from Mohammad Ghori's tomb. In this tomb, there is much less dependence on the demolished temple components. Arches and semi–domes raised over the squinches were laid in a corbelled fashion. Illtutmish tomb's exterior is simple but intricately carved and has a lavish ornamentation on the entrance and the interior. It depicts geometrical and Arabesque patterns in Saracenic tradition. Famous historian, Ferguson described it as "One of the richest example of Hindu art applied to Mohammadan purpose."

Illtutmish, nominated his daughter Razia Sultan to succeed him. She is remembered one of the earlist woman rulers in India. Her tomb exists at Turkman gate. This is intriguing and leads to speculation that river Yamuna was flowing near Turkman gate, which shifted its course towards the east. However the capital city was not confined to Mehrauli, but it extended much beyond during her reign.

Nasru'd-din,' the last Sultan, left the state affairs in the hands of his father-in-law, Balban, who succeeded him in absence of an heir. A rubble built square tomb near Qutab Minar, which is now in a dilapidated condition and domeless, is a reminder of the riegn of Balban. Here first real Muslim arch had been employed for construction.

Muizzuddin Khilji succeeded the Sultanate of Delhi in 1286 AD. He shifted his capital to Kilokari on the bank of the Yamuna, near the present Jamia Milia Islamia, close to the Okhla village. There are two mounds and a lonely structure as the monuments of that era. The slave dynasty came to an end in 1290.

The Qutab Minar complex has been declared as a 'World 'heritage zone'. It includes the Zafar Mahal, The palace of Bahadur Shah where the emperor wished to be buried; the remains of palace enclosures; the 16th century Chaumachi tomb, the Hauz Shamsi, 10th century water tank, Jahaẓ Mahal, and the Jharna, a terrace Mughal garden with a cascade.

The heritage zone also covers the adjacent park in the Qutab Complex which is to be devloped as an archaeological park. This sprawling area has about 70 monuments, including the ornamented Jamali-Kamali mosque and tomb, Dil Khusha, Quli Khan's tomb, historic orchards and gardens ranging fron the earliest slave period to colonial times. This also includes the British Resident Thomas Metcalfe's terrace garden with a pond and palm trees. It is proposed to revive old gardens and pathways and to conserve various structures of the old capital. This covers about 100 acres of Mehrauli Archaeological Park.

Mehrauli Archaeological Park

The park has some 80 monuments belonging to different eras, the oldest dating back to the 11th century pre-Islamic Rajput settlements. The monuments range from grand structures like

Quli Khan's tomb to slave ruler Balban's tomb and several minor monuments that together denote a huge cultural resource for the city. 100–acre park in the shadow of the Qutub Minar, is being developed as a buffer zone to the world heritage site. Some of the prominent historical structures include the following:

Balban's Tomb

The 13th century tomb of Slave Dynasty ruler Balban lies in a square chamber built with arched openings on all sides. It is the first major building in India where the true arch and dome were constructed.

Khan Shaheed's Tomb

Ruined rectangular chamber; is believed to have contained grave of Balban's son, Muhammad, who died fighting Mongol invaders near Multan in 1285.

Metcalfe's Bridge

A grand staircase led to Quli Khan's tomb from the bridge, which Thomas Metcalfe erecterd to provide access to his estate which had gardens, terraces and guesthouses.

Jamali Kamali's Mosque and Tomb

Jamali was a famous court poet of the Lodi and Mughal Period. The mosque was built in 1528 as was the tomb. The tomb of Jamali is inscribed with some of his verses. It has a well preserved interior with coloured tiles and richly decorated plaster works.

Quli Khan's Tomb

The tomb of Quli Khan lies just beyond the walled enclosure of Qutub Complex. Muhammad Quli Khan was the brother of Adham Khan and the foster brother of Emperor Akbar. The octagonal large domed tomb, built in early 17th century was originally decorated with tilework.

Adam Khan's Tomb

Adam Khan's Tomb in Mehrauli is a protected monument. Adam Khan, whose mother Mahim Anga was a nurse for Akbar, killed Atgah Khan, a minister. The enraged emperor had Khan thrown from the ramparts of Agra Fort. His mother got the tomb built for him.

City Gates of Mehrauli

The City Gates of Mehrauli depict its historical importance and

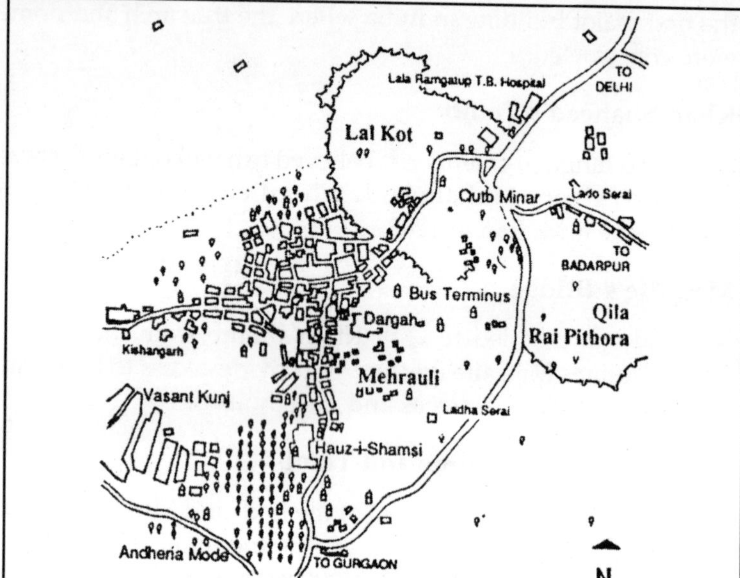

Lal Kot, Qila Rai Pithora and Mehrauli
Source: Delhi Guide Map, Survey of India, 1985

connectivity with the other cities of importance.The darwazas-Chaumukha, Sohan, Ranjit, Fateh, Hauz Rani, Barka, Badaun and Badayuni – can be traced back to the 11th century citadel of Lal Kot which was later extended by the Chauhans into the Qila Rai Pithora, in Mehrauli. The Chaumukha Darwaza near the Qutb complex which was the gateway of Lal Kot with "horned" outwork has been graded by INTACH of archaeological value B. Of all the Khilji darwazas, Alai Darwaza stands at the southern end of the Qutub complex. Built in 1311, it was part of

Alauddin Khilji's grandlose plans of building four gateways; the other three could not be completed because of his death.Verses from Koran and Hadis can still be seen on the windows which are enclosed by ractangular bands made of red sandstone and marble. Hauz Rani and Budayuni Gates were two prominent gates. History has it that at the Budayuni Gate, Alauddin Khilji had ordered his wine caskets to be emptied and his fabulous China dashed to ground to cease the consumption of alcohol. Here the guilty were tortured and beheaded in public view. The gate was under construction watch fearing of Mongol invasions. Ibn Batuta, who visited India in the 14th century, mentions the Badaun Gate as being the "principal gate of the city reached by a populous street occupied by the cloth merchants of Old Delhi." Most of these gates are now only giant gaps in the long stretches of the walls of Lal Kot.

Zafar Mahal: Mehrauli had been an important and evolving seat of the rulers. Zafar Mahal palace identified by its lofty gateway (popularly called the Sheesh Mahal), is an important landmark in Mehrauli. Originally built by Akbar Shah II (1806-37), the main gateway was reconstruced by Bahadur Shah II (1837-57) to enable elephants to enter. It is of a more refined construction than earlier structures, ornamented in red sandstone and marble. The main piers are three-storeyed, splayed at the corners with protecting windows covered by Bengali domes. The broad chajja on the upper floor is an elegant mehfil-Khana overlooking the entrance forecourt. It is a large hall noteworthy for its slender, double, Shahjahani columns and engrailed arches. There is a marked colonial influence in the form of plasters and mouldings.
Source: INTACH

Photograph of 'The Kutb Minar with the great arch, from the West, Delhi' by Bourne, Samuel, 1866.

Source: Victoria and Albert Museum

Tomb of Illtutmish, drawn by John Luard

Ruins of the Alai Darwaza that lie in the Qutub Minar Complex. Built around 1300 A.D., It was the southern Gateway to the Quwwatu'l Islam Mosque.

Quwwat ul-Islam Masjid, Qutab, Delhi: Qutubuddin Aibak calls the mosque Jami-Masjid in an inscription on the main eastern entrance. He writes that the mosque was built with the carved columns and other architectural remnants of 27 Hindu and Jain temples that were demolished.

The Western portion of the mosque's courtyard is where one of the demolished temples originally stood. At the two ends of its eastern cloisters, an intermediate storey was raised to provide compartments for women. To later rulers enlarged the mosque. Shamsud-din doubled the size of the mosque in 1230 by extending its colonnades and prayer hall outside the original enclosure, with the result that the Qutab Minar fell within the mosque premises. Alaud-din Khilji (1296-1316) again extended the mosque substantially by enlarging the enclosure. He provided two gateways on the longer eastern side and one each on the north and south.

Gate of Alauddin Qutab drawn by E.Therond

Source: Archaeological Survey of India

Rajon ki Baoli

Rajon Ki Baoli

Built during the reign of Sikander Lodi in 1506, this three-storeyed step-well was also called the Sukhi (dry) Baoli. This baoli near a well, along with a tomb and a mosque was built during the reign of Sikandar Lodi in 1506 and its name derives from the word meaning masons. Although originally there were four storeys, due to the continuous silting, only three storeys remain.

Gandhak Ki Baoli

The five-storeyed Gandhak ki Baoli, named after its strong sulphur smell is located nearby. These baolis once supplied water to the area. There are several ruins including a walled enclosure to the south and an arched colonnade to the south-east of the baoli.

Quli Khan's Tomb

Source: INTACH

Metcalfe's Guesthouse

An Old sketch of Dilkusha

Dilkusha

Formerly Known as Dilkusha, the tomb of Quli Khan lies just beyond the walled enclosure of the Qutb Complex. Muhammad Quil Khan was the brother of Adam Khan was the foster brother of Mughal Emperor Akbar. The octagonal, large domed tomb, built in the early 17th century was originally decorated with tilework now visible only the eastern facade. In the early 1840's, Sir Thomas Metcalfe, the British Resident at Delhi, converted the tomb into a country residence with landscaped gardens, terraces and guest houses.

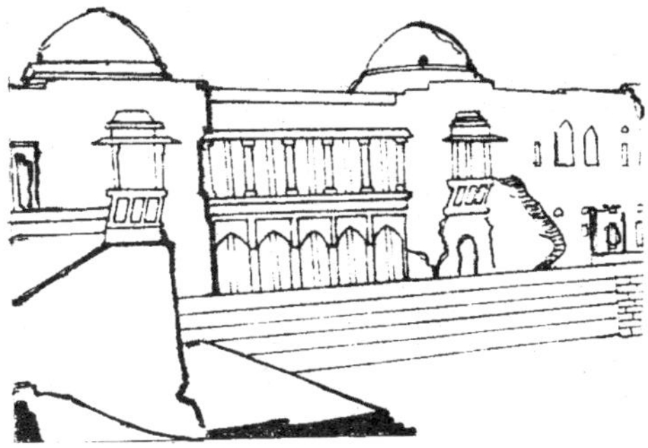

6. Siri—the City of Khiljis

When one goes through the history, one wonders why so many Delhis? In the Indian context, it may be said that there are two major factors which govern the founding of the cities. First, the existance of a river, or a water body, and second, the will of the ruler. Besides these, there are some other factors. The invasion and destruction of a living settlement, the changing course and floods in the river Yamuna and the ambition of the rulers, wishing to outdo their predecessors in glory and power. These have also played important roles in the creation and rebuilding of the city time and again.

The pressure of attacks from the Mongols forced Alau'd-din Khilji to take refuge at Siri where he constructed another Delhi. Alau'd-din Khilji, son of Jalaluddin Khilji, was an ambitious man who was not only known for his political exploits but also for architectural achievements. He succeeded into power through embattled events. He built his capital at Siri in 1303 AD, adjacent to the scene of massacre of the Mongols, at Chor Minar in Hauz Khas. The eastern portion of Siri is cut across by a wide road connecting Moolchand Hospital and Chiragh Delhi. Its rubble built high wall is over in plan. It is said to have possessed seven gates, one towards south-east may be seen even today. The Siri Fort was built with a magnificient palace, and a hall of thousand pillars called Hazar Satun. The vast reservoir called Hauz Khas which was originally known as Hauz-e-Ala'i was built to meet the needs of water. Alai Darwaza was also constructed by him at Mehrauli in finely carved sandstone, inlaid with marble bands. This gateway has a semi-circular horseshoe arch with lotus motif. The Tarikh-e-Alahi of Amir Khusro states that Alau'd-din ordered the construction of another minarat by the side of Qutab Minar which was abandoned. One of the Nagri inscription at Qutab Minar mentions that "Alau'd-din carried out some repairs to the tower. However, Allauddin had to abandon the construction at its initial stage, due to his departure to Chittor and Ranthambor for wars."

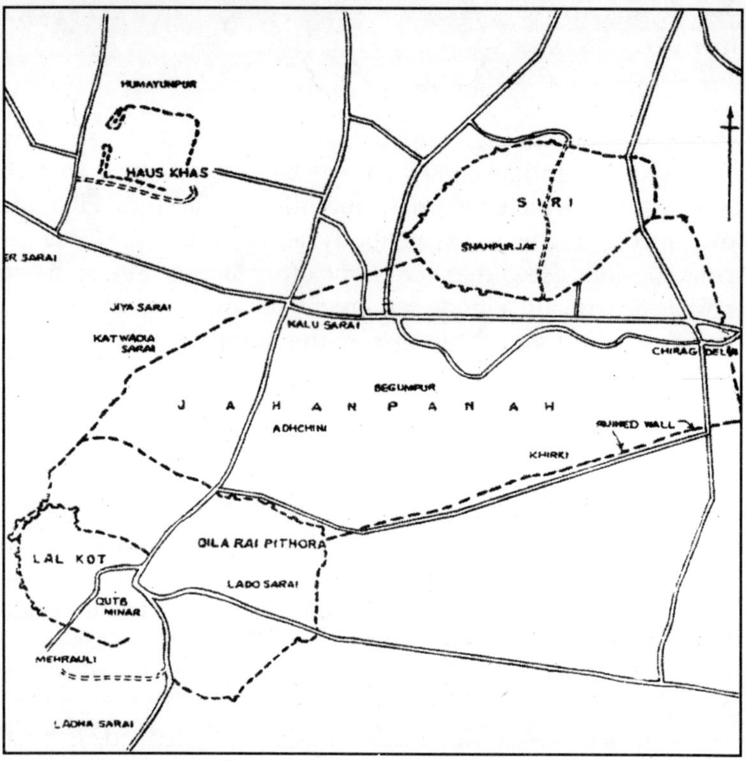

Siri—the City of Khilji Dynasty

Source: Survey of India, 1985.

(a) entrance to shrine complex and tank
(b) tomb of Sheikh Nizam-u-din Auliya
(c) Jamat Khana
(d) Tomb of Atgah Khan
(e) Tomb of Khan-i-Jahan Tilangani
(f) Kalan Masjid
(g) Chaunshath Khamba
(h) Lal Mahal

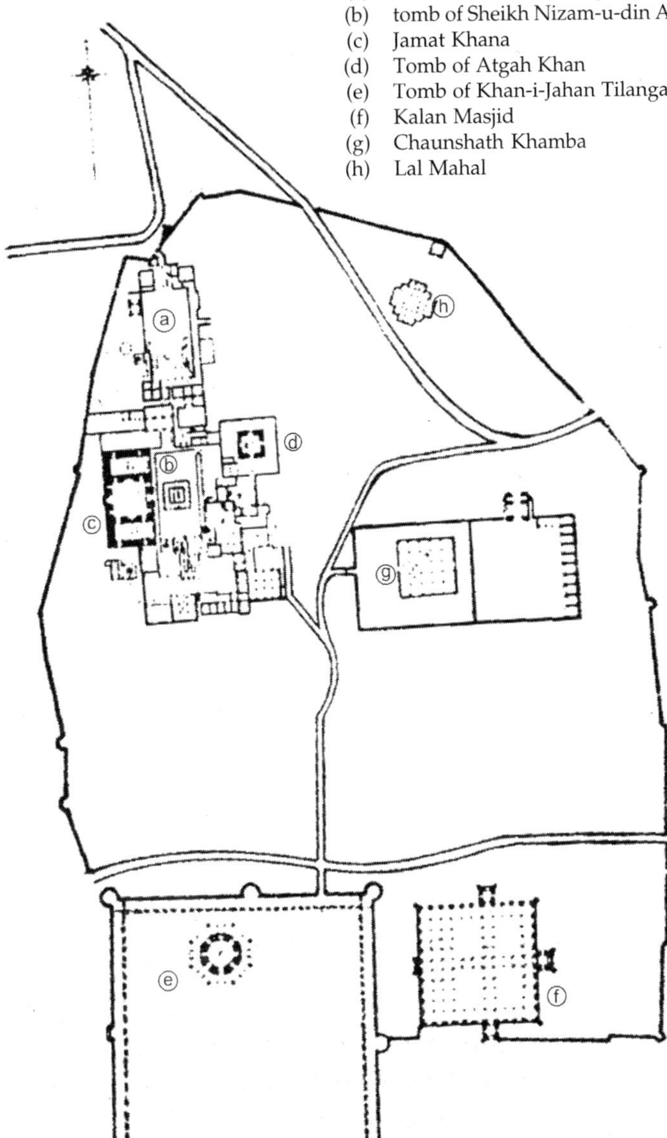

Nizamuddin

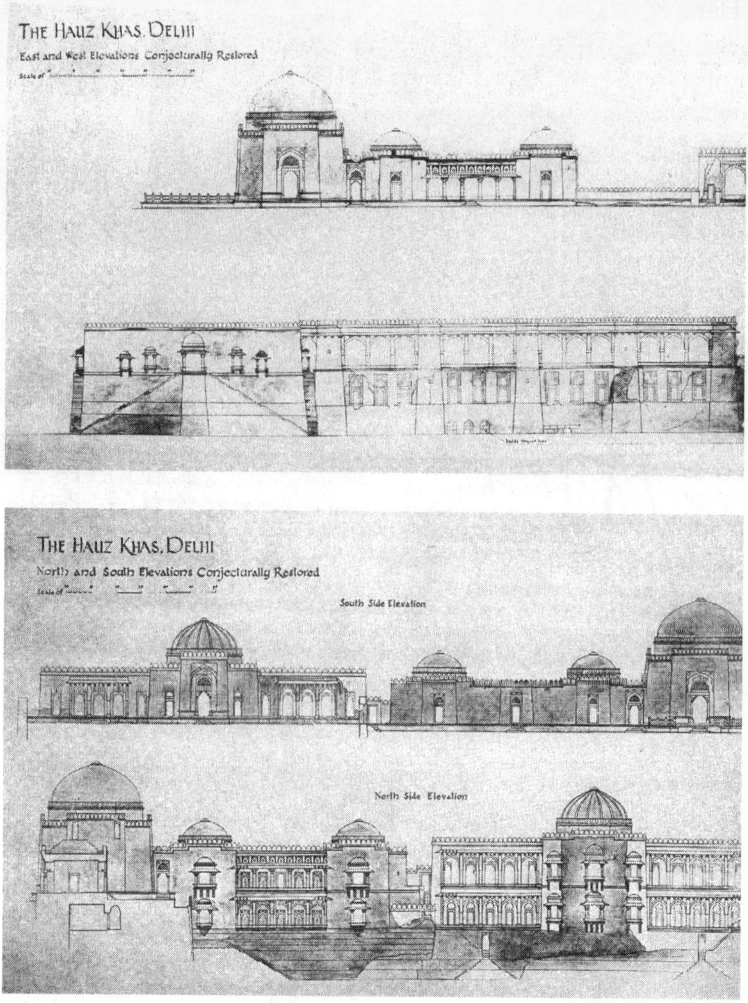

Elevations of the diferent wings of the Hauz Khas Complex.

Source: Archaeological Survey of India

Huaz Khas Madarsa

Built around a large tank believed to have been dug by Alauddin Khilji around 1296 AD, it is also known as Hauz-e-Alai. The madarsa remains almost hidden behind the ethnic village of Hauz Khas. The madarsa used to be a residential one. It has a beautiful architectural fusion of Persian and Indian styles. The corbelling is Indian, sometimes referred as the Hindu style whereas the arch had its origins in West Asian and Central Asian countries.

'Hauz-e-Khas' was built by Alauddin Khilji for his new city Siri. This tank attracted the attention of Batuta and he wrote in detail about it. This is a very scenic tank with grand buildings all around it and wonderful trees. The tomb of Sultan Feroz Shah lies at the western side of the tank.

Abdur Rahim Khan-I-Khanan's Tomb

Nizammuddin draws its name from the revered saint Hazrat Nizamuddin Auliya. In its vicinity are the his dargah. Humayun's tomb and the tomb of Mughal nobleman, Abdur Rahim Khan-i-Khanan. The relative anonymity of his tomb is in stark contrast to his lifetime, in which he towered above his contemporaries. The son of Akbar's regent Balram Khan and later one of the navratnas at Akbar's court, Khan-i-Khanan was an accomplished scholar and poet. A truly diverse man, he translated Babar's memoirs into Persian, commanded Akbar's armies, acted as patron to the numerous men of letters who appeared in the Mughal court and was tutor to future Emperor Jahangir.

The story soured later. Jahangir executed two sons of Khan-i-Khanan, possibly to settle scores for their father, who had opposed his ascendancy to the throne. To add insult to injury, Khan-i-Khanan's tomb was stripped of its marble cladding decades later, possibly to face lift Safdarjung's Tomb.

Contemporary to Allauddin, Durgah of Amir Khusro and Hazrat Nizamuddin Aulia have been notable in the history of Delhi. Nizamuddin's status as a saint courted by the Royal Durbar is evident from Dargah Nizamuddin having a cluster of 7 royal tombs. The Dargah built by Allauddin's eldest son Khizr Khan was maintained and renovated by the succeeding emperors; from Feroz Shah to Mohammad Shah. The tomb of Amir Khusro, a celebrated poet is also located in the vicinity of the main shrine.

Jama-at Khana Masjid which lies close to the Tomb of Hazrat Nizamu'd-Din Auliya was built by Khizr Khan in 1325. It has a red sandstone facing, low dome, the 'lotus bud' fringe of arches, squinch arches with frames bearing Quranic inscriptions. The features of Ala'i-Darwaza seem to have influenced the design of the Mosque. Khizr Khan was the hero of one Amir Khusro's love poem.

The salient feature of Khilji architecture is that it developed its own style, methods and idioms. Khilji buildings are of red sandstone which are relieved by marble. For the first time, the arch had been employed, which are generally in the shape of horseshoe. Broad dome, recessed arches under the squinch, decorative moulding are some of the characteristics of Khilji architecture.

In 1320, Khilji rule was usurped by Khusro Shah in a bloody coup. Owing to the resistance of the military governor of Multan same year Ghyasuddin Tughluq Shah I became the Sultan of Delhi.

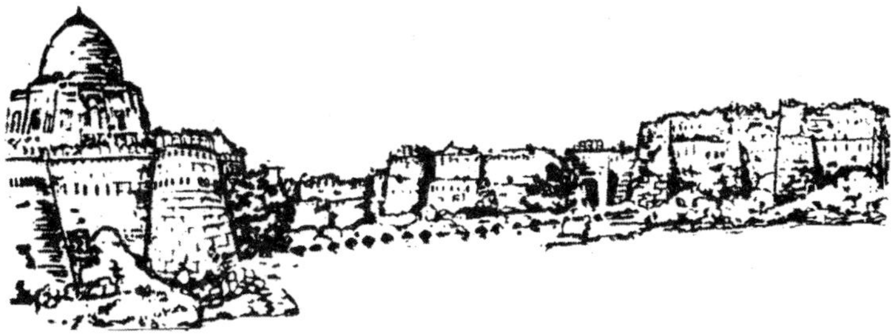

7. Tughlaqabad of Tughlaqs

Once the celebrated poet, Galib asked what is Delhi, and then replied himself, "if the world is the body, Delhi is its soul." Delhi had been the capital of several empires and dynasties. Its countryside is scattered with the ruins, monuments, mausoleums, mosques, temples, forts, etc. Delhi is a curious destiny through the ages of which now remain only the remnants. Tughlaqabad is one of the formidable reminders of Delhi's embattled past and the terror and valour of that era. Ghyasuddin came to power in 1321 by beheading Khurso Khan, who had also snatched power in a bloody coup. Ghyasuddin Tughluq in order to counter attack the invading Mongols raised pyramids of enemies' heads and used the elephants to crush the captives to death. The massive fortification of Tughlaqabad with immense circular bastions and more than 250 gateway was raised by Ghyasuddin who routed the Mongols in 24 pitched battles. Location was strategic, so as to get a natural advantage over the invaders. On the south side, a vast reservoir was created for harvesting rainwater for the city. Wide embankments near south-east corner of the fort, provide access to the Adilabad fort. This was built later on, over an adjoining hill.

The fortification of city is in two parts. The central citadel and the main city within the outer wall. Ghyasuddin was familiar with the construction of big tombs in Multan region, built with sloping walls. This style was adopted for

Towers of Tughlaqabad, Robert Elliot, 1834

Tughlaqabad. Located five miles east of Qutub Minar, Tughlaqabad Fort was built with amazing speed by Ghyasuddin Tughlaq in just four years of his rule. Ghyasuddin's tomb lies within the citadel. To south lies Adilabad, a subsidiary fort built by his son and successor Muhammad bin Tughlaq, and to the east is a small fortress known as Nai-ka-Fort or Barbers' fort. The sloping walls are built at an angle of 75° with the ground. The outer walls of Tughlaqabad are over 6.5 km long and 10 to 15 metres high. Rubble built walls are reinforced with sloping battlements and circular bastion. There are at least 13 secret ways. For drinking water there were 7 water tanks in the Fort complex. Across the main entrance on the south Ghyasuddin's tomb was built in 1325 AD. It has sloping walls and a marble dome crowned by a Kalash finial. This was originally surrounded by a large lake. Its underground walls are said to have concealed enormous treasures. The openings have horseshoe shaped arches. Each arch is complemented by a lintel installed beneath the springing point. This became the hallmark of Tughlaq style. The mausoleum is about 8 metre square, raised on an octagonal drum. There are three graves inside. The central one is of Ghyasuddin and other two are believed to be of his wife and son.

Tughlaqabad had a short span of life and was abandoned in less than 10 years. Legend asserts that the Fort was deserted because of the curse of Saint Sheikh Nizamuddin Auliya, whom Ghyasuddin did not allow to make a Baoli. He prophessed that the city would be inhabited either by the Gujars or would be abandoned. Ghyasuddin died in an accident. Tughlaqabad continues to remain a dead city. One wonders that this city was once full of life. Ibn Batuta praised it and said that it is made of gold bricks. In sunshine it glows to an extent that nobody can look at it for a long time. Though the excavations point to a brief period when the city had come to be abandoned, it suggests that the site was not deserted soon after Ghyasuddin's death. The layers of excavation show that though Tughlaqabad lost its status as capital to later cities like Ferozabad and Shahjahanabad, people continued to live here. Pottery from the late Mughal period and an anna coin belonging to the British period are some pointers.

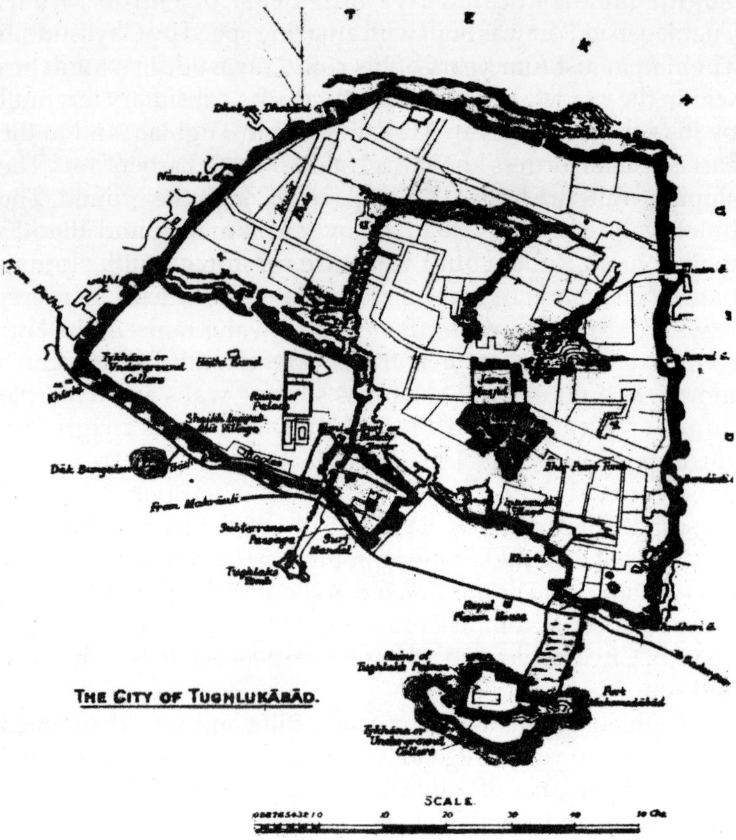

Tughlakabad Fort by John Luard

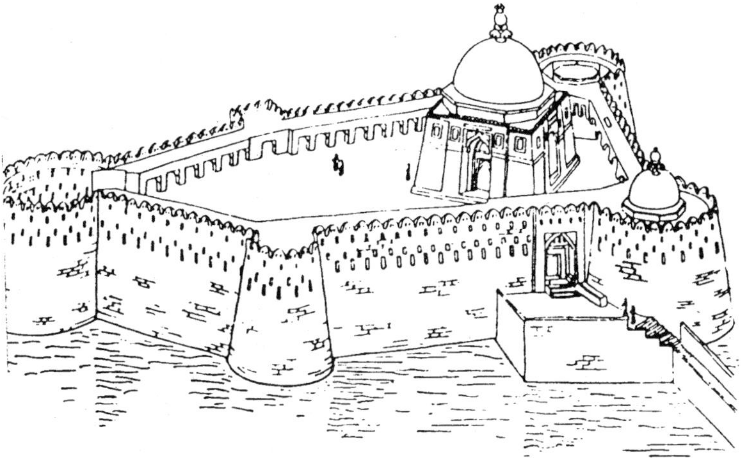

Tomb of Ghyasuddin Tughlaq

During the time of Alauddin Khilji, the tank was repaired and renovated. Feroz Shah further built a dam around it and connected it to Tughlaqabad in 1355-56. The entire water system was based on the principle of gravity with storage tanks and underground tunnels being a part of that. It is believed that about 75,000 litres of water was released every day from these mysterious water systems that extended upto the 'Sat Pula' bridge. Moroccan traveller Iban-e-Batuta in his 'Safarnama-e-Ibn-e-Batuta' writes that the tank was filled with rain water and that it stretched around two miles in length and about a half mile in breadth. The reservoir at 'Shamai Talab' was connected to the Tughalaqabad Fort by a canal known as 'Nau Lakhia Nala'.

Photograph of 'Ruins inside the Fort, Tughlaqabad, Delhi' by Bourne Samuel, 1860s.
Source: Victoria and Albert Museum

Till about two decades ago Tughlaqabad was surrounded by the forests. It was lifeless except wild animals and an isolated tiny village within the Fort. Today it is engulfed by various developments, housing and large unauthorised colonies, named after Tughlaqabad, The stones from the walls of the Fort have been plagarised by the unscruplous builders. There is a need to check indiscriminate and the unplanned developments within and outside the Fort. Besides the maintenance of the Fort by the Archaeological Survey of India, there is a need to conserve its pristine surroundings.

8. Jahanpanah: the Habitat of the World

As one of the most important and historic cities of the world, Delhi has witnessed a cycle of destruction and reconstruction. The city has emerged like the legendary phoenix from ashes to one of the most powerful kingdoms, dominating the history of India. Each ruler has left his mark. More than elsewhere, the history of Delhi highlights the variety of temporal and the living imprints.

After the death of Ghyasuddin Tughlaq, Mohammad Bin Tughlaq ruled from Tughlaqabad for 7 years and then brought disaster to Delhi. He forcefully moved the capital to Daulatabad, towards south India, and ejected all the population from his city. He was a furious tyrant, though also one of the most accomplished prince. Forced shifting of the people of Delhi to Daulatabad had been like making fish to live out of water. Tughlak's grandoise but insensitive and brutal action caused widespread suffering and avoidable torture among his countrymen. Obviously, the scheme was a complete failure. After he realised his mistake, in 1334, he returned the capital again to Delhi. Mohammad Bin Tughlaq built a new city, known as Jahanpanah which was located between Mehrauli and Siri. Jahanpanah which means "World's Asylum", was altogether a new city, different from Tughlaqabad. He did not return to the abandoned Tughlaqabad most likely because he was convinced that it was a cursed city. Jahanpanah was located close to the inhabitated areas between Qila Rai Pithora and Siri. In order to protect the city from incursions, he built defensive fortified walls all around, most of which have disappeared. The north-west wall was stated to be 2.5 Kms long, the east wall about 1 km and the south wall more than 3 kms long. There were thirteen gates; six to the north and seven to the south. A considerable amount of the wall is still existing, which can be seen in Malviya Nagar, Saket, Panchsheel, Asian Games Village, Masjid Moth, Shahpur Jat and many other areas. In an excavation carried out during 1964–65, the eastern wall of Qila Rai Pithora joining with a part of city wall of Jahanpanah was exposed. The excavations revealed three stages of construction and additions.

Hauz Khas Madarsa

There exist several monuments, which are the reminder of the Jahanpanah and the reign of Mohammad bin Tughlaq. Several mosques, tombs and water tanks, now engulfed by the posh urban settlements, still remind the magnificience of the capital. In between the villages of Kalu Sarai and Begumpur lies rubble built octagonal structure called Bijai Mandal or Badee Manjil. It is built on a high platform, with sloping walls. It has lofty doorways at the cardinal points, built in the Tughlaq Style. Towards its east lies the remains of an arcaded residential building, which apparently formed part of the mansion. It is regarded as a bastion of Jahanpanah and was used as the residence by Sheikh Hasan Tahir, a saint during

Sikandar Lodhi's reign (1489–1517). Mohammad bin Tughlaq is said to have used it as a tower for reviewing his troops.

Satpula lying about 800 metre east of the Khirki Masjid is a reservoir built by Mohammad bin Tughlaq to harvest and regulate rain water for irrigation purpose. It has eleven openings, two on each end and seven on the bridge. Satpula means a bridge with seven openings. As each end there is a tower, which is still being used as a school.

Another important monument of Jahanpanah's Delhi is Chirag-i-Dilli's Dargah situated on Malviya Nagar-Kalkaji Road at Village Chiragh. The village was enclosed by a large rubble built rectangular wall. On both the sides, there was a gateway. The Dargah is a square chamber, having a dome supported over twelve pillars. It is enclosed by perforated screens. The main dome is surrounded by smaller domes and turrets on the four

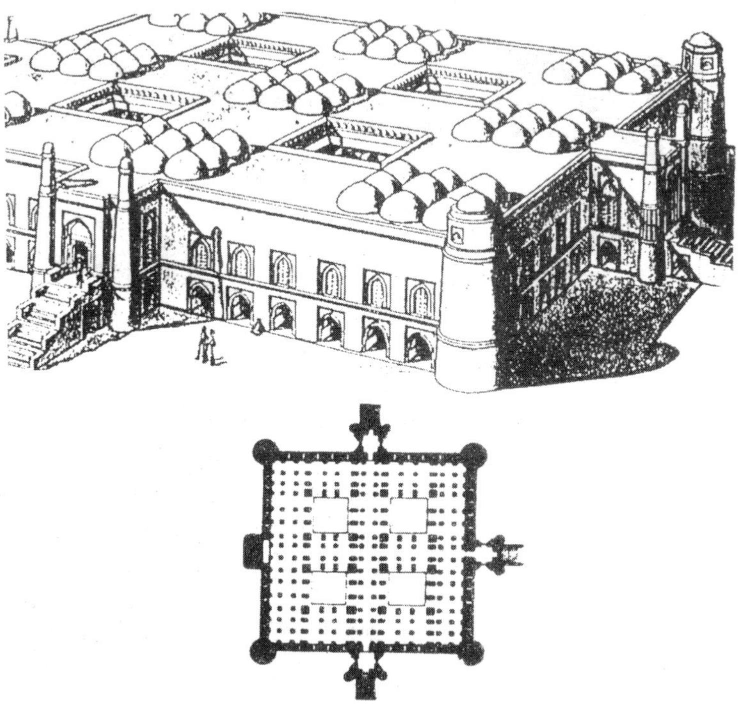

Khirki Masjid (C. 1375)

corners. Besides these, the Jahanpanah area is strewn with many tombs, graves and monuments as its souvenirs.

The tyrant ruler Tamoor Lang recorded following quaint description of the Jahanpanah :

"When my mind was no longer occupied with the destruction of the people of Delhi, I took a ride round the cities. Siri is a round city. Its buildings are lofty, surrounded by strong fortification of stone and brick, Old Delhi has a similar fort, but larger. From one to another—at considerable distance—runs a strong wall built of stone and lime. The city called Jahanpanah is in the centre of the inhabitated area. The fortifications of Jahanpanah had thirteen, Siri seven and Old Delhi (Rai Pithora) ten gates."

Vijay Mandal (Badee Manzil) Jahanpanah

Vijay Mandal (Badee Manzil) and Begumpur Mosque

The city of Jahanpanah built by Muhammad bin Tughlaq, was situated between Qila Rai Pithora and Siri. Parts of the stone built walls of the city and some of the monuments can still be seen at several points. Some of these monuments are now surrounded by the urban village of Begumpur. One such monument is the Vijay Mandal.

Mohammad bin Tughlaq succeeded his father in 1325 AD. His new capital, Jahanpanah had Vijay Mandal for Sultan's public appearances. He was known for implementing ground-breaking ideas. Much ahead of time, he was the one who first introduced the concept of promissory value of currency through introduction of copper coins. Though nothing recognizable remains of this city, the Begumpur Mosque is almost intact, which built on a later date, and marks the heart of Jahanpanah.

Mohammad Shah sat atop the palace to review his troops and cavalry. Aside from the hamams and the zenana, traces of which have been excavated, the palace also included Qasr-e-Hazaar Sutoon—a thousand pillar hall where Mohammad Shah Tughlaq heard his subjects. According to archaeologists, the hall was a two-storeyed structure that rested on huge wooden

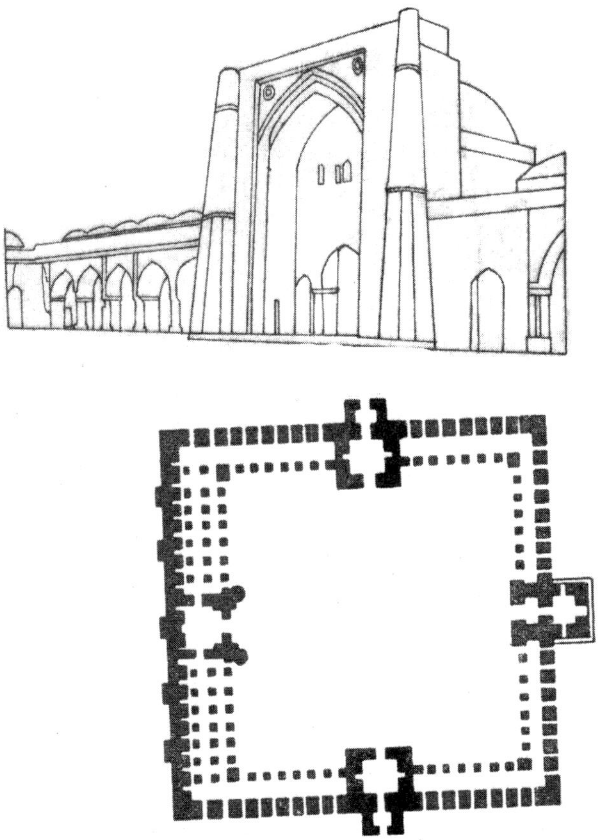

Begumpur Mosque, Jahanpanah

pillars. Over the centuries, the pillars crumbled and the roof collapsed. The only evidence of the structure ever having existed are pillar bases. To the South-east, the beautiful Begumpur Mosque can be seen.

Hidden behind the ungainly structures that have overrun the centuries old Begumpur village, is one of the finest examples of Afghan architecture in Delhi—the little known Begumpur Mosque. This is one of the six mosques built by Juna Shah also known as Khan-e-Jahan, an important minister during the reign of Ferozshah Tuglaq. One has to climb 15 steps from the East to enter the almost square mosque (93 metres x 90 metres). The mosque has two other gates to the north and south as well. All along the parameter of the mosque, there are covered corridors surmounted with small domes, 64 in all. Nine of these are bigger and taller than the rest in the style of the Khirki Mosque—also built by Khan-e-Jahan.

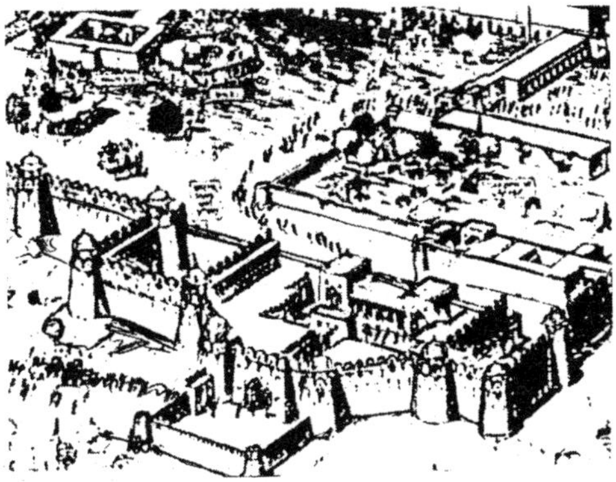

9. Ferozabad—the Rome of Asia

The historians have been fascinated by Delhi. Someone called Delhi "the Rome of Asia" while some believed it to be the most glorious and beautiful empire in the Orient. The fact remains that Delhi offers a rich and interesting anthology of history and architecture. Lying on the bank of Yamuna, the settlement had always been well watered and sheltered from dust storms. According to Martiner Finch, who visited Delhi in 1611, the town (Delhi) comprised of "seven castles and fifty-two gates". He adds that its ruins were sprawling over in miles.

After the death of Mohammad bin Tughlaq, his cousin Ferozeshah succeeded the throne of Delhi empire. The life in the city that time was shattered. The people were adjusting themselves after forcible migration to Daulatabad and then having been brought back to Jahanpanah. Due to the relocation of the capital from Delhi to Daulatabad by his predecessor, there was an acute shortage of skilled masons and builders, who at one time were concentrated in Delhi. This is discernible in the early building of Ferozeshah which comprised of random rubble work and random stone work or ashler. There was hardly any carved building. The Multani influence can be seen in the battered and sloping walls and conical towers crowned by low domes. However, his energetic and dynamic personality revived Delhi and the Tughlaq style came to fruition.

Ferozshah, who was a renowned builder of medieval times, extended the city from old Indraprastha to the ridge and then new capital known as Ferozabad flourished. For the first time Yamuna Canal was constructed to irrigate and for transportation. In 1354, he brought two sandstone pillars bearing Ashokan inscriptions from Meerut and Ambala and placed one at the ridge (Jahanuma) and another at Kotla Ferozeshah (Ferozabad). The third century B.C. Ashoka Pillar in polished sandstone with Brahmi script inscriptions is 43 metres high and weighs 23 Tons. The edicts promulgate religious observance against killing and eating of animals listed in detail, (ants, queen ants, terapins and prawns, for example). He built Khirki Masjid, tomb and Madarsa at Hauz Khas which is a beautiful complex of mosque, open classrooms, spacious garden and a large water tank. Another embankment built by him is found at Mahipalpur, where he also raised a hunting place. Kalan Masjid and Chausanth Khamba are the other notable monuments built by Ferozshah. Chausanth Khamba was built in Nizamuddin with carved marble pillars and trellises. Out of its original 64 pillars only 36 are discernible. Ferozshah also repaired Qutab Minar and is credited to have built other significant monuments, viz., Begumpur mosque (near Malviya Nagar) and adjacent Bijai Mandal and Bara Khamba. He is also credited for building several hunting lodges in the forests of the ridge. Among these lodges, Bhooli Bhatiyari Ka Mahal, Pir Ghalib and Malcha Mahal are still surviving.

Ferozshah's reign also witnessed construction of several important mosques. His Prime Minister Khan-i-Jahan Junan Shah built seven famous mosques in Delhi. Kali or Kalan Masjid at Turkman Gate, another at Nizamuddin, Khirki Masjid, Ferozshah mosque, Begumpur mosque and Kalusarai Masjid still remain important and well known mosques of Delhi. These mosques are characterised by robust rubble walls, chajjas, low domes, simple design, sloping minarates at the corners and at the entrances. The most prominent feature is massive arch and buttressed pylons which support the entire composition including the dome.

Source : Archaeological Survey of India.

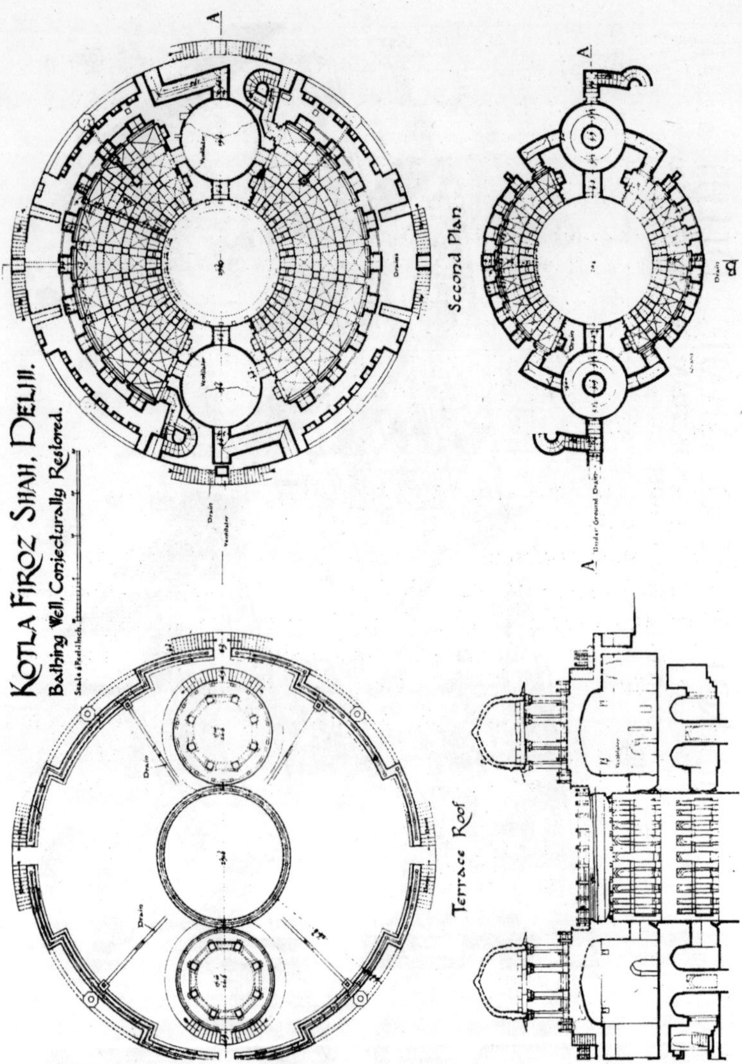

Source : Archaeological Survey of India.

Two tombs of that period are quite significant, which are the tomb of Ferozshah Tughlaq and the tomb of Khan-i-Jahan Tilangani, his prime minister, who died in 1369. Ferozshah Tomb is situated within Hauz-i-Khas at the junction of the two wings of Madarsa and is built in Tughlaq style. It is a powerful, restrained and austere building with sloping walls and a contoured dome. The Tilangani tomb is remarkable for its elegant conception and octagon shape. It has projecting chajjas and a series of eight small cupolas over the parapet. It dominated the tomb architecture and remained a model for more then 200 years. The chajja was a new concept in Islamic architecture, introducing an opportunity for playful effect of light and shade on the facade.

Due to the shortage of water at Mehrauli, Ferozshah moved his capital to the new city called Ferozabad which is now known as Ferozshah Kotla. Its grandeur surpassed the earlier capitals and it was much larger and sophisticated than Tughlaqabad. It is a large enclosure of high walls along which then flowed the river Yamuna. Though Ferozshah Kotla is now in ruins, it originally contained a larger palace facing the river Yamuna, besides public halls, gardens, mosques, a pigeon tower and a baoli (tank). Towards the centre of the complex, raised high on a pyramidical structure, is the Ashoka's famous pillar, which was brought from Topra (Ambala).

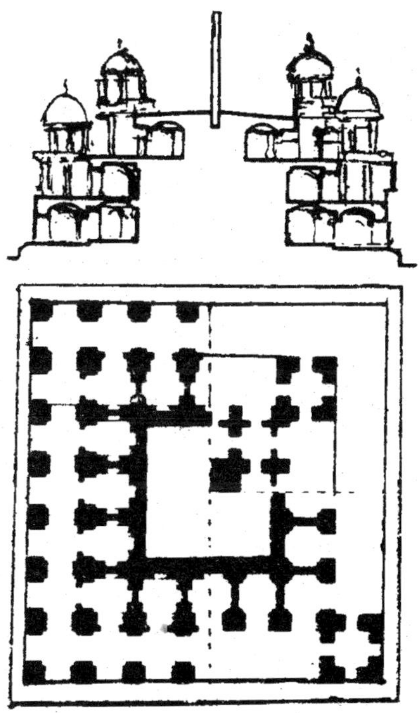

Kotla Feroz Shah, Delhi

Inscription on Ashokan Pillar at Kotla Feroz Shah

Ferozshah's rich heritage of buildings brought much glory and fame to the capital city. At the same time its riches, splendour and beauty inflicted danger from the plunderers. During a brief interlude of two weeks in December 1398 Delhi passed through a nightmare when Tamoor Lang plundered Delhi. He proceeded to Meerut on 1st January 1399. This brought an abrupt end of the Tughlaq dynasty.

The Saiyyad dynasty followed the Tughlaqs, who did not leave behind much historical evidence in the form of monuments.

10. Delhi of Saiyyads and Lodhis

Delhi with its strong ethnic and cultural characteristics acted as a chohesive super-regional force. Its culture, literature and history had been cosmopolitan and diverse. The chequered history of Delhi presents a spectrum of continuing tension between diversifying and unifying cultural forces. The alien rulers assorted their individual identities, while absorbing the local customs and rich culture. Persistent invasions from the north-west dominate the history of Delhi from early sultanate period. After the death of Ferozshah Tughlaq became the ruler of Delhi. In 1398, Tamoor Lang invaded India and Delhi suffered his wrath. There was merciless killings and indiscriminate looting. Although Tamoor retreated back, but Delhi could not recover from the onslaught. There was infighting between various rulers and provincial governors. After the death of Mohammad Tughlaq, in 1413, Khizr Khan, the governor of Punjab ascended the throne of Delhi. He founded the Saiyyad dynasty. During his reign, it was a dark age for city building and architecture. No cities, palaces or mosques were built, but only countless tombs and mausoleums were in the field of funerary architecture. Two types of tombs came into existance, that is, octagonal and square. The octagonal tombs were usually the style and pattern of Tilangani tombs, of these three were stately tombs, and had some significance. These include the tomb of Mubarakpur, the tomb of Mohammad Saiyyad and Sikandar Lodhi in the Lodhi Garden.

Bridge of old Delhi. Behind a bridge that now stands on the north-eastern edge of Lodi Gardens, lies the octagonal tomb of Sikander Lodhi. The Lodhi dynasty was last in a series of five (Mamluk, Khilji, Tughlaq, Saiyyad, Lodhi) that ruled from Delhi before it was conquered by the Mughals. The mausoleum is surrounded by a square garden, enclosed within high walls.

Another type of tombs of the period are square in plan with hemisphere boat keel domes. Most of these are isolated structures, without enclosing walls, which are popularly called, 'Gumbad'. These tombs are double-storeyed. The central portion of each side is projected thus forming a vertical rectangle. The sides of the rectangle and the corner of the structure are provided with the pinnacles. These square tombs are higher than the octagonal tombs, but cover less area. The most notable of these tombs are Kale Khan's Gumbad (1491), Bhure Khan's Gumbad (1497), and Chotte Khan's Gumbad (1496), Bare Khan's Gumbad (1497). The Sheesh Gumbad in Lodhi Garden was decorated with glazed tiles, from which it derives its name 'dome of glass' Sikander Lodhi in 1501 built Shihabu'd-din Khan's tomb known as Bagh-I-Alam Ka Gumbad. This is one of the most beautiful domes of that era. Khizr Khan's son and successor Muizu'd-din Mubarak Shah found the city Mubarakbad, along the river

Yamuna, but no trace of it remains. He died in 1434 and his tomb is in Kotla Mubarakpur. It is octagonal, with a central chamber and varandahs around it. The tomb of Mohammad Shah which lies in the Lodhi Garden is more impressive than the tomb of Mubarak Shah. It has a raised drum and high chattries, which make it spectacular. The tomb of Sikandar Lodhi is at the northwest corner of Lodhi Garden. It is octagonal on plan with Persian double dome and Hindu decoration of lotus motif. The mosque and a square garden enclosure were later adopted widely by Mughals in their tomb architecture.

Bahlul Lodhi's tomb at Chiragh Delhi is an ordinary square structure, each side broken by three arched openings. Its roof is surmounted by five domes. Although the public mosques were built during this period, several private structure incorporate interesting changes, which paved the way in the design of great mosques of the following Mughal period. Two mosques deserve special mention. The Bara Gumbad mosque in Lodhi Garden,

Lodhi Tomb by Capt. James Luard. The tomb stands on a large plinth having several graves.

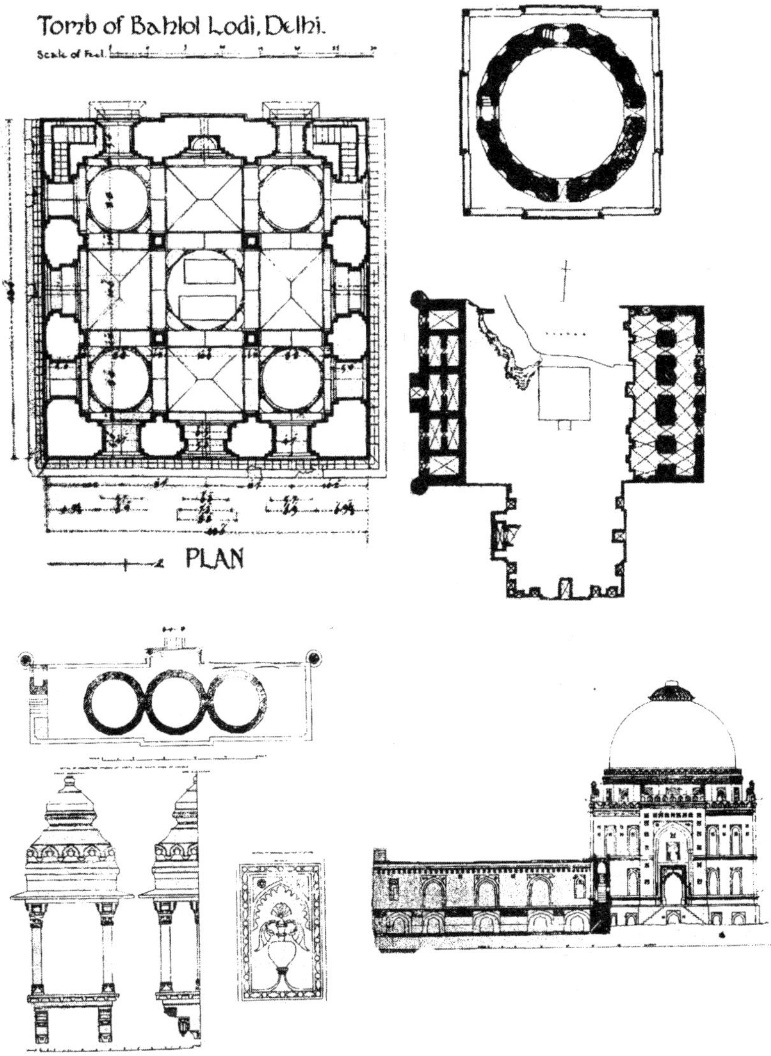

Above Left: Bahlol Lodhi's Tomb. Above centre and right-Bara Gumbad mosque.

Source: Archaeological Survey of India.

Tomb of Sikandar Lodhi: Built in 1518 is set in a square garden enclosed within high walls. The concept of an enclosed tomb garden was later refined to perfection in Humayun's Tomb and the Taj Mahal.

Sheesh Gumbad named after the glazed turquoise tiles which once adorned its facade.

Tomb of Mohammad Shah: The oldest tomb in the garden, built in 1450 for the last of the Saiyyad rulers. The octagonal plan on which it is constructed is typical Mughal.

Athpula: built during Akbar's reign, it was on eight-piered bridge.

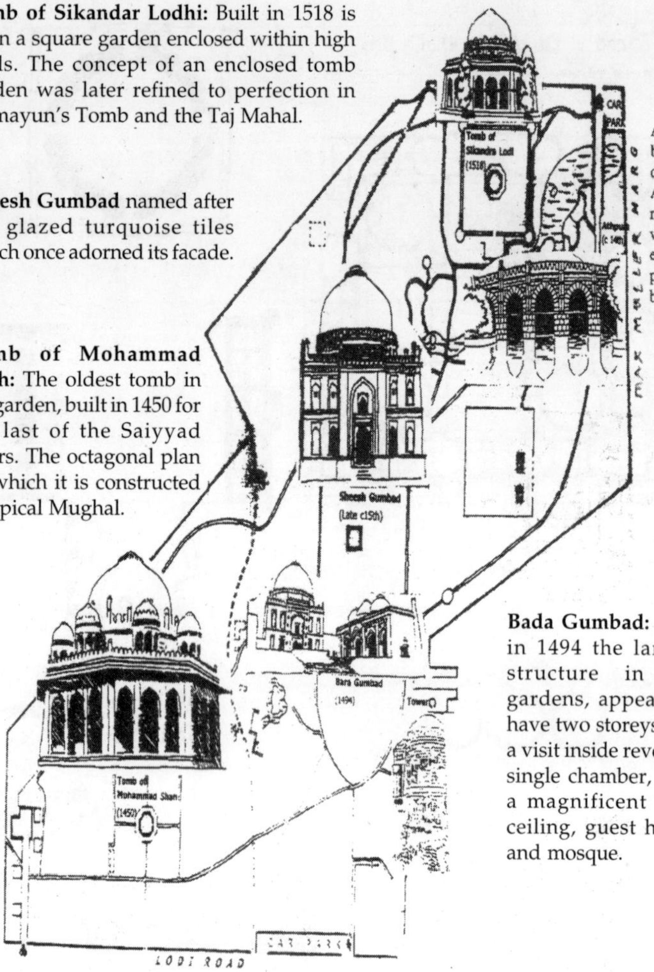

Bada Gumbad: Built in 1494 the largest structure in the gardens, appears to have two storeys. But a visit inside reveals a single chamber, with a magnificent high ceiling, guest house and mosque.

Lodhi Garden manifests the climax of landscape and architecture of the Saiyyads and Lodhis was built in 1494. Bara Gumbad mosque is divided into five bays with end beys roofed by low vaults. It is surmounted by three domes, which are resting on corbelled pendentives. It has a double storey facade. It is ornamented with coloured tiles and foliage. It had sloping buttresses, double storey corner tower and oriel windows.

In 1931 when New Delhi was nearing completion, the Lodhi Tombs stood in the village of Khairpur, on the outskirts of New Delhi. In 1936 the villagers were moved from Khairpur and the garden was laid out with native and exotic trees and plants around the monuments. It was at first called Lady Willingdon Park, after the wife of the then British Viceroy. This was changed to Lodhi Garden after 1947. The Lodhi Gardens were designed in 1936 as a setting for a group of fine, five hundred year old buildings.

Kotla Mubarakpur

Kotla Mubarakpur is named after Mubarak Shah the second ruler of the Saiyyad dynasty who built Mubarakabad. Around his tomb are an adjoining mosque, a closed up Baoli and a Gumti that have survived the ravages of time. The tomb of Mubarak Shah dated 1433 AD, stands on an octagonal platform. A wall surrounding the tomb does not exist now except for the western and southern gateways.

Adjoining to Mubarak Shah's tomb is a mosque, which is enclosed within the walls which originally surrounded the tomb. The two way deep mosque is divided into five compartments. The mosque has a big courtyard. According to local people there was a well in the courtyard of the mosque that has been filled up.

Tomb at Kotla Mubarakpur

Source: Zafar Hasan / ASI

About 50 yards to the north-west of the tomb is a closed-up Baoli, measuring 90 feet from north to south and 38 feet from east to west. It was built in five stages, each growing narrower towards the bottom. At the southern end lay a circular well. At the upper ground level there were arched dalans on the eastern, western and the southern sides. The Baoli is now being used for storing fruit crates. There is also a Gumti standing on a raised platform, in this area which is kind of domed octagonal pavilion made of rubble. These Gumtis belong to the Lodhi period.

Tomb of Sikandar Lodhi

Source: Zafar Hasan/ASI

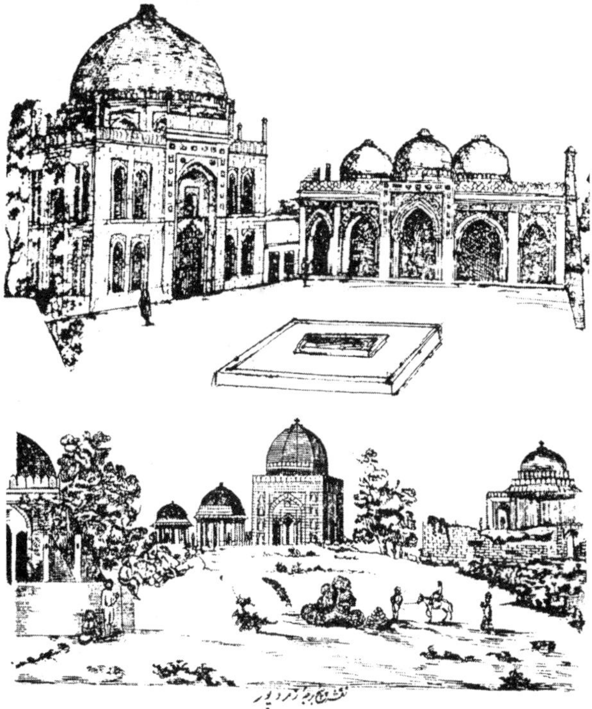

Zamrudpur ruins and tombs

Source: Zafar Hasan / ASI

Barakhamba Tomb (17th Century) in Delhi Golf Course.

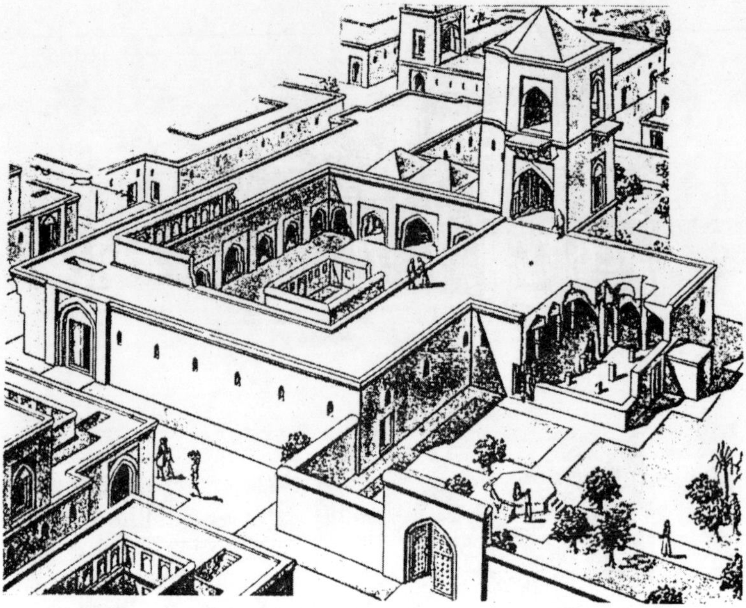

Mansion at Begumpur, the residence of a nobleman of Lodhi Dynasty (1451-1517)

The Moth-ki-masjid, built by Miyan Bhuwa has a more open, robust style. It is raised on a platform with underground halls. Its prayer chambers are surmounted by three domes over five arched openings. The central dome is the highest and is faced with tiled medallions. It was constructed in a very bold and bare manner, unadorned by any carvings, mouldings, or refinement in the masonry.

With its little achievement, the Lodhi reign came to an abrupt end. After the death of Sikandar Lodhi, his son Ibrahim Lodhi came to power, who was a suspicious and capricious person. He is said to maltreat nobles and provincial governors. As a result there were continuous rebellions. His uncle, Daulat Khan Lodhi, the governor of Lahore, invited Babar, the great Mughal, to attack Delhi. In the battle of Panipat in 1526, Babar humbled and killed Ibrahim and occupied Delhi and Agra. Thus came the end of Sultanate era in Delhi. It also heralded the beginning of a new chapter in the glory of the city which acquired a cosmopolitan character.

11. Din-panah—the Abode of the Poor

Whereas the annals of Sultanate era in Delhi present a picture of violence, treachery, fanaticism, the great Mughals brought artistic and cultural sophistication. Babar, the descendent of Tamoor and Genghiz Khan, invaded India and founded the dynasty of the great Mughals in India. He was man of culture and taste, though most of the time he was engaged in the wars. He was very fond of gardens and laid two formal gardens—one at Panipat and another at Agra. He constructed a small mosque in Palam Village, which was built in brick with three arched opening. Another mosque which is much more refined, is Jamali-Kamali mosque in Mehrauli. This was started by Babar, but could only be completed during the reign of Humayun. Humayun ascended the throne after the death of his father Babar in 1530. In 1533, he laid the foundation of his city Din-Panah, on the western bank of river Yamuna. It took him less than ten months to complete the walls, bastions and gates of the city. The building material from the Alau'd-din-Khilji's abandoned city Siri was used for Din-Panah. It is said that Humayun took a long time to decide the site and consulted learned men and astrologers.

In 1540 Shershah Suri defeated Humayun, who fled to Iran. Shershah Suri raised his own city at the site of Purana Qila. He pulled down the walls, gates and bastions of Din-Panah systematically to reconstruct the Purana Qila. There is no trace of the city of Din-Panah now. In July 1555, Humayun defeated Shershah Suri and returned to the throne of Delhi. He completed the remaining city at the Purana Qila which was left unfinished by Shershah. He also completed the mosque of Jamali-Kamali. Jamali's Tomb, lying next to the Mosque was ornamented by glazed tiles. Surmounted by single high dome, oriel windows and octagonal towers, it has an important place in the evolution of the Mughal architecture. Both architecturally and administratively the Mughal empire was in debt to Shershah Suri who laid the foundation on which they built. It was the beginning of the glorious Islamic architecture in India, which developed in two distinct phases.

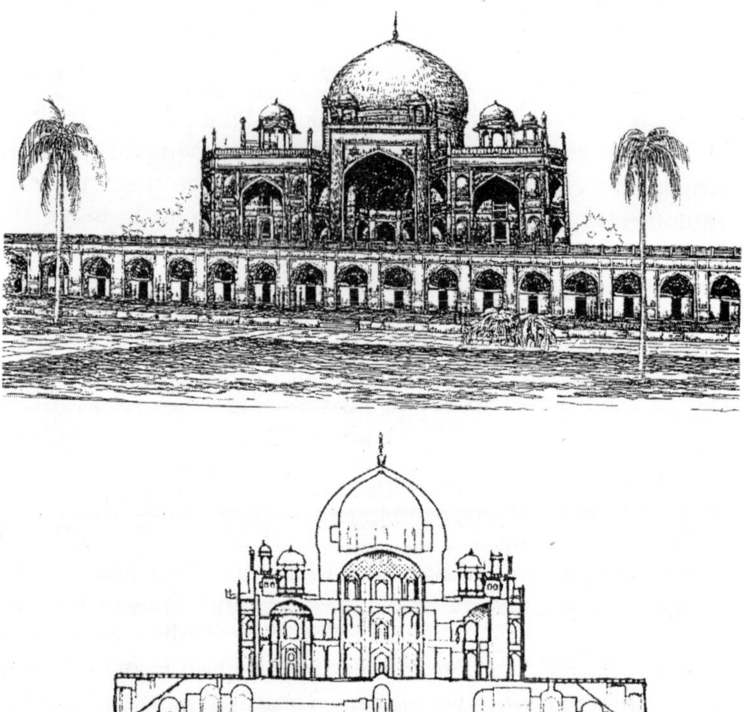

The Humayun Tomb

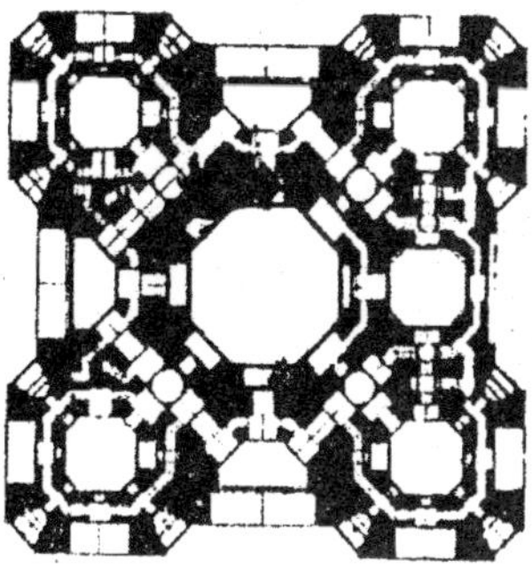

Plan of Tomb

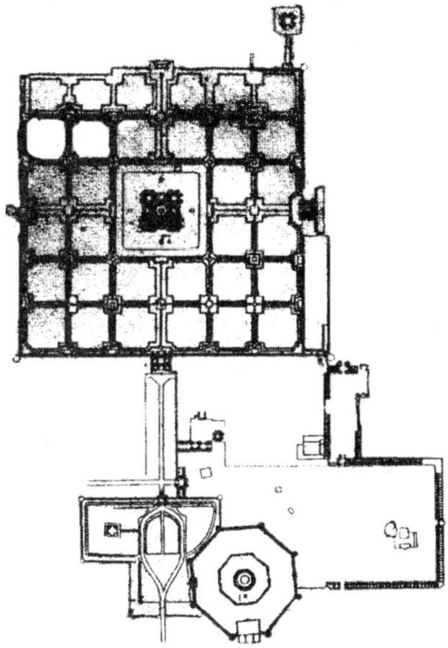

The layout showing the tomb surrounded by Charbagh garden.

Humayun Tomb and Surrounding Park: The Humayun Tomb presages the development of a mature style of a garden tomb, which culminated seventy years later in the incomparable Taj Mahal.

The earlier buildings were constructed in red sandstone with marble relief and were masculine in outlook. In the later era, particularly during the Shahjahan reign, the style reached its apogee. White marble, bulbous domes, high minarates and feminine beauty are the hallmarks of the second phase. Though Humayun reign lasted only about a year, yet it was fruitful. He brought from Persia its decorative arts, culture and religion. With the help of Persian craftsmen and artists, he set up a royal school of building and painting. This helped in cross breeding of Indian architecture with the arts of Persia. He died in 1556, while descending from the stairs of Sher Mandal, which is believed to have been used by him as a library.

Humayun's Tomb on Mathura Road is an outstanding landmark in the development of the Mughal architecture. It was designed in 1564, eight years after his death. This was built by his widow Bega Begum, popularly known as Haji Begum. Some historians believe that Humayun himself planned the tomb on the basis of the ideas he acquired during his exile in Persia. But, there is no such concrete evidence. The architect Mirak Mirza of Persia chose the site near river Yamuna and employed Persian crafts and techniques. It is a careful synthesis of the Persian and Indian traditions in architecture. The plan comprised of a central octagon, surrounded by four chambers in each corner. The dome is a double shell. The shape of these arches and alcoves reflect the Persian influence, whereas kiosks, cupola, chattris, marble inlay work on sandstone elevation of the tomb were designed according to the traditional Indian concept. The integration of the two concepts presage the development of a mature and sophisticated style. It is also the first mature example of the idea of garden tomb, which can be seen almost seventy years later in the incomparable Taj Mahal.

Within the compound of the Humayun Tomb, on its south-east lies the tomb of a Babar, built in late 16th century. Another important drum domed tomb, with its blue tiles, known as Nila Gumbad was built in 1625 by Abdul Rahim Khan-i-Khana. It is said to contain the remains of his faithful attendant Rahim Khan. Arab Sarai, adjoining the South-West corner of the Humayun Tomb, was built to lodge the Persian workers and craftmen,

Tomb of Abdur Rahim Khan-I-Khanan

On the main road that connects Nizamuddin to Jangpura stands a large, domed tomb that looks vandalised. Unlike the dressed stone or plaster finishes of other structures, the tomb has much of its rubble masonry exposed. The Tomb of Abdur Rahim Khan-i-Khanan is striking, its history is interesting, and the man himself was highly accomplished.

Mausoleum of Nizamuddin. The Tomb of the Sufi Saint Hazrat Nizamuddin Aulia with the Jamaat Khana Mosque in the background.

Sufi Shrine of Nizamuddin the Chishti saint (circa 1325). This is a devotional poster from the collection of Yousef Saeed.

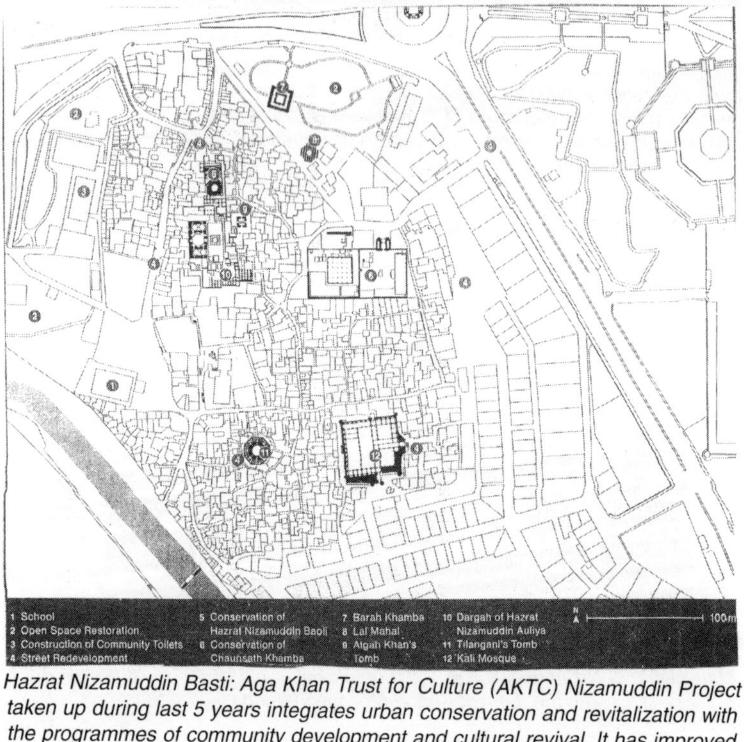

Hazrat Nizamuddin Basti: Aga Khan Trust for Culture (AKTC) Nizamuddin Project taken up during last 5 years integrates urban conservation and revitalization with the programmes of community development and cultural revival. It has improved the conditions of education, health and employment.

Source: Aga Khan Trust for Culture, New Delhi.

who were engaged in building the Humayun Tomb. Afsar Wala Mosque and Tomb, Bua Halima's garden, Sunderwala Mahal and Burj, Lakkarwala Burj, Subj Burj, Nili Chattri and Bare Batashewala Mahal remind about the grandeur of the early Mughal architecture.

Humayun's son, Akbar succeeded Humayun in 1556 and shifted the capital to Agra. During Akbar's reign Adam Khan's Tomb near Mehrauli was built in 1562. Adam Khan who had enraged Akbar, was dashed to death from the Fort. The tomb has an interesting Bhul Bhulaiya inside. Another reminder of Akbar is the tomb of Atgah Khan, Akbar's foster father and that of his sons Mirza Aziz, both located in Nizamuddin. The beautiful tombs are built to red sandstone with marble tiles and perforated screens (1566–67). Close to Lal Darwaza is Maham Anka's Madarsa which was the scene of an attempted assassination of Akbar. Its high walls and brilliant tiles evoke a sense of quientness and grace. Another remarkable monument of this period is Ugrasen-ki-Baoli, situated on Hailey Road. It is a stepped water tank built by the Hindu noble Ugra Sen.

Jahangir, son of Akbar, succeeded to throne in 1603. He shifted the capital to Lahore and Delhi lapsed into oblivion.

12. Shergarh—the Citadel of Shershah Suri

History repeats itself. The ancient site of historical Purana Qila had been the venue of the capital of several eras of history. Beginning with the Indraprastha, the capital of Pandavas, the excavations reveal inhabitations of the vicinity time and again. It had been a living city during the Kushan, Saka, Gupta, Sultanate and Mughal periods. Mughal Emperor Humayun, laid the foundation of Din-Panah near Purana Qila in 1533. In 1540, he was deposed by Shershah of the Afgan dynasty. Shershah constructed a new city in the vicinity, extending upto Ferozabad. Amid the greenery, the relics of his city lie scattered.

The architectural heritage of Suri dynasty discerns two distinct styles. The first phase emerged between 1530–40 during his reign from Sasaram and Narnaul in Bihar. There he built magnificient tombs, forts and mosques. The second phase occurred between 1540–45 when he overthrew the Mughal emperor Humayun and raised a citadel at Delhi. He rebuilt his city mainly in and around the Purana Qila which was also the site of Humayun's Din-panah. He built a sprawling city on the bank of river Yamuna and gave it the name—'Shergarh'. The extensive city of Shergarh was fortified with an entrance gate—Khuni Darwaza on the west. The northern gate was called 'Talaqi Darwaza' (Forbidden gate). It has oriel windows on its facade. The gate is decorated with carved leographs, engaged in combat with men. Originally, the exterior was decorated with coloured tiles. The southern gate, called Humayun Darwaza, has similar panels with elephants. It faces the Delhi zoo. The design of these gateways reveals an interesting mixture of Hindu and Muslim styles of architecture. The pointed Islamic arch is blended with Hindu Chattris and brackets.

Purana Qila Gateway

"O God preserve the house (of Humayun) from damage", says one of the ink transcriptions on the Talaqi Gate at the northern gate of the fort. This Forbidden Gate, as it is also known, is made of grey and red sandstone, and is replete with history. Legend has it that a certain king sallied out of this gate to fight a rebel and vowed he would never enter the city unless he vanquished the enemy. The king fell in battle, never returned and the gate remained closed till 1912 AD. It is flanked by two huge bastions and has a hole in the arch head, with a frame of yellow sandstone, through which missiles, hot oil or quicklime could be dropped on the attacking forces. The front portion of the gate is decorated with marble with sculptures in which a leopard has been engaged in a mortal combat with a man.

The Qila-i-kuhna Masjid, also known as Shershah mosque was built in 1542. It is in front of the Purana Qila. It was a product of his extraordinary egotism, influenced by anticipatory Mughal architecture with the ornamentation of Afghan architecture. It illustrates the skill and expertise of Suri craftsmen. The mosque exhibits a disciplined and balanced composition of geometry. Its prayer hall has a large dome, which is flanked by chattris. The cloister under the dome has five arched openings. The dome of the mosque is skillfully raised over four central arches, set in a rectangular frame. The dome is fringed with lotus cusps and is articulated by the horizontal lines of projecting chajja. The Mihrab on the western hall is uniquely designed by sinking one arch into another. It is richly decorated with relief. The double-storeyed mosque has oriel windows and three-storeyed towers on the rear.

To the south of the mosque is Sher Mandal, which is double-storeyed octagonal tower. It is built in red stone relieved by marble. The interior is decorated with glazed tiles. The purpose of the tower is not known. May be it was originally intended as a pleasure tower, but it was used by Humayun as a library. After the death of Shershah, his son, Islam Shah, also known as Salim Shah succeeded to the throne. Salim Garh, which is situated on the north east of the Red Fort, on the bank of river Yamuna is believed to have been built by him. It is triangular in plan, and is built with thick rubble ramparts and circular bastions. This small fort remained abandoned and was used for building the railway and road bridge during the middle of nineteenth century.

In 1547, octagonal tomb of Isa Khan was built, which is near Humayun Tomb. This is another small remain of Shershah's reign in Delhi. Isa Khan was a nobleman during the reign of Shershah and his son Islam Shah.

The Old Fort, Delhi
Source: Painting by Thomas and William Daniel in 1796, (INTACH, 2010)

In July 1555, Humayun recaptured the throne by defeating Sikandar Shah Suri, the last descendent of Shershah. Humayun who died in January 1556 completed parts of the Purana Qila, i.e., Shergarh and maintained the buildings erected by his predecessors.

Babur stormed India in 1526 AD and established the Mughal (Persian for Mongol) dynasty. In 1530 AD, Humayun on being enthroned on his father's death, shifted from Agra and made Din-panah his new capital. The Old Fort stands evidence to the fact, though major structures that lie within the precincts today were constructed by Sher Shah who dethroned Humayun. After the death of Sher Shah, Humayun recaptured Delhi and ruled till his death due to a fall from the staircase of Sher Mandal, which still exists. The Quila-i-Kuhran Mosque, or Mosque of Shershah, lies just beyond it and is in a fairly reasonable condition.

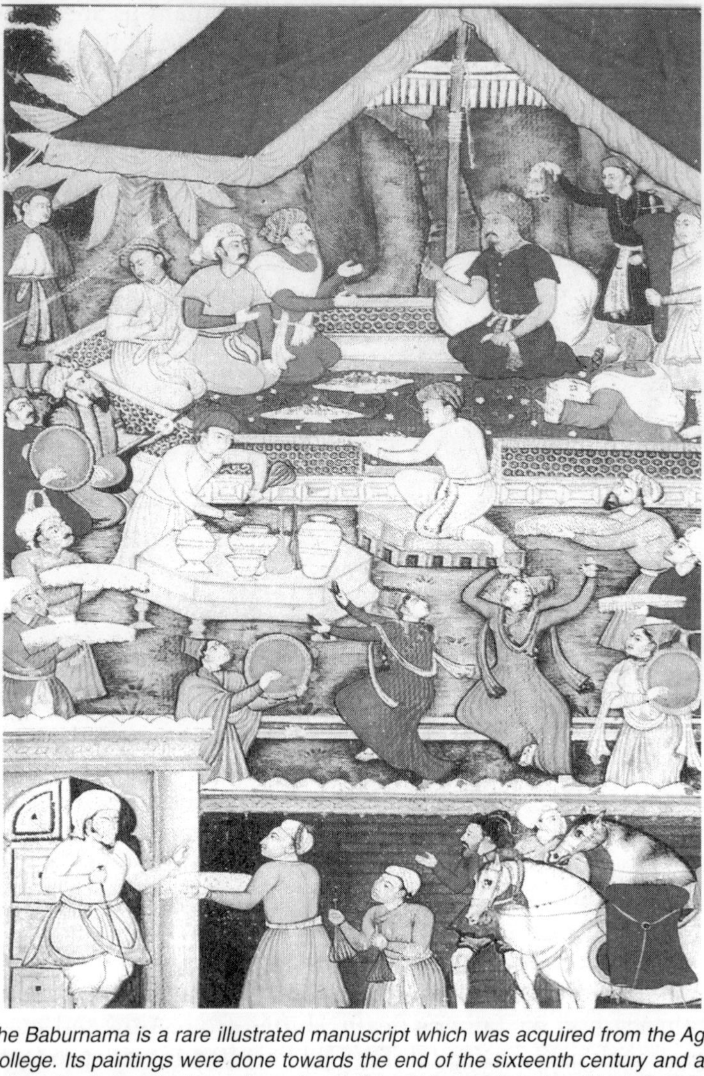

The Baburnama is a rare illustrated manuscript which was acquired from the Agra College. Its paintings were done towards the end of the sixteenth century and are believed to belong to the mature phase of the Akbar period when Mughal art was still deeply influenced by Persian art. This beautifully illustrated manuscript in the Nasta', liq script is dated 1598 and consists of 378 folios with 145 illustrations. Its cover page bears the signature of the Mughal Emperor Shahjahan. Forty-nine artists worked on this set, including great names such as Daulat, Bhawani, Mansur, Miskin and Farrukh Chela.

Source: National Museum, New Delhi

The Khooni Darwaza, Opposite Ferozshah Kotla

The Khooni Darwaza (Near Delhi Gate)

The Gate came to be known as the Khooni Darwaza during the Mughal days. It was constructed in 1540s during Sher Shah's reign. Since it was an the outskirts of the city, it was used presumably both as an outpost and the place where heads of criminals were exhibited. Emperor Jahangir in the early decades of the 17th century ordered the killing of the two sons of Abdur Rahim Khan-e-Khanan here on a trumped-up charge that they were traitors. Aurangzeb had his elder brother, Dara Shikoh's head displayed at this gate. Later, on September 22, 1857 the sons of Bahadur Shah Zafar, Mirza Mughal and Mirza Khizr Sultan and grandson Mirza Abu Bakar, were murdered at the gate by Major Hudson after the king surrendered to the British. During the riots of 1947 the Khooni Darwaza again saw much bloodshed. The refugees were murdered here while proceeding to Purana Quila for safety.

After the death of Humayun, Salim Shah (1550–55) built Salimgarh Fort on the bank of river Yamuna, towards the north of Ferozshah Kotla. In 1556, Akbar shifted the capital of Agra and in 1603, Jahangir shifted the capital further, from Agra to Lahore. As a result Delhi went into the oblivion, until Shahjahan brought back the capital to Delhi and founded Shahjahanabad in 1638.

13. Shahjahanabad—the Glory of the Orient

Agar firdaus bar roo-e-zameen ast, Hameen ast- o hameen ast- o hameen ast.

If there is a paradise of earth, It is here, it is here, it is here.

– Amir Khushro

From the ancient times, Delhi had been a seat of power. There is a saying—"He who rules Delhi, rules India." The influence of Delhi has dominated over other regions. Geographically its location has been suitable from the point of view of protection. It had also been a convergence point of strategic land routes. The site of Shahjahanabad had been chosen mainly for two reasons. Firstly, the availability of high land on the western bank of river Yamuna and secondly the natural fortification provided by the two arms of Aravali ranges and the river Yamuna, forming three sides of the triangular site.

After Delhi, then known as Shergarh and Din-panah, had been in oblivion for some 80 years, Shahjahan in 1638, brought back the capital of Mughals from Lahore to Delhi and ordered the construction of a totally new city. He selected its site on the western bank of the Yamuna to the north of the Purana Qila. He called the city after his own name, Shahjahan-abad, which means the settlement created by the ruler of the universe.

Shahjahanabad along River Yamuna
Drawing by A Maclure, 1857

The Persian engineer Ali Murdan Khan supervised the works. He made immaculate and novel arrangements for water supply to the city. A canal system was laid linking the river Yamuna to fulfil the need of water. Shahjahanabad was secured and enclosed by about ten kilometer long wall. Ten gates connected the city with the surrounding region. Lahore gate was the main entrance for the Red Fort, besides Delhi Gate. The Kashmere Gate, Calcutta Gate, Mori Gate, Kabul Gate, Farash Khana Gate, Ajmere Gate and the Turkman Gate were the other major links of the city with the highways.

Shahjahanabad Chronology

1627	:	Shahjahan as the emperor
1638–48	:	Capital shifted from Lahore/Agra to Delhi (Shahjahanabad)
1707–12	:	Bahadur Shah (Lahore as capital)
1714–17	:	Embassy of East India Company
1713–37	:	Emperor Farrukhsiyar and Bahadur Shah Zafar
1724	:	Jantar Mantar built by Maharaja Jai Singh
9.4.1737	:	Baji Rao, defeated at Kalka Devi Temple
9.4.1739	:	Nadirshah defeats Mohammad Shah at Panipat and enters Delhi
1754	:	Safdarjung (Safdarjung Tomb)
1782	:	Famine in Delhi
1786–88	:	Nazaf Khan as the ruler

Shahjahanabad is a climax of city planning of the Mughal era. It was designed as a major trading centre of the Mughals with Chandni Chowk as its centrepiece. Its structure was conceived with a network of landmarks, focal points, linear markets and a spatial subdivision. The Red Fort, the Royal Palace was the head of the city, and a focal point for the fashionable Chandni Chowk. It was located on the bank of the river so as to dominate the cityscape. The accommodation on eastern and northern sides was provided to the rich and noble class. The proximity of the house to the palace determined the status of a person. Two commercial boulevards, Chandni Chowk and Faiz Bazaar were created, of which Chandni Chowk was the central axis of the city. The original bazaar had octagonal chowks, with a water channel excavated by Ali Mardan, running through the centre of the road. Its wide boulevard was an instantaneous success and created a scale of its own. The vista of the boulevard terminated at the Fatehpuri Mosque. Jama Masjid, was located on the Bhoja Pahari so as to dominate the whole city visually. The geometry of the layout of Jama Masjid, Red Fort, Chandni Chowk and Faiz Bazaar was formal, while the rest of the city was planned in an organic pattern. A system of Mohallas and Katras was developed to suit the homogeneous community structure.

The Red Fort, built of red sandstone was commenced in May 1639 and is a masterpiece of Mughal architecture. The Fort was originally surrounded by a wide moat and contained numerous buildings. Inside the fort there were many gardens, fountains and a canal known as Nehar-i-Bahisht (The stream of paradise). The Red Fort is entered through the Lahori Gate. Chatta Chowk, the adjacent shopping arcade was once the hub of world famous Indian handicrafts and commercial transactions. Naubat Khana is the next in the sequence, where court musicians were seated. Diwan-i-Aam and Diwan-i-Khas and the flanking Rang Mahal are the exclusive and sumptuous pavilions in the Red Fort. The red sandstone walls of the fort are decorated with marble pietra-dura, inlaid with precious stones. Diwan-i-Khas contained the famous peacock throne which eventually was carried off to Persia by Nadirshah.

Other notable features in Red Fort are the Hayat Baksh Garden and Sawan and Bhadon pavilions, Hamam Khana, Mumtaz Mahal and Moti Masjid. Across the Red Fort, Jama Masjid, the Royal Mosque was built. It was designed by Ustad Khalil. It remained the largest mosque in the world for 300 years and its grandeur and splendour still attract the visitors and pilgrims from all over the world.

During the reign of Emperor Shahjahan, many large gardens were also laid and planted. Of these, Roshanara Garden, Shalimar Bagh and Begum Bagh (Queen's Garden) are still surviving. In 1670 Aurangzeb took over the rule from Shahjahan. He built 12 metre high defensive barbican in from of the Red Fort and also built Moti Masjid which is among one of the finest examples of Mughal architecture.

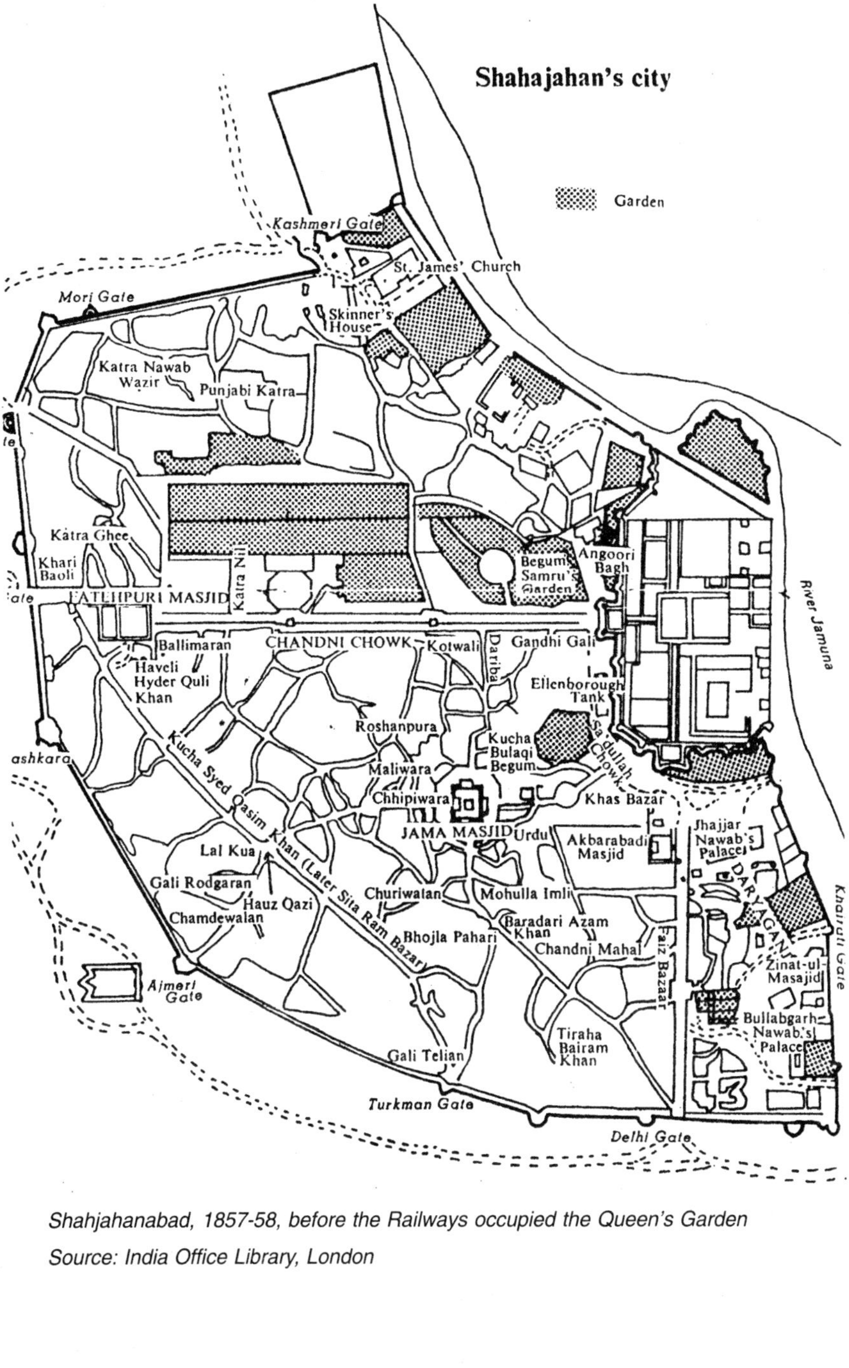

Shahjahanabad, 1857-58, before the Railways occupied the Queen's Garden

Source: India Office Library, London

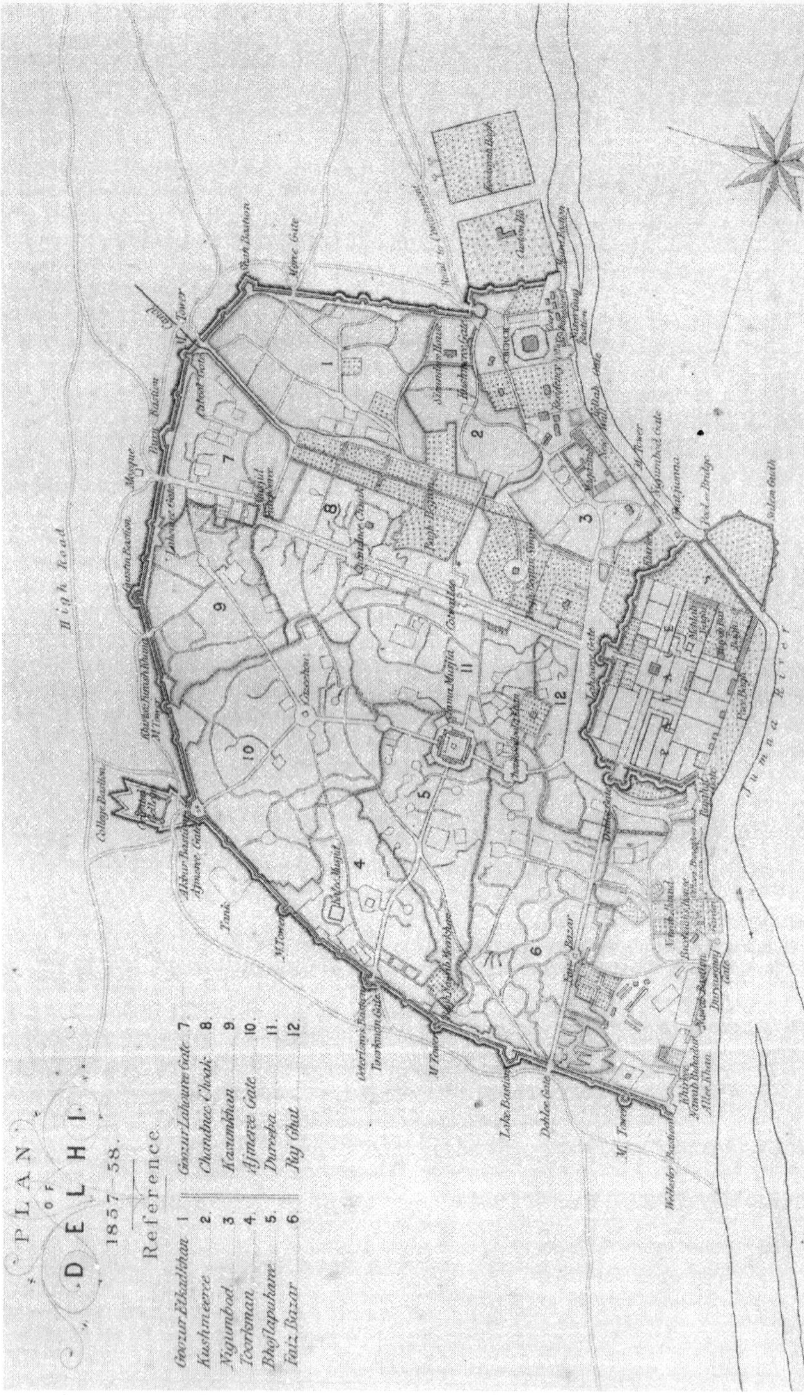

Shahjahanabad Map (1857-58)
Source: INTACH, Delhi A Living Heritage, 2010

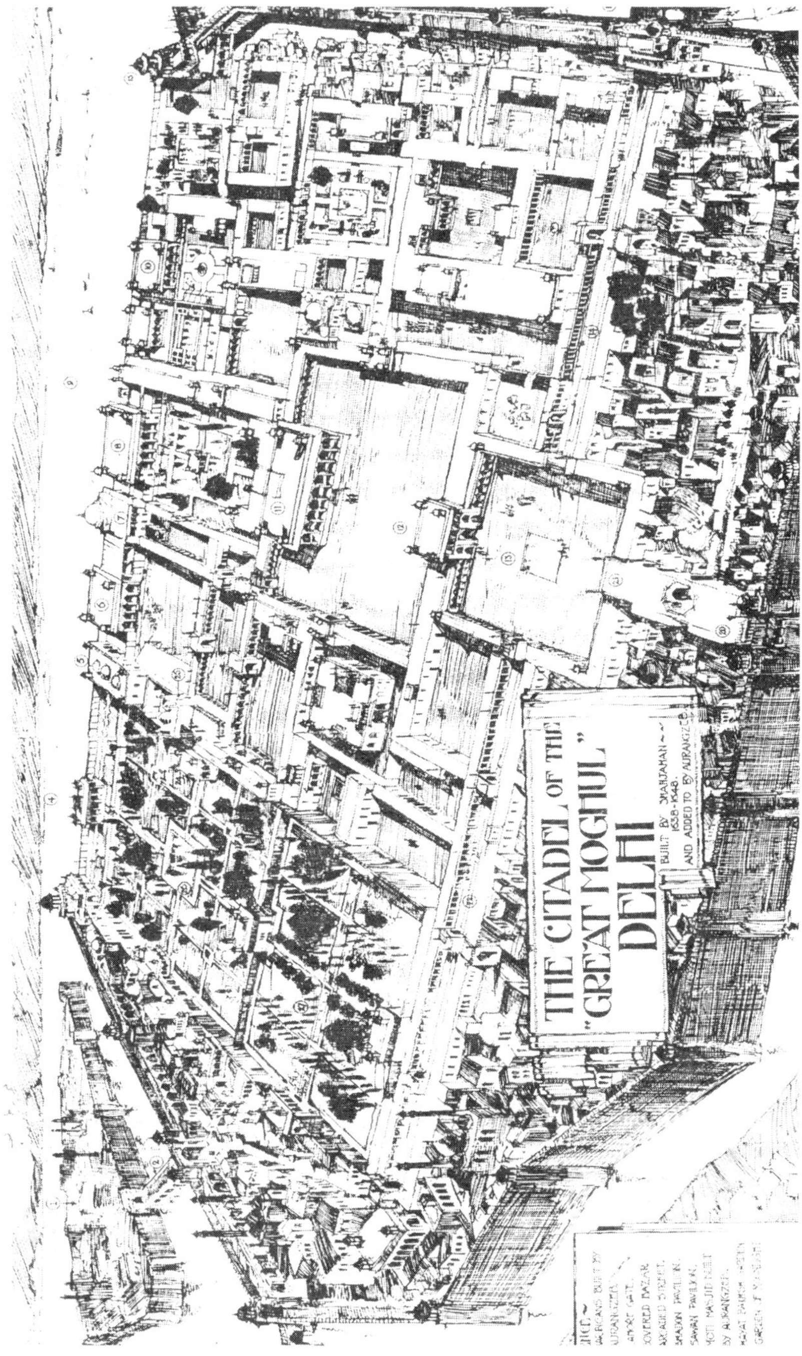

Red Fort–the citadel of the Great Moghul, Delhi
Source: Archaeological Survey of India

Skyline of Shahjahanabad from River Yamuna, 1843,. For the construction of Ring Road the low lying river bed and moat were filled up during 1950s, which buried about one third height of the Fort wall.
Source: Victoria and Albert Musuem/INTACH, 2010, Delhi- A Living Heritage.

Erstwhile canal between Red Fort and Salim Garh, Delhi
Source: Phillips Antiques, Mumbai, Artist: Capt. N.J. Luard

Chandni Chowk used to be a popular meeting place.

The Red Fort

The Quila-I-Mubarak (the auspicious fortress) was inaugurated in 1648 with much fanfare by Emperor Shah Jahan. Prince Dara Shikoh is said to have scattered gold and silver coins as he walked through the entrance of the Khizri Gate that faces the Yamuna. The palaces inside were decorated, the courtyards draped with rich carpets and colorful hangings. There was opulence everywhere. Some of the grandeur, and the opulence, are still evident. It is now familiar as Lal Qila, Red Fort.

River Yamuna had been an important element in the design of Shahjahanabad and in locating the Royal Fort.

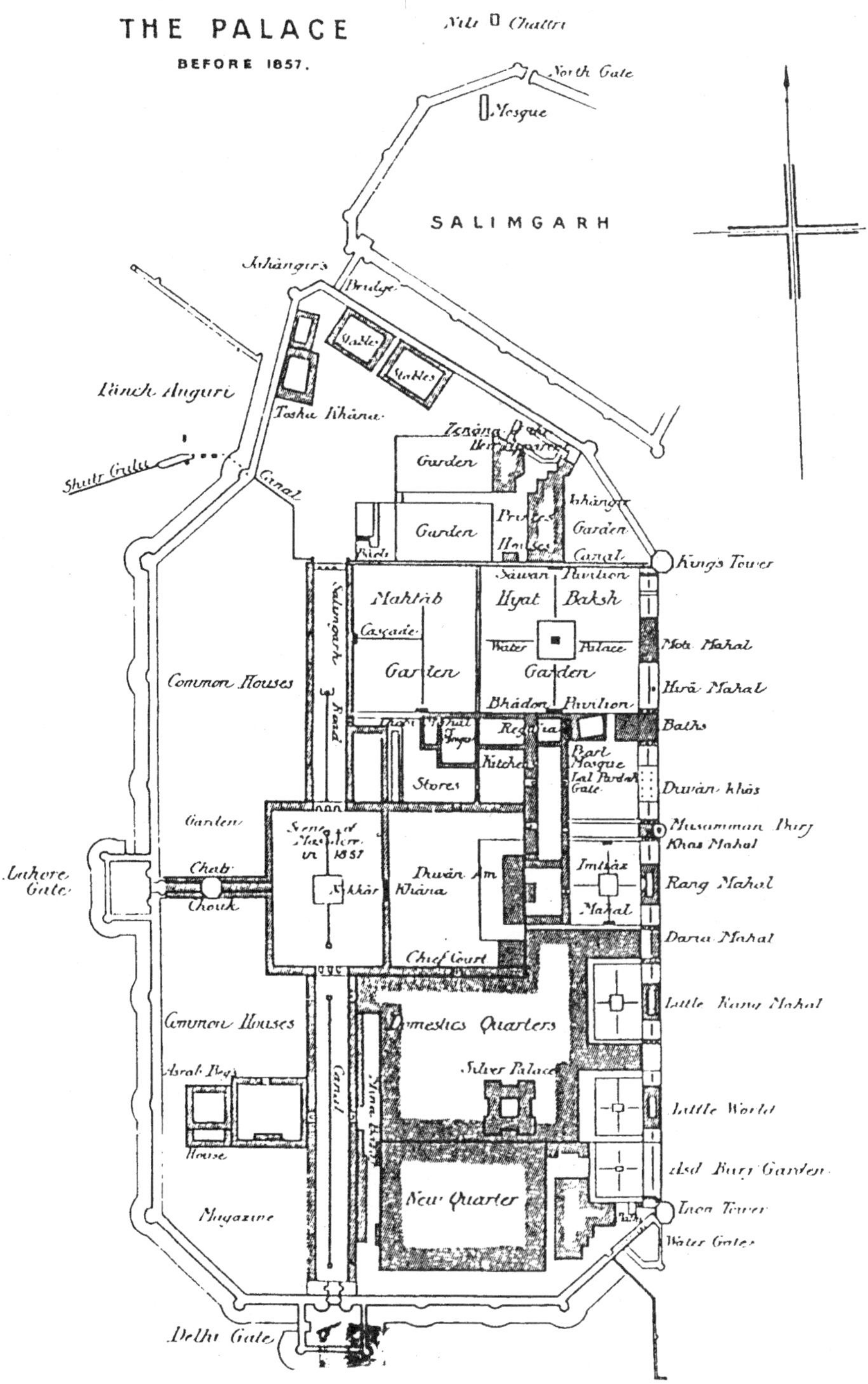

The Red Fort Plan

Source: Archaeological Survey of India

The King's Palace, is called Lal Qila or the Red Fort. However, in the time of Shah Jahan, its founder, it was called Urdu-i-Mu'alla. Under the later Mughuls it came to be known as Qila-i-Mu'alla. It took nine years to be completed and cost around one crore rupees.

Red Fort—A Jali (Stone screen)

Inside Red Fort is Diwan-i-Khas or the hall of private audience. The peacock throne sat in this room until 1739 when it was carried off to Persia by Nadir Shah. The peacock throne was solid gold and encrusted with a large number of jewels. Cabinet meetings took place in the Diwan-i-Khas.

In the design of the Red Fort, Shahjahan balanced everything perfectly: building and landscape, space and texture, light and shade, colour and scent. In the realm its siting on the bank of River Yamuna and the canals flowing with the new city every detail was considered. It was a city of gardens.

The deeper symbolism and the poetic nature of the gardens is reaffirmed in an inscription in the Red Fort describing the water garden of the palace: "The Hayat Bakhsh (life bestowing) garden, which is to these buildings as the soul is to the body, and the lamp to an assembly; and of the pure canal, the limpid water of which is to the person possessing sight, as a mirror showing the world; and of the water cascades, each of which you may see is the whitener of the dawn.... and of the fountain each of which is a hand of light inclined to shake hands with the inhabitants of heavens, or a string of bright pearls made to descend to reward the inhabitants of earth: and of the tank, full to the brim of water of life and in its purity the envy of light and the spring of the sun."

The garden made Shahjahanabad cool and attractive, with the stream of flowing water and the sound of water falls and fountains. As a place for the emperor to sit in his Hall of Public audience, the Diwan-i-Aam, its ceiling reflected the surrounding pool. The courtly aspect of these garden is carried through by their linear progression from the Hall of Public Audience to the Hall of Private Audience, to the living and women's quarters, the *zenana,* to which only the emperor himself had access. Each building is surrounded by its own garden area.

The French doctor, Bernier, wrote an amusing description of a visit he made to the private quarters within Shahjahanabad. It is probably the best contemporary description of this lovely purdah palace.

"Who is the traveller that can describe from ocular observation the interior of that building? I have sometimes gone

Diwan-i-Khas inside the Red Fort

into it when the King was absent from Delhi, and once pretty far I thought, for the purpose of giving my professional advice in the case of a great lady so externely ill that she could not be moved to the outward gate, according to the customs observed upon similar occasions; but a Kachemire shawl covered my head hanging like a large scarf down to my feet, and an eunuch led me by the hamams if I had been a blind man. You must be content, there for with such a general description as I have received from some of the eunuch who inform me that the Seraglio contains beautiful apartments, spacious and splendid, according to the rank and income. Every chamber has its reservoir of running water at the door; on every side are gardens, delightful alleys, shady retreats, streams, fountains, grottoes, deep excavations that afford shelter from the sun by day, lofty divans and terraces, on which to sleep coolly at night. Within the walls of this enchanting place, in fine, no oppressive or inconvenient heat is felt. "

Moti Masjid, Red Fort

Chandni Chowk was the centrepiece of Shahjahanabad and an engine of its economy, attracting merchants from all over the world for jewelry, spices, clothes and handicrafts.

Source: Photograph by Felice Beato, 1858, (INTACH, 2010)

Qudsiya Bagh

Delhi and Surrounding Country by A.Maclure, 1857.

The beautiful Zinatul Masjid, i.e. Ghata Masjid, was built by Aurangzeb's daughter, Zinatul Nisa Begum in 1711 A.D. It is a smaller version of the Jama Masjid, which was built by his grandfather. It is a beautiful structure with red sandstone facing, white marble dome, black marble flutings and tall minarets. After the death of Aurangzeb in 1707, the desolation of the Mughal empire began. Bahadur Shah shifted the capital to Lahore. With the decline of the power of the Mughals and their confinement to Lahore, the reins of control were overtaken by the Nawabs of Lucknow.

Zinat'ul Masjid

1714 is a milestone in the Indian history as the Britishers succeeded in establishing in Delhi an Embassy of the East India Company. This planted the seeds of British rule.

Chandni Chowk (Dariba) during 19th century.

A Delhi street at the back of Jama Masjid. (1857)

Jama Masjid–a view from the north
Drawing by Mazhar Khan (19th cent.)

Source: INTACH, 2010, Delhi A Living Heritage

Chawri Bazaar behind the Jama Masjid, 19th century photograph by S.C.Sen. Source: INTACH, Delhi–A Living Heritage, 2010.

Chatta Chowk–double storeyed market with arcaded shops on two levels inside Red Fort.
Source: ASI/INTACH, Delhi–A Living Heritage, 2010

The river Yamuna was a major element of the city design. The river was also used for navigation, connecting Agra, where the earlier Mughal capital existed. Ali Mardan Canal supplied water to the city and the river had numerous ghats all along for the people of Shahjahanabad. It provided water to the city besides protecting it.

"Shahjahanabad had a network of canals emanating from Yamuna river. ......The canals brought greenness to Delhi. It ran in all of the city from lane to lane, and the wells became full from it... it followed into the imperial fort and around the moat. Having flowed into the city to Chandini Chowk to the Chowk of Saddullah Khan, to Paharganj, to Ajmeri Gate, to the grazing places, to other mahallahs and to all the lanes and bazzars of the city."

Chaturma Rai, Chahar Gulshan,
Persian manuscript Collection.

Chandni Chowk – A view from Red Fort (2012)

Chandni Chowk in 1857, drawn by Capt. Luard

The Walled City of Shahjahanabad encloses an area about 1500 acres having Jama Masjid and Red Fort as the nodal points. Three main boulevards radiated from Red Fort. The first was Chandni Chowk with a canal in the middle; the second was the Jama Masjid while the third one led to Delhi Gate. The other three main streets radiated from Jama Masjid towards Chandni Chowk, Ajmeri Gate and Turkman Gate. It was reputed to be one of the most beautiful cities in orient. The spatial form of the Shahjahanabad is comprised of introvert open spaces, narrow lanes, compact and high density. The variety of land uses has richness of activities round the clock. The organic character of the city is striking, strongly reminiscent of pattern of nature. The indigenous form of the Shahjahanabad derives from a spatial context where the intimacy of physical expression results from a close packing of components. Behind blank walls and narrow alleys 30 to 40 per cent of the spatial envelope is in the series of internal courtyards, where most of the activities of living take place. The spatial structure of the community corresponds to its occupational division. The unclean occupations cluster on the periphery-low lying areas or in the west. The trade and business of the dominant groups occupy the prime locations, usually high lands, central areas or north side. The patches of occupational clusters are separated by open ground and community facilities, e.g. chowk, chopal, temple and bazaar, allowing all levels to interact. Sometimes the boundaries are simply common walls of houses, courtyards, or streets between groups of houses.

The settlement structure represents a closely knit orthogonal fabric with an introvert character. The clusters were defined in terms of social structure, which traditionally relate to mohalla, i.e. a geographical area that manifests the spatial pattern of the community. Increasing social mobility now makes it difficult to relate the occupation to a mohalla, but groups related by practice or customs and geographic origin continue to cluster in specific mohalla. The traditional spatial structure has a sieve like porous form. Closely knit fabric of structures helps to keep out the harsh sun and provides shaded courtyards and streets. During the night, the open courtyards radiate out the heat and creating a cooling effect. Thus the form, based upon the principle of thermal comfort through passive means, presents a framework of energy conscious design. The indigenous settlement is a working model of closely knit and self-contained community. Its spatial structure is a logical outgrowth of viable set of social and economic norms governing the community and individual behaviour.

During last 350 years Shahjahanabad has evolved into a compact maze of mixed use, where residential, commercial and industrial activities mingle and formal and informal sectors of trade operate in harmony. The buildings reflect the absorption of colonial and modern features of design and present an interesting portfolio of cross-breeded architecture.

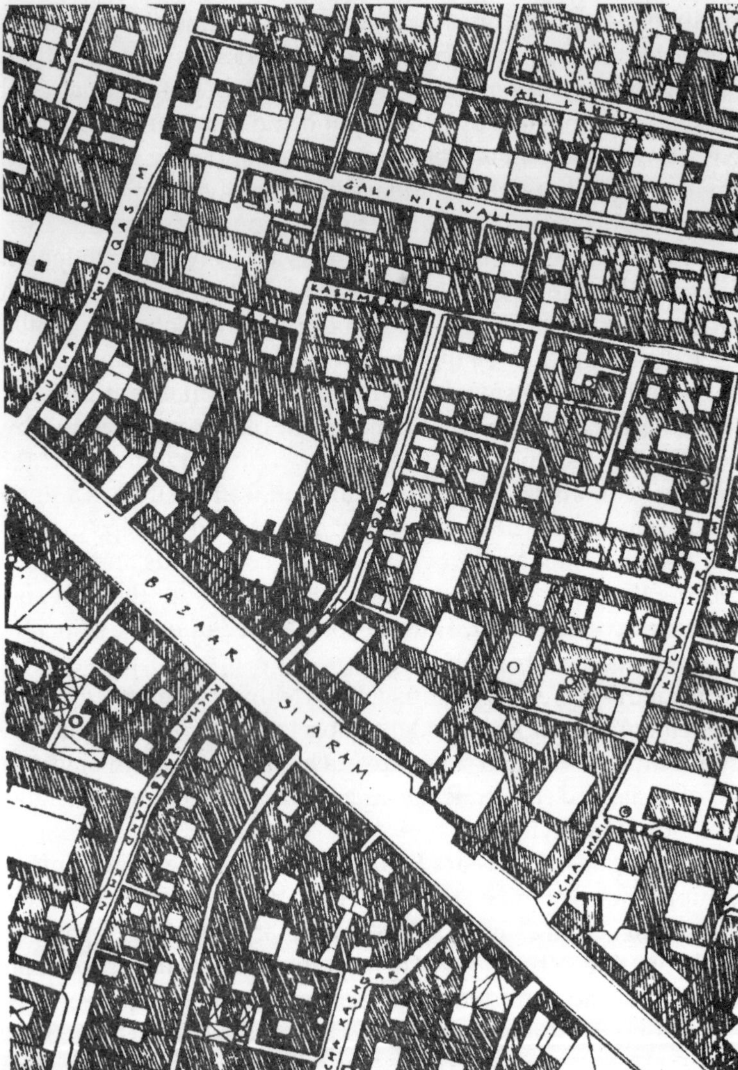

The Pattern of Shahjahanabad. The power of indigneous form of Shahjahanabad derives from a spatial context where the intimacy of physical expression results from a close packing of components. Self generated settlements at high densities have achieved a rich spatial form, which are often *viewed as slums*

Source: Rory Fonseca, The Walled City of Delhi, in Shelter and Societies.

Features of old buildings at Chawri Bazaar, Ajmeri, Gate

The custom of purdah required that women be shielded from the gaze of passersby, so that a street view presented high blank walls and katras/housing units invariably have the courtyards. The privacy is protected by a series of envelopes according to the accessibility and spatial continuum. First degree of privacy is provided by the interior courtyard which is the exclusive domain of women. Second degree of privacy is defined by the land outside the door, which is accessible to the members of family and their relations. Third level of privacy is the boundary of the mohalla, which is the domain of the local residents. These zones of privacy are reflected in a sequence of public, semi-public and private domains of space, including streets, chowks and chopal.

The Decline of Shahjahanabad

After 1717, during the reign of Emperor Farruksiyar and his successor Mohammad Shah, the political situation remained turbulent and no important landmarks were built. In 1719 Maharaja Jai Singh of Jaipur was entrusted with the task of revising the calender. He built the Jantar Mantar, a complex composition of pure geometrical forms of massive masonry astronomical instruments of chart the movement of the planets. The observatory was modelled on the general pattern laid down by Ulugh Baigh of Samarkand during the 14th Century. In 1737 the Maratha invader Baji Rao was defeated at Kalka Devi Temple.

On 9th March 1739 Nadir Shah defeated Mohammad Shah at Panipat and entered Delhi. He massacred the inhabitants and carried away vast quantities of gold, jewels, the celebrated peacock throne and Kohinoor diamond, beside many fine craftsmen. This was perhaps the darkest period in the history of Shahjahanabad.

Safdarjung Tomb is perhaps the last Mughal mausoleum built in Delhi. The tomb of the Wazir of Emperor Mohammad Shah, erected in 1753 is a son's tribute to father. It is built in red buff sandstone with marble panels and domes.

The Safdarjung Mausoleum

Safdarjung Tomb was modelled on the design of Humayun Tomb and Taj Mahal

Source: Zafar Hasan / ASI

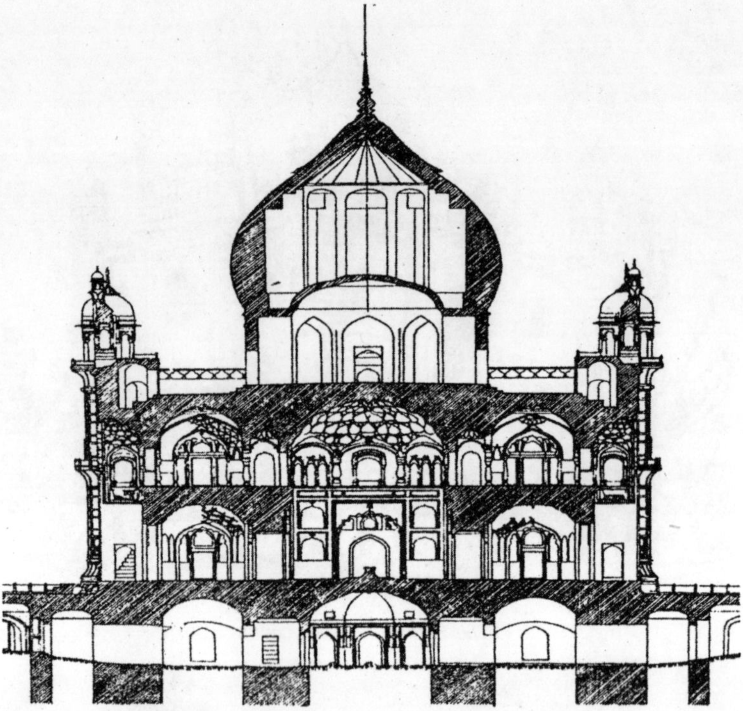

Section drawing of Safdarjung Tomb (1739-53)

During the rule of Afghan adventurer Ahmad Shah Abdali, his successors, Mohammad Shah Alam and Nazaf Khan, (1757–1788), Delhi set into a decline. 1782 was a terrible year of famine. Nazafgarh about 20 km west of Mehrauli was established by Nazaf Khan during 1786–88. Delhi empire was pathetically reduced in importance, wealth, power, glory and jurisdiction. Even the local folk ridiculed—"Shah Alam—the ruler with empire from Delhi to Palam."

The Kashmir Gate, Delhi, 1860

Gateways to Shahjahanabad

When Shahjahan transferred his capital from Agra to Delhi Shahjahanabad had 14 gates. Of these, the Kashmiri and Mori Gates opened to the north, Kabul and Lahori gates opened to the west, Ajmeri and Delhi gates to the south, and through Calcutta gate the Grand Trunk Road passed. The names of these gates conjured visions of the cities—Lahore, Ajmer, Kabul, Kashmir, Calcutta. Delhi Gate was built between 1638–48 and went by this name because it opened towards the old city of Delhi. It had a simple design and was made out of local stone. History says that post 1857, about 4000 women, half of them widows, were given rations at this gate. In 1857, the British used Kashmiri Gate in order to prevent the mutineers from entering the city. It was that the gate gained importance. The Ajmeri Gate is a single-arched structure with semi-octagonal turrets. Mori Gate had been inhabited by the poor, and post-1857, it became more crowded, chiefly with the survivors of Bahadur Shah Zafar's court.

The Mori and Kabul gates were demolished in 1867 though Viceroy Lawrence had said that the wall was not to be breached. Now the ruins of Mori Gate are only visible from the gaps in the walls which flank the road, laid by the British, from Calcutta to Delhi.

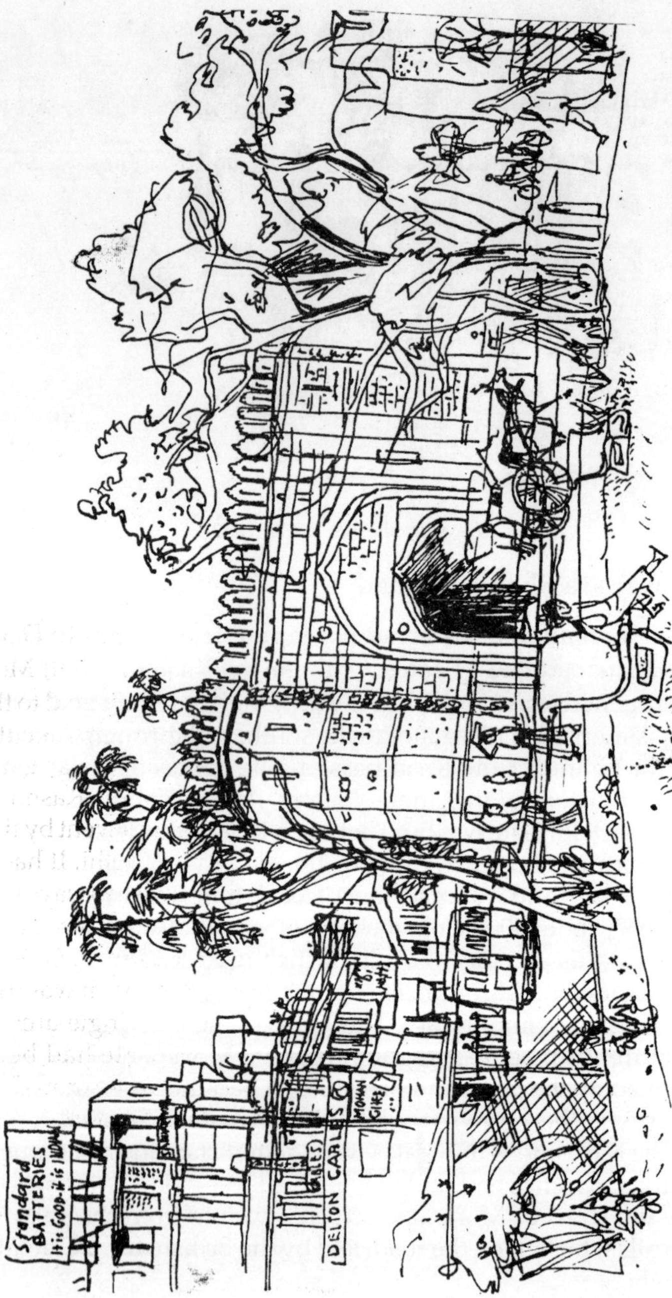

Turkman Gate

Jantar Mantar

Jantar Mantar

Jantar (yantra–meaning instrument) – Mantar (formula) was built in 1724 by Maharaja Jai Singh of Jaipur, who later built observatories on the same lines in Jaipur, Ujjain, Varanasi, and Mathura. The instruments at Jantar Mantar are fascinating for their novel architecture.

Kadam Sharif

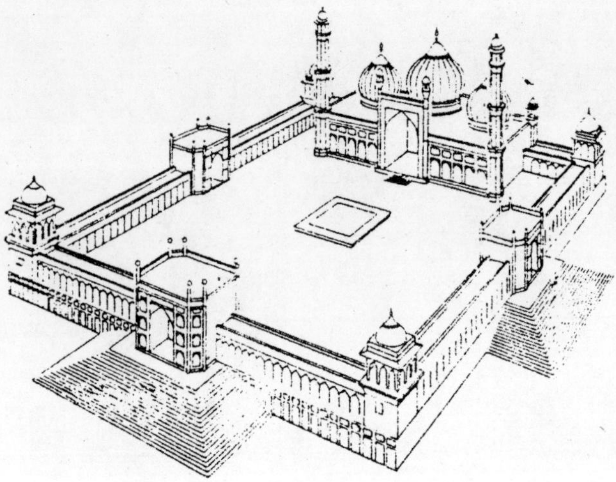

The Jama Masjid

Redevelopment of Jama Masjid

A Redevelopment Plan for Jama Masjid area has been prepared by Architect Pradeep Sachdeva for the Municipal Corporation of Delhi. The Redevelopment Plan seeks to integrate heritage conservation, urban renewal, mobility management and landscape into a composite whole keeping in focus the Jama Masjid. It also provides for in-situ rehabilitation of many informal trades, bazars, cultural and traditional festivities. According to the broad contours of the plan, the entire area in front of the Jama Masjid will be a pedestrian zone. Parking will be fully underground and *wuzu* facilities will serve the worshippers. All the scattered offices of public utilities, like BSES and Delhi Jal Board, will be relocated into planned buildings. The entire area will be lit up properly.

The redevelopment will also cater to the major bazaars the Meena Bazar and the Urdu Bazaar. The Red Fort will be visible clearly from the Jama Masjid, and a direct walkway will connect the two monuments. All structures which block the view of Red Fort will be brought below Jama Masjid's plinth. The pedestrian link will follow the path used by Shah Jahan to go to the mosque from the Fort.

Facade of the Jama Masjid

Elevation–Jama Masjid, Delhi

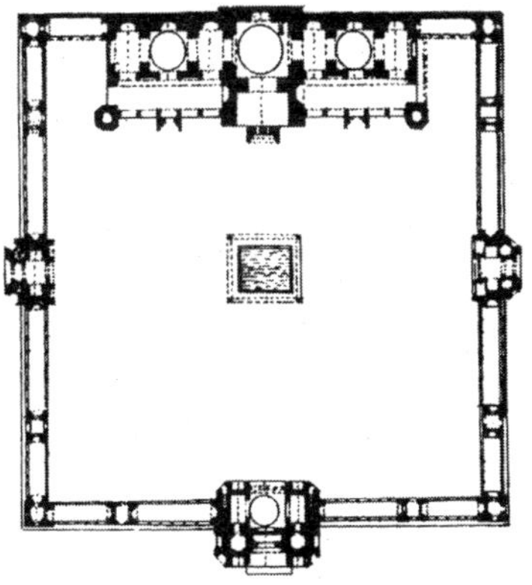

Plan of Jama Masjid

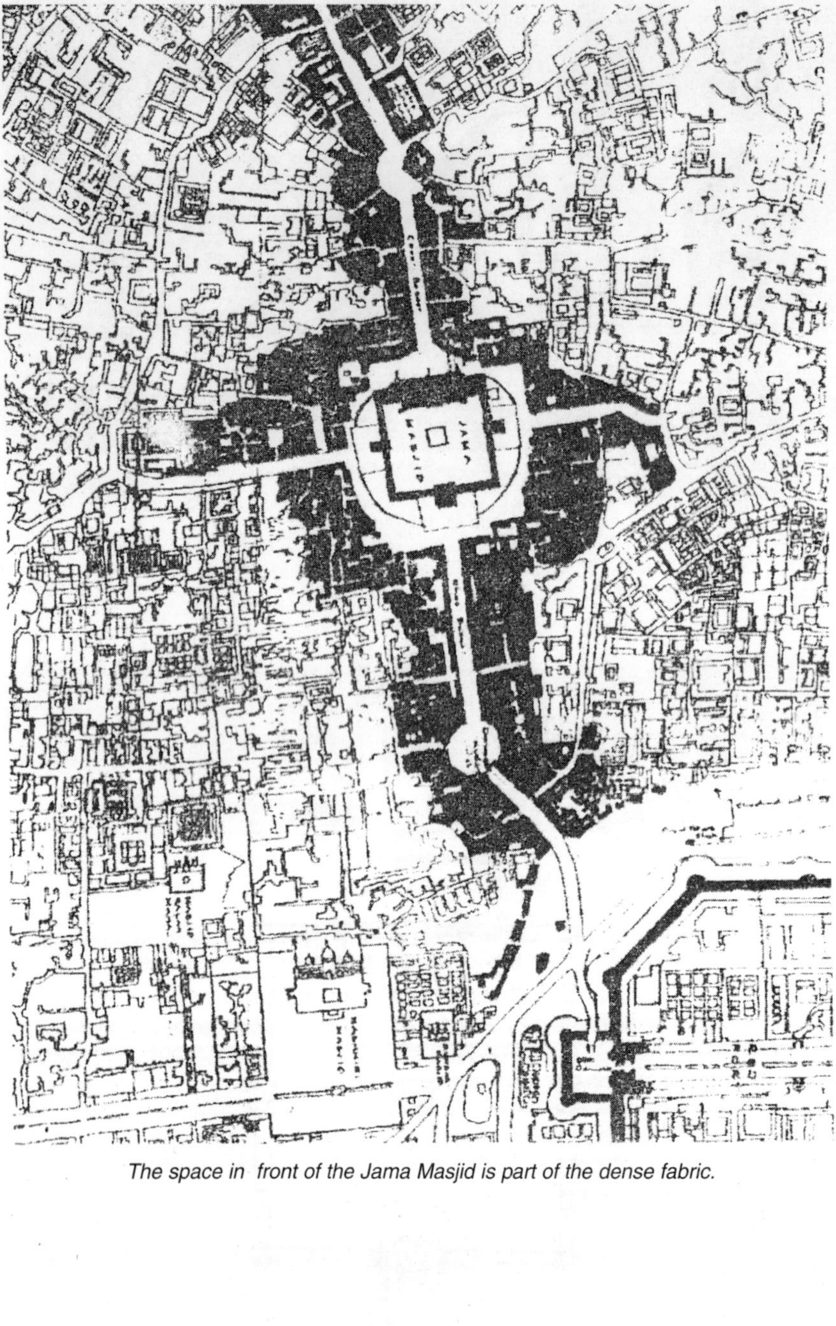

The space in front of the Jama Masjid is part of the dense fabric.

Jama Musjid Aquatint by Thomas Deniell, 1795

The redeveloped area will be a barrier-free environment, accessible to the physically challenged. There will be well-designed toilets, kerb cuts, warning blocks, ramps for transition of level changes, Braille guide maps and handrails.

The Meena Bazaar will have a green roof that will merge with the treescape, framing the Lahori Gate of the Red Fort. The Nukkad Faiz Bazaar will be redeveloped with Subhash Chandra Bose statue in front of it. However, recent claims of finding the remains of disputed Akbarbadi mosque and raising of an unauthorised structure have stalled the work of redevelopment.

14. Delhi of East India Company

Delhi! the name sums up the pomp and power of bygone days.
—*Count Hans von Koenigsmarck, 1910*

The European connections with Delhi had been very old. As back as 327 B.C., Alexander the Great invaded India and left social and cultural traces which are visible even today. However, after the presence of the East India Company in 1714 in Delhi, the English influence became pronounced. Throughout the late 17th and 18th centuries, European style buildings started coming up, which intercepted the facade of Mughal and Indian architecture. Besides, quite a few town houses, bungalows, churches and cemeteries were built in European style. Even the narrow streets of Shahjahanabad witnessed the imported architecture.

In 1739, Nadir Shah, the emperor of Persia invaded India and defeated Mohammad Shah and siezed the throne. When he returned to Persia he took the treasures and the famous diamond, Koh-i-noor. By 1740 the unifying power of the Mughal empire began to shake. The Sikhs, Rajputs, Jats, Marathas,

Rohillas and Pindaris formed regional alliances against each other. In conjunction with the European trading companies each wanted to succeed the Mughals. In 1757, the Afghan adventurer Ahmed Shah Abdali attacked India and four years later defeated the combined forces of Mughals and Marathas at the battle of Panipat. He had to retreat back due to the mutiny. After the war of Panipat the country was divided and Delhi became a ravaged city. The famous poet Mir reflected the sad state of affairs in 1782, in the following couplet:

> *"Why do you mock at me and ask yourselves*
> *Where in the world I come from, easterners?*
> *There was a city, famed throughout the world.*
> *Where dwelt the chosen spirits of the age:*
> *Delhi its name, fairest among the fair.*
> *Fate looted it and laid in desolate*
> *And to that ravaged city I belong."* —Mir, 1782

At this juncture the intervention the European companies occurred. In this melee the English East India Company emerged victorious. The year 1803 was a milestone in the history of Delhi, when East India Company wrangled a foothold in the crumbling Mughal empire. The Mughal dynasty practically came to an end when in 1803, the native rulers were defeated by General Lake of East India Company near Patparganj. The East India Company appointed the first Resident of Delhi as the 'protector' of battered Mughal crown. That time Delhi territory comprised of Delhi Division and Hissar Division. In the early years, the British and their troops settled within the walled city, around the Red Fort and Kashmere Gate. They improved and partly reconstructed the old city wall and developed a residential colony named Mubarak Bagh. To provide drinking water to the old city, Ali Mardan canal was lined and reopened.

In 1824, Town Duties Committee was established which was perhaps the first town improvement agency in Delhi. In 1828, British troops shifted from the old city to Ridge cantonment, referred as Rajput Cantonment and Khyber Pass. At the same time the Civil Lines, outside the walled city, in the north came up. The first census of Delhi in 1833 counted 1,19,800 persons.

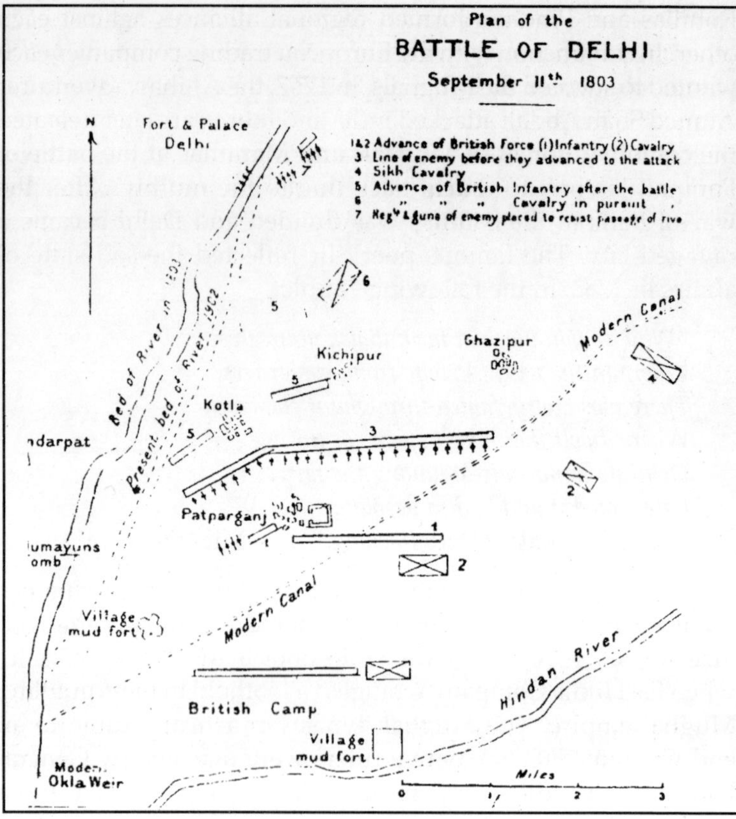

Battle of Delhi at Patparganj, September 11th, 1803

Subsequently, several schemes to meet the growing demands were undertaken outside the walled city. These included the development of Sadar Bazaar, Kishanganj and Deputyganj. The census of 1836 recorded a population of 1,30,662 and the census of 1843 recorded a population of 1.31 lakh. In the same year water sources were surveyed. It was found that water in 555 wells out of city's total 607 wells was brackish and drinking water from the river was considered necessary.

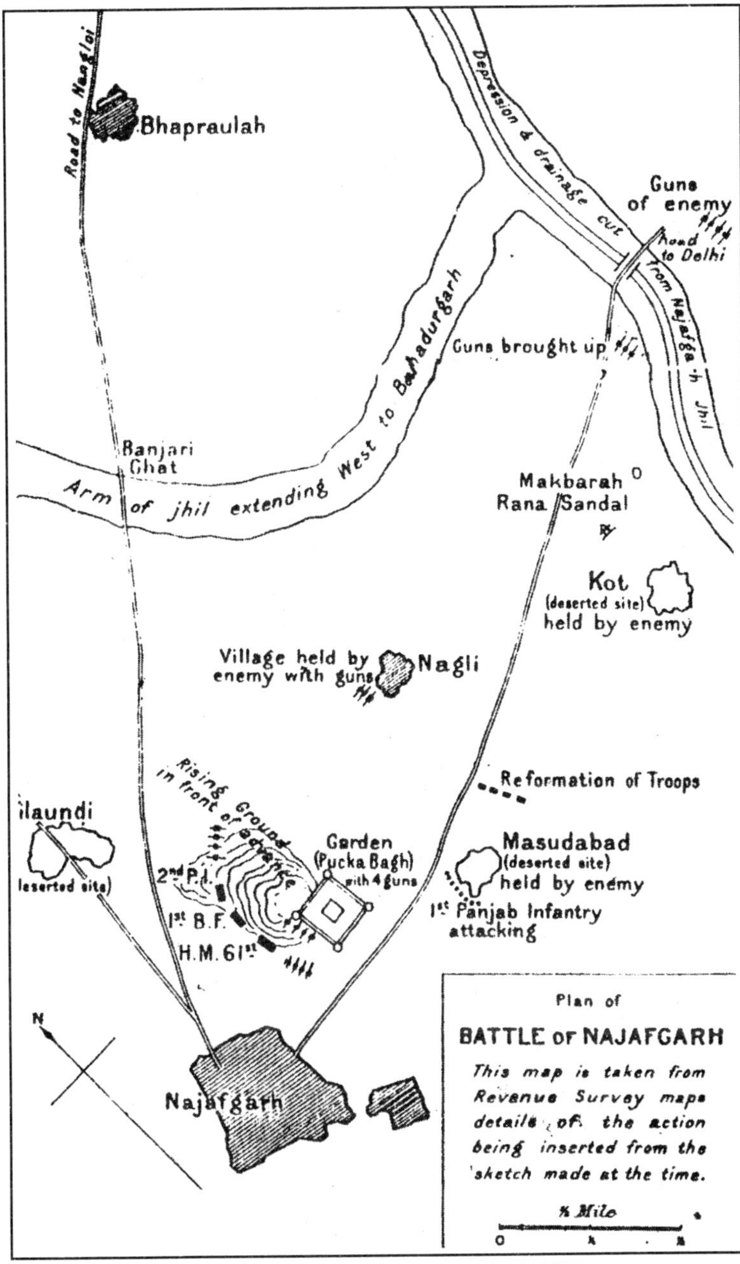

Plan of the Battle of Delhi at Nazafgarh 1803

The Census of Delhi (October 1836)

	Males	*Females*
Musalman adults	21,865	23,314
Musalman children	10,098	8,890
Hindoo adults	24,339	24,311
Hindoo children	9,866	7,989
Grand Total	66,158	64,504

The total population in 1836 was 1,30,662, who lived in 28,006 houses.

In early eighteen-fifties ambitious development schemes were mooted. Salient among them had been report on "Drainage in Delhi" by Greathead. The proposals for Grand Trunk Road to cross through the Walled City, removal of city wall, reclamation of land under the ditch near Mori Gate and linking Delhi with the railways were discussed. To decongest the grain market (Khari Baoli) 11 acres of land outside the city walls (Naya Bazaar) was gifted to grain merchants. The census of 1853 recorded a population of 1.51 lakh. In 1848, 193 sq. miles from Meerut and Bulandshahar District, across the river were included in Delhi territory. This necessitated the construction of a permanent bridge on the river Yamuna. However, the city underwent drastic transformations after the war of 1857. One-third of the city was razed to rubble. In 1858, the East India Company transferred the rule to the British Crown.

The first war of Independence (1857) at the Kashmere Gate

The heavily built-up area surrounding the Red Fort was completely cleared. Almost the entire population of the walled city was ejected. Muslims tried to settle down in the suburbs at Motia Khan, Idgah, Qadam Sharif, Nizamuddin, Mehrauli and Paharganj and many of them migrated to far off cities, as Lucknow, Hyderabad and Jaipur. Red Fort and Jama Masjid were used as military camps. Initially there were proposals to blow up the entire city including the Red Fort. There were the suggestions to build Fort Victoria in place of Red Fort and a

A lithograph of a battle scene outside the ramparts of the Red Fort, Delhi, by Thomas and William Daniell
Source: Philips Antiques, Mumbai.

cathedral by replacing the Jama Masjid. However, the destructive proposals were stalled by the Secretary of State who decided that "the political object to be gained by destroying the palace will be gained by occupying it." Work started in early 1858 for the removal of the city wall, which was discontinued after 10 months. When the city was returned to civil authorities in 1859, it was annexed to Punjab. The infantry was centralised in Daryaganj and Kashmere Gate, where sections of the city wall were demolished and several roads were widened or constructed. In 1859, it was ordered to clear buildings within 500 yard radius around the Red Fort, but Dariba and small temples falling in the clearance zone were spared. Jama Masjid continued to be a military camp till 1862, when it was released on the condition that no political meetings would take place and it would function under a government controlled committee. Fatehpuri mosque which was sold to a banker in 1860 could be restored to the Muslims in 1877.

Lahore and Delhi Gates of the Red Fort were renamed as Victoria and Alexandra Gates and Town Hall was built in Chandni Chowk. The proposal to demolish the city wall was dropped in favour of military control of the city wall and an area upto 450 metres outside it. In 1861, Calcutta Gate and the area between Kashmere Gate and Mori Gate were demolished for construction of the railways.

In 1863, Delhi Municipal Committee was given control and jurisdiction over the walls and adjacent areas were transferred to civil authority. One of the earliest scheme undertaken by the Municipal Committee was shifting of the vegetable market outside the walled city. In 1866, the railway lines, railway station, and their road links were constructed piercing the walled city in and around Mori Gate and Kashmere Gate. The effected population was shifted to Sadar Bazaar, Katra Ghee and Kishanganj. In 1867, Delhi was given the status of a first class municipality. The cholera epidemic in Paharganj resulted into shifting of the tanners to Regharpura (Karol Bagh). In 1874, Delhi Municipal Committee was given control of nazul (government) lands upto three mile radius of the city walls, which enlarged its functions and jurisdiction.

Delhi after East India Company Takeover

14.9.1803	East India Company defeated Marathas near Humayun Tomb
1806	Shah Alam died
1820	Canal of Ali Mardan Khan cleared
1824	First Improvement and development agency set up as the Town Duty
1829	St. Jame's Church built
1832	Delhi included in North-West province
1845	Metcalfe appointed Resident of Delhi
1853	Delhi population 1,51,000
11.5.1857	First War of Independence (Mutiny)
21.9.1857	Surrender of Bahadur Shah to East India Company
1857	East India Railways
11.1.1858	Delhi Civil Government
6.2.1858	Delhi Transferred from North-West province to Punjab, Delhi District
1.11.1858	The British Crown assumes the Government of India
1863	First Municipal Committee for Delhi constituted
1865-67	St. Stephen's Church built
1.1.1867	Delhi linked with Railways
1870	Mutiny memorial at Ridge
1873	Rajputana State Railway (Delhi-Bombay)
1876	Prince of Wales visited Delhi
1881	Municipal Committee passed Building Bye Laws
1891	Delhi-Ambala- Kalka Railway opened
1892	Introduction of piped water supply
1895	Construction of sewerage in Chandni Chowk
1897	Karachi-Delhi Railway link
1900	Ghaziabad-Moradabad Railway link
1901	First Notified Area Committee for Mehrauli formed
1905	Delhi Agra Railway link
1907	Lord Curzon—Delhi Durbar, Delhi Railway Station.
1910	Willson Survey of city carried out the Municipal Committee

Delhi Durbar of 1877 signified the importance attached to Delhi and boosted the development and expansion of Civil Lines and the area towards north of the Walled City. In the following years several schemes for drainage, water supply, irrigation, road construction and development of residential suburbs were undertaken. With the growing building activity, the Municipal Committee in 1881 passed the 'building bye-laws'. Another dimension added to Delhi was introduction of industries during the eighties. In 1888 there were scores of factories mainly comprised of cotton spinning, ice factory and flour mills. In 1889, the major industry established in Delhi was Delhi Cloth Mills. With the railways, the industrialisation of Delhi became rapid and factories started coming up at Sadar Bazaar, Subzi Mandi and other suburbs. Consequently with the increase in trade, population growth and introduction of automobiles, the traffic situation became acute. Free plots were offered to the dairymen outside the city to discourage animals within the city.

Old Delhi Railway Station: Built by Sir Ronald MacDonald Stephenson of the East India Company in 1864, this is among the earliest railway stations in India. This was rebuilt in 1910-11 during the preparations of the visit of Emperor King George V.

In 1892, a water works at Chandrawal was opened which introduced in Delhi piped water supply in the building. In 1895, the construction of sewer in the Chandni Chowk area was undertaken. Piped water supply and sewerage in the walled city had been significant modernisation of services, which was almost parallel to such efforts in the cities of the Western world. In 1901 electric lighting was introduced in Shahjahanabad.

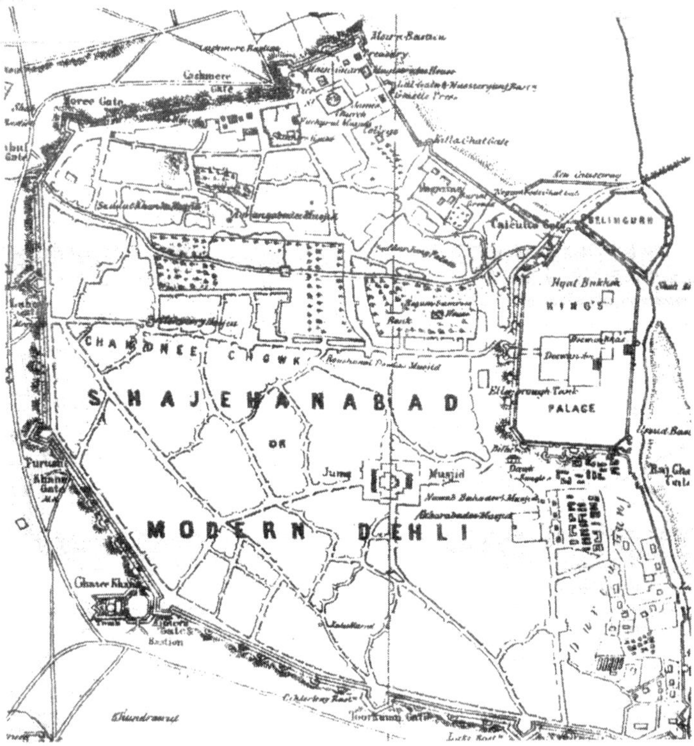

Shahjahanabad or Modern Delhi, 1849-50

Source: *India Office, Library, London: The Fort and Cantonment of Delhi, taken from Lieut. 'Burgess' Survey of 1849-50 and Surveyor General's Office, Calcutta, October 1857, Thomas Krafft and E. Ehlers, Imperial Design and Military Security, Erdkunde, Band 49/1995.*

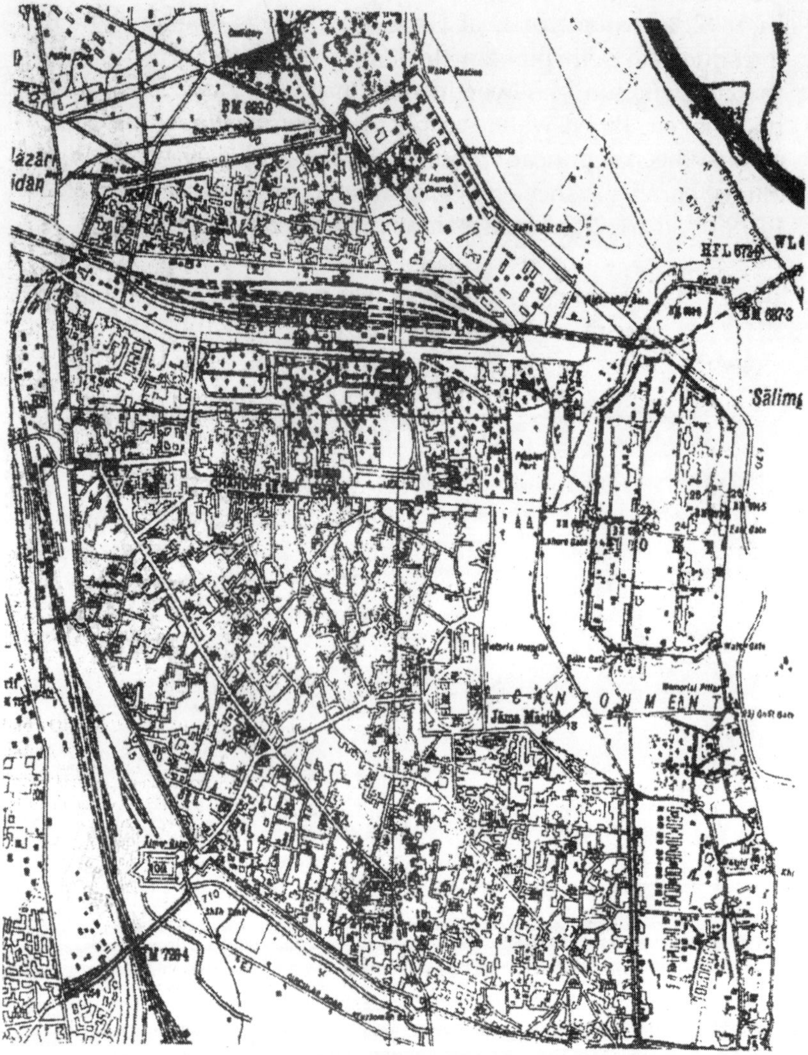

Shahjahanabad (Old Delhi) at the turn of the Century (1912), Railway Lines and Station laid at Begum-ka-Bagh, Shahjahanabad

Source: *India Office, Library, London: Delhi prepared from the Delhi and Hissar Revenue Surveys, 1870-1872, revised in 1912. Surveyor General of India 1912. Thomas Krafft and E. Ehlers: Imperial Design and Military Security, Erdkunde, 49/1995.*

Poetry of the Last Mughal Emperor of Delhi
Bahadur Shah (1775-1858)

Umer-e-daraaze se maang ke laye the char din
Do aarzu mein guzar gaye, do intezaar mein
Hai Kitna badnaseeb Zafar dafn ke liye
Do gaz zameen bhi na mili koo-e-yaar mein
(I had requested for a long life, a life of four days)
Two passed by in pining, and two in waiting
How unlucky is Zafar! For burial
Even two yards of land were not to be had, in
the land of the beloved.

Na kisii kii ankh ka nur hun na kisii ke dil ka qarar hun
Jo kisii ke kam na aa sake main vo ek musht-e-Gubar hun
Na to main kissi ka habiib hun na to main kisii ka raqiib hun
Jo bigar gaya vo nasib hun to ujar gaya vodayar hun
(My life give no ray of light. I bring no solace to heart or eye
Out of dust to dust again, of no use to any one am I
Barred the door of fate for me, bereft of my dear ones am I
The spring of a flower garden ruined
Alas, autumn wind am I)

hamane duniya mein ake kya dekha
dekhaa jo kuchh so Khvab sa dekha
hai to insan Khak kaa putala
lekin paani ka bulbula dekha
(I came into the world and what did I see?
Whatever I saw was just like a dream
Man is moulded from clay but I saw him as a bubble of water)

During the reign of East India Company and the British crown (November 1858 onwards), the architecture underwent a slow transformation, sometimes referred as 'colonial', 'Indo-Saracenic', 'Victorian neo-classical 'mixed' style. Some of the following structures bear testimony to this.

The Mutiny Memorial, Ajitgarh 1863 (Near old Sabzi Mandi)

Ajeet Garh: On the road from the Bara Hindu Rao Hospital to Delhi University exists Ajeet Garh. The memorial was built in 1863 by the Britishers "in the memory of the soldiers of the

Delhi Field Force who were killed in 1857". It was kept under wraps after Independence, finally converted to a memorial for Indian soldiers and opened on August 15, 1972. "The word enemy had been used for the Indian soldiers," says the new plaque. The monument stands in the forested area of the ridge, but the engravings are covered by graffiti and there is no guard.

Jama Masjid, Delhi, Traces of the Uprising, 1857; Photo by Samuel Bourne

Repulse of a sortie by the Sepoys on the British troops before Delhi; lithograph, 1857. (Flagstaff Tower is on the escarpment, top right)

Flagstaff Tower: Flagstaff Tower was erected by the British. The tower is situated on the ridge in the Delhi University area. It is constructed of plastered bricks. The building contains three arched opening on the north, east and west. The flagstaff tower was the spot where ladies of the cantonment gathered with the children and servants on the 11th may, 1857. From here they fled to Karnal after they gave up hope of succour from Meerut.

St. James Church: The Church was built by James Skinner, an important and colourful personage of 19th century Delhi. The building of the church was commenced in the year 1823 and was completed by Bishop Daniel Wilson in 1836. The building was built at a cost of $ 10,000. St James is a centrally planned church, based on a Greek Cross Plan. The Church consisted of an altar at the east end with porticoes on the three other sides. The Greek cross plan was, extended on two sides and a pointed 'Florentine' dome surmounted by a heavy lanter covered the central octagonal space. The Church was plastered to facilitate a uniform Neoclassical expression, through a two shade colour scheme differentiated the classical elements from the plain wall surfaces.

St. James Church

St. James Church is a fine example of the colonial classical architecture and is a subtle synthesis of "classical" and late Mughal styles. Visually the 'classical' look dominated styles, can be observed on closer examination. The floral pattern of the plinth which one can discern at the west portico is typically late Mughal. Many additions have been done to the Church building. After 1857 repair was necessitated by the extensive damage to the Church. Two stained glass windows were placed behind the altar and a third was placed in the newly built vestry.

Ghazi-ud-din Madrasa, Ajmeri Gate.

Ghazi-ud-din Madrasa, Ajmeri Gate: Ghazi-ud-din Khan's Madrasa is one of the rare surviving specimens of the typical Mughal school of architecture. It was erected in 1692 at its present site, which was then just outside Shahjahanabad's Ajmeri Darwaza. Unlike other similar madrasas, this one has been conceived as separate from the traditional mausoleum. It still houses the Anglo Arabic School, and until a few years ago, also hosted the Zakir Hussain College. The building complex is a feast of Indo-Saracenic architectural design, and features a mosque, a "makhtab", a library, as well as double-tiered "hujras" to seat the students. The Madrasa is a glowing example of enduring religio-educational endowment. Additions, modifications and regular upkeep have been tastefully implemented to preserve the original architectural style and character.

Ugarsen Ki Baoli

Maharaja Ugar Sen built a Baoli which provides water till date and has been located at Hailey Road near Connaught Place. It has two rows of arched building without a roof. Today, it is buried under the shadow of the skyscrapers. There are two other famous water works known as Athpula and Barapula. Athpula was built by Nawab Akbar and is now situated in Lodhi Gardens beside the tomb of Sikandar Lodhi.

Ugarsen-Ki-Baoli

Source: Dastan-e-Dilli, ICCR, 2011

Anglo-Sanskrit Senior Secondary School, Darya Ganj: Formerly known as Anglo Sanskrit Victoria Jubilee High School, the institution came into being with the unique objective of synthesising Sanskrit "pathshala" culture and the English system of higher education. The School's present building at Darya Ganj was constructed in 1919. It features architecture in

Western architecture in Shahjahanabad as depicted in Begum Samru's Palace (1840)

Anglo Sanskrit Senior Secondary School, Darya Ganj.

Source: DDA, New Delhi

the Victorian neo-classical style–with distinctive semi-circular arches in the lower structure. The upper floor has Doric order columns of changed proportions. The School has made additions and modifications to the original building over time, however, the changes have been tastefully executed. Excellent maintenance has contributed to the preservation of the original architectural flavour.

Saint Mary's Home, Rajpur Road: St. Mary's Home is an expression of philanthropic initiative. Born 125 years ago, and then called the "Refuge Home", the institution was conceived to provide shelter to abandoned women and children. The present building, constructed in 1925, also houses two girls' schools: Victoria Girls Senior Secondary School, and the Saint Annie's Diocesan Preparatory School. Built with distinctive stone and brick masonry, the architecture features semi-circular brick arches supported by blue stone pillars, rugged walls and a compact verandah. The use of local materials and a functional construction technique enhance the building's simple heritage and beauty.

Saint Mary's Home, Rajpur Road

Source: DDA, New Delhi

Ayurvedic and Unani Tibbia College Ajmal Khan Road.

Source: DDA, New Delhi

Ayurvedic and Unani Tibbia College, Ajmal Khan Road: The only institution in the country to offer training in both Ayurvedic and Unani Systems of medicine, Tibbia College is a unique example of living history. Its foundation stone was laid in 1916 by Lord Hardinge, the then Viceroy of India. And the College was inaugurated by Mahatma Gandhi himself—a rare distinction no other building in Delhi can lay claim to. The structures on the College's sprawling campus reflect a fusion of neo-classical, colonial and Mughal architectural styles. The complex is well maintained, and continues to be used as both college and hospital to this day.

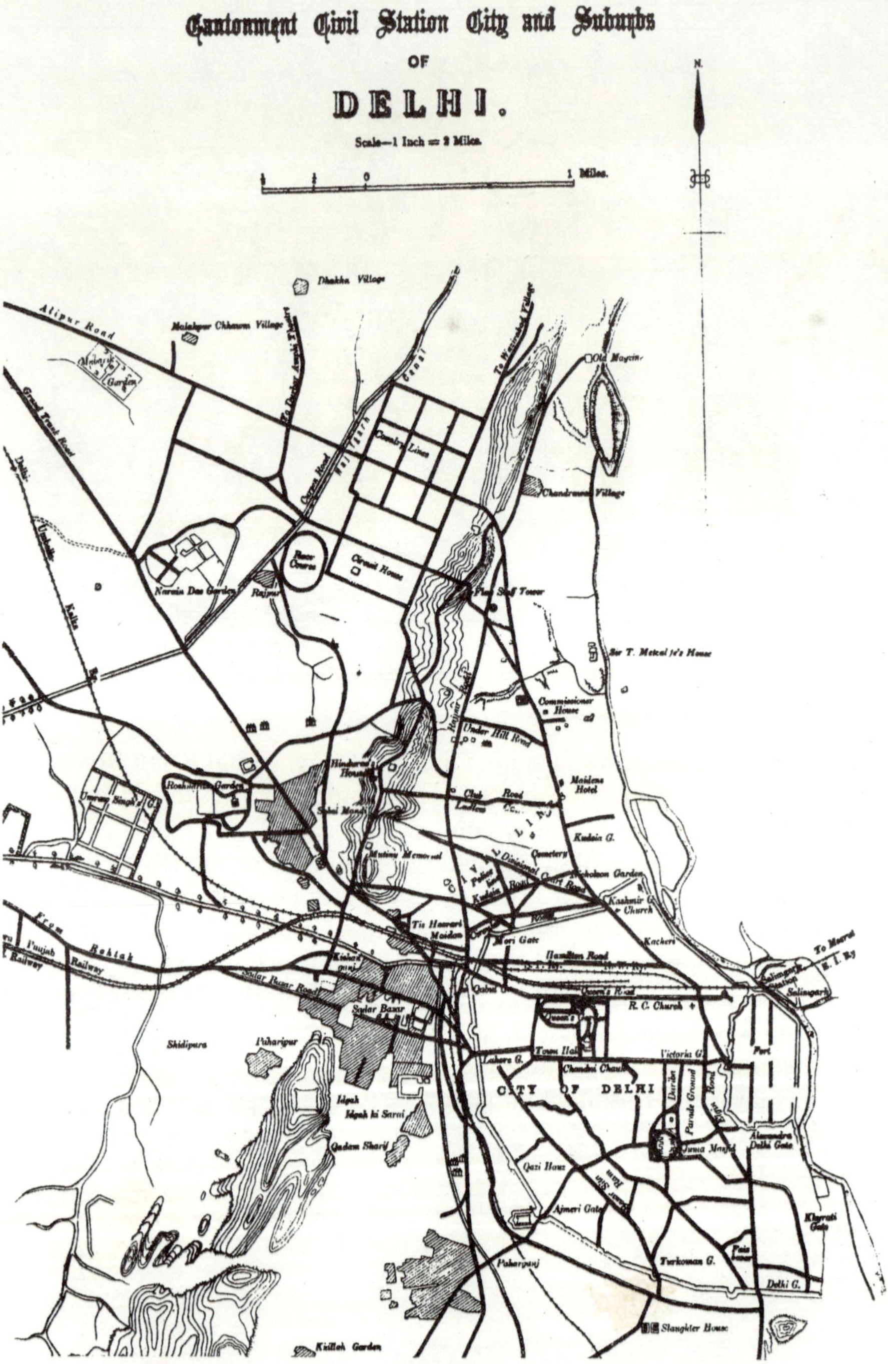

Delhi Survey of India Map, 1913, Showing the expanse of Sadar Bazar, Civil Lines and Cantonment / Cavalary Lines in the North.

15. Imperial Delhi—the Anglo-Indian Rome

During the early phase of their reign in India, the British faced numerous political, social and economic problems. The empire was preoccupied with law and order problem and in

In 1911, the British government shifted capital from Calcutta to Delhi. This was announced at the great Delhi Durbar to celebrate the accession of King George V, for which a huge procession moved to Red Fort.

Source: Getty Images, Exhibition on New Delhi (2011)

consolidation of its control over scattered regional powers in the vast subcontinent. In 1905, when Lord Curzon partitioned Bengal, he had little idea about the turbulence it would create. There was total anarchy, communal strife, continuous resistance and violence by the Bengali nationalists. Therefore, in 1911 the Coronation Durbar in Delhi was seen as an opportunity to demonstrate Anglo-Indian unity. The intention was to unite Bihar and Orissa under a new governorship; with a legislative council at Patna. The main project was to create a wholly new capital at Delhi. The choice to shift the Imperial capital from Calcutta to Delhi had many reasons. Delhi had a deep rooted historical association as the seat of the government. It was much closer to the summer capital, Shimla. Delhi lied on the major routes of roads and railways and was close to Punjab and the United Provinces.

Procession during Delhi Durbar, 1911
Source: Alkazi collection exhibited during century celebrations of New Delhi (2011)

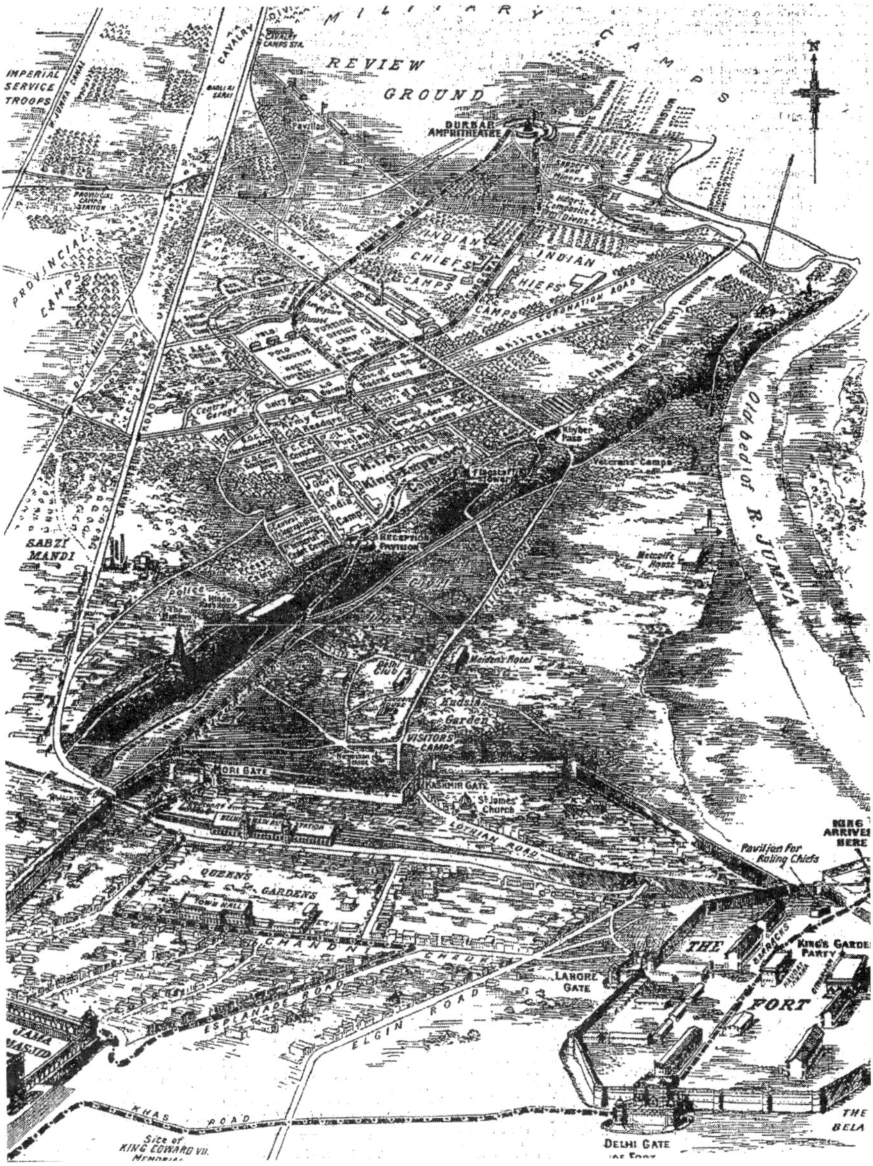

The State Entry of the King-Emperor into Delhi

The above bird's eye view shows the route taken by the King-Emperor through the Fort, across the Maidan, round the Jama Masjid, along the Chandni Chowk, the main thorough of Delhi, through the Mori Gate, and over the historic Ridge to his Camp. The whole route is five miles long. From the Delhi Gate to the Jama Masjid is 400 yards. The whole camp covers 25 square miles. The Pavilion for ruling Chiefs, inside the Fort and facing the Salimgarh station where his Majesty arrived, was destroyed by fire on Tuesday, but the presentation took place in a marquee erected on this site. From this point to the Delhi Gate the distance is three fifths of a mile.

Source: Getty Images, exhibited during century celebrations of New Delhi (2011).

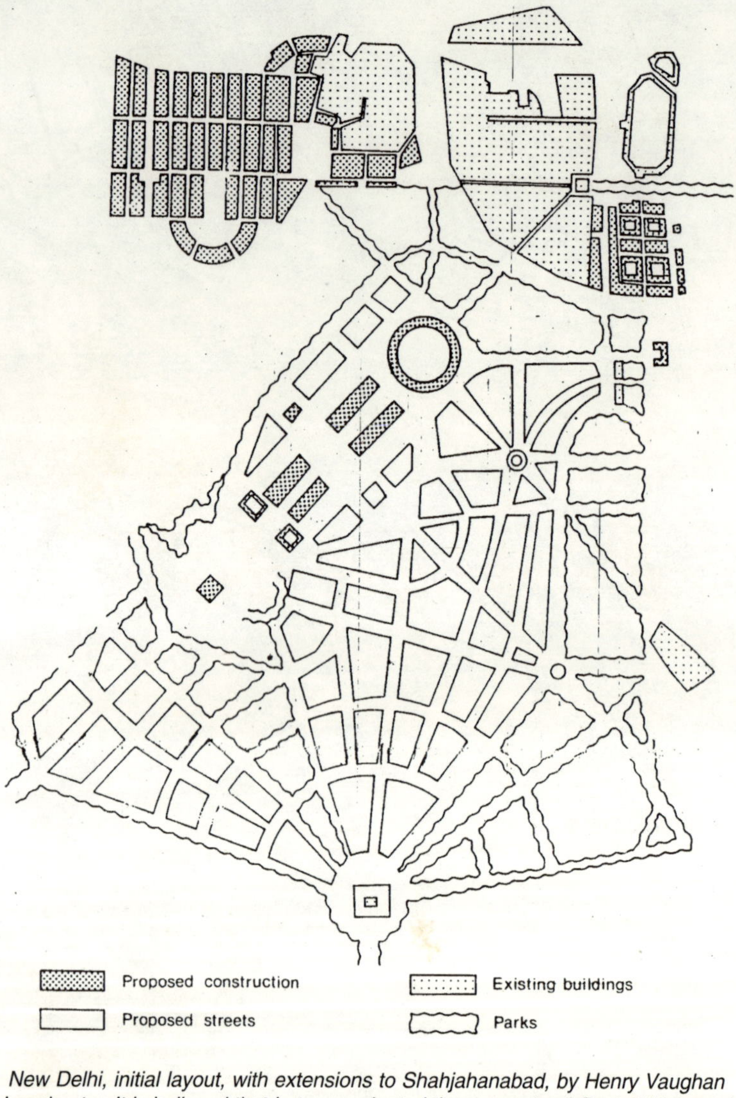

New Delhi, initial layout, with extensions to Shahjahanabad, by Henry Vaughan Lanchester. It is believed that Lutyens adopted the concepts of Central Vista and historical monuments as the nodal points in his plan, which he developed later. However, Lutyens' ignored close interface of new city with Shahjahanabad as was conceived by Lanchester.

The Durbar Dais

Source: The Historical Record of Imperial visit to India (1911), London, Published in 1914.

On the 12th of December 1911 at the Delhi Durbar, King George V, Emperor of the British Empire, proclaimed his decision to move the capital of India from Calcutta back to Delhi. That the new city be worthy of its predecessors, the Emperor expressed his desire that the planning and design of the public buildings be considered with great deliberation and care.

Lutyens, the architect was given the task to build the city of his dreams, an "Anglo Indian Rome", which would reflect the might, glory and vastness of an Empire on which the sun never set.

Delhi Coronation Durbar (1911)

The Viceroy, Hardinge, chose the Kingsway Camp for coronation Durbar of 1911 where the earlier Durbars had also been held. Exquisite shamianas were borrowed from the native rules. The Durbar area had 475 camps with arterial roads, a polo ground, football and hockey fields, a two-square mile parade ground, a band stand, a power house and many other amenities. Lakhs of Indian were lured to Delhi to witness the greatest star-studded drama in Delhi, under the direction of Lord Hardinge and supported the Marquis of Crew, Duchess of Deveonshire, Earl of Durham, Earl of Shaftesbury, Duke of Tock, and others.

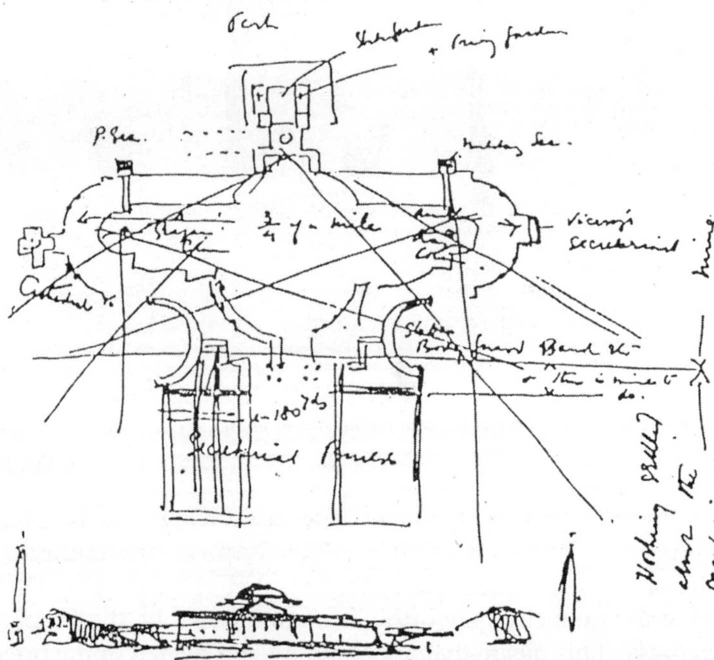

Edwin Lutyens' initial sketch of Capital Complex (June 1912)

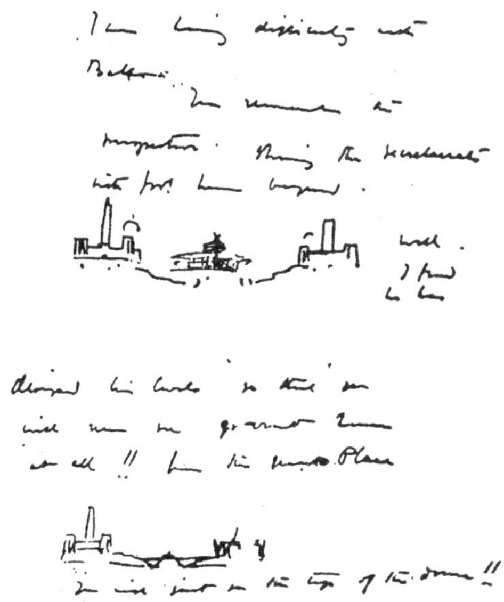

Lutyens' letter to his wife, Lady Emily Lutyens with his initial concept sketches of the new capital.

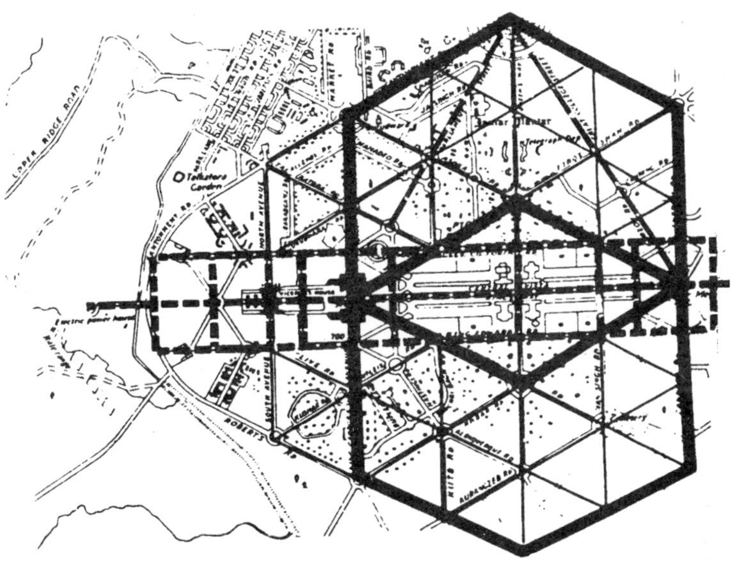

The plan of New Delhi is formed by the superimposition of two separate and distinct geometric systems. The narrow rectangular grid is monumental and relates to the major scale of the region and Government buildings. The other, the hexagonal system is local and devoted to the residential city.

Source: A Greenburg, 1969, Lutyens' Architecture Restudied, in Perspecta, 12, Connecticut

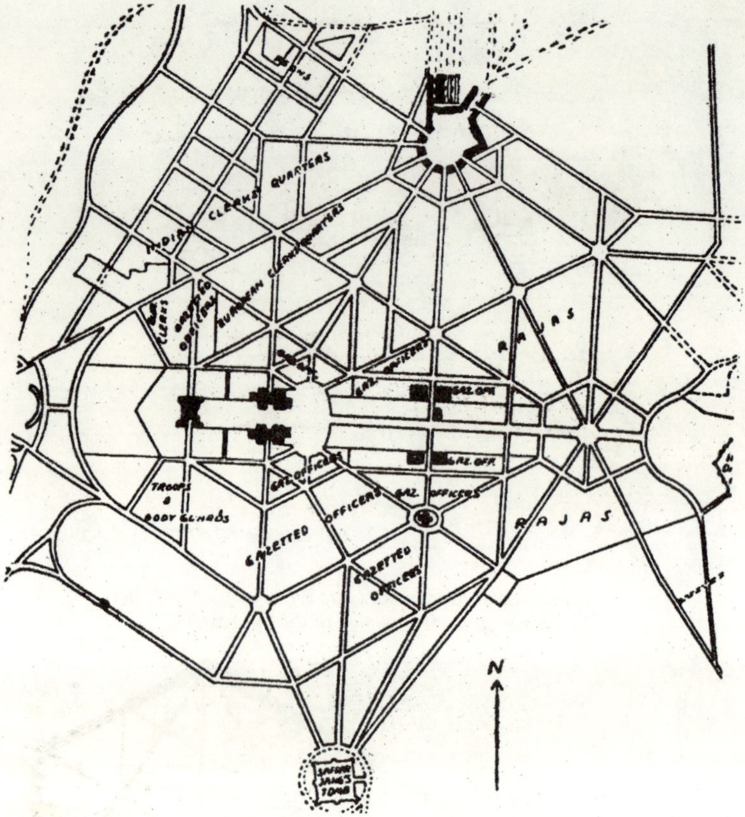

Imperial Delhi: Plan by Lutyens (1913)

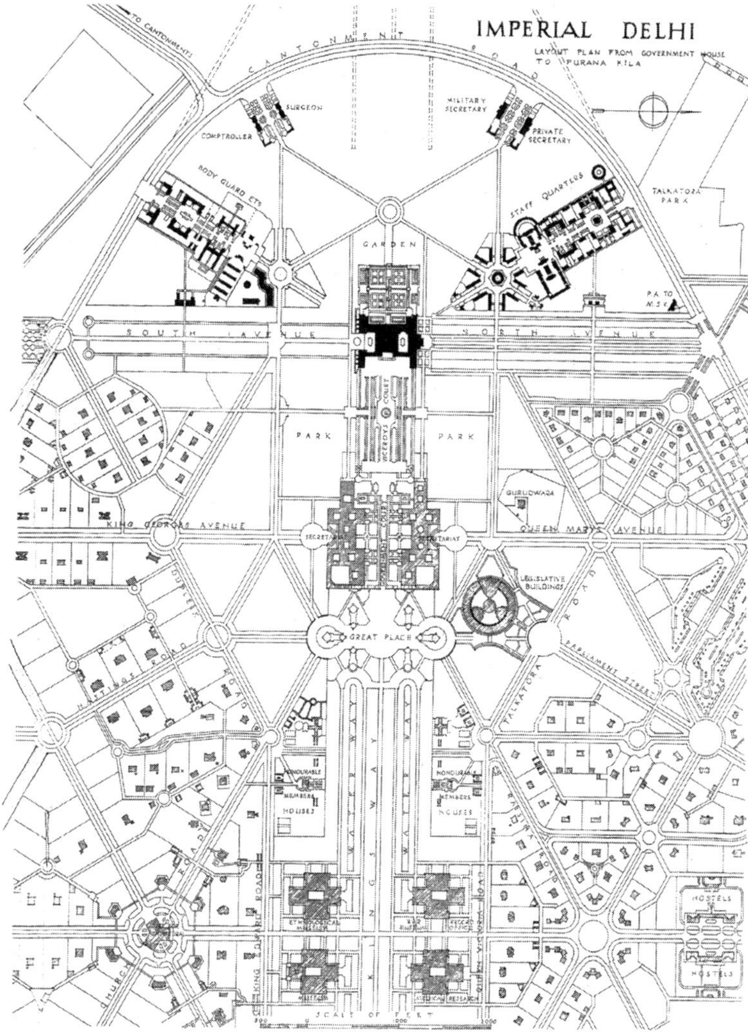

Detail of the layout of Capital Complex at Raisina, including the Viceregal Estate. Source: Central PWD, New Delhi.

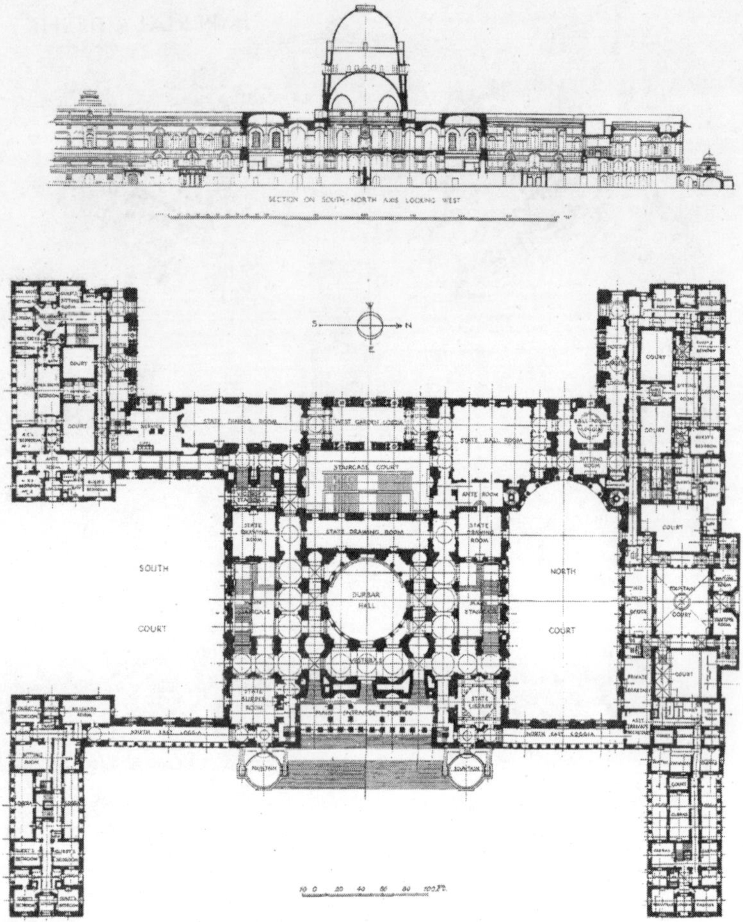

Plan of Viceroy House Architect: Edwin Lutyens

Source: Central PWD, New Delhi

On Dec. 7, 1911, Lord Hardinge, the Viceroy, welcomed the King George V and Queen in Delhi: The King on a horse, the Queen in an open carriage, the Viceroy and Vicerine, the royal guest, Indian rulers, Governors, top army brass, 10,000 troops and escorts of rulers left the Red Fort in a procession of horses and 3,000 cars. The procession passed around Jama Masjid, Fatehpuri Bazaar, Dufferin Bridge, Mori Gate and then entered

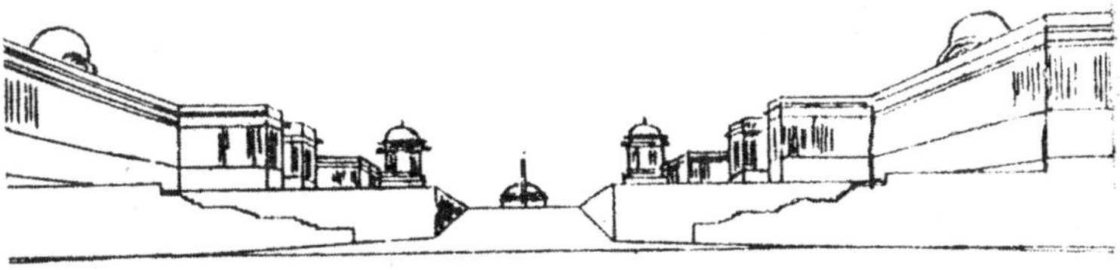

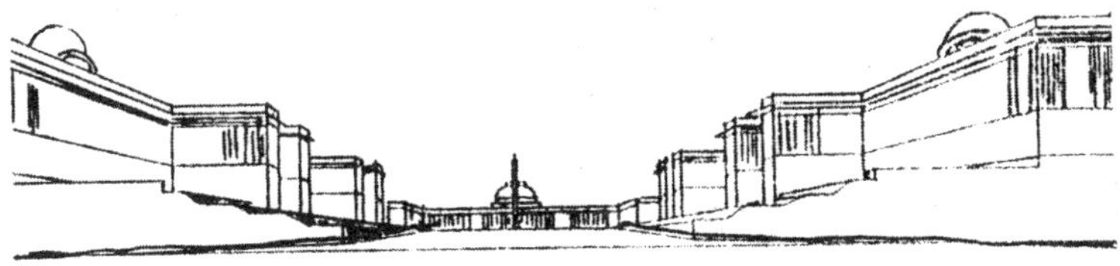

Top sketch shows actual view from the centre of the Great Court; bottom sketch shows Lutyens' proposal to cut back the slope and reveal Government House.

the ridge. In a spacious Shamiana in front of the Flagstaff House, the Royal Couple was given a civic reception. Sir Lawrence Jenkins, Vice President of the Imperial Legislative Council read out the address. King George expressed his happiness to be in India where people admired him and his consort. The King inaugurated the Edward Park and unveiled the statue of the late King between Jama Masjid and Red Fort.

On December 12th, the King Emperor and the Queen arrived in the great arena. They sat on thrones under a canopy which was adorned by a Mughal style golden dome. One lakh privileged people witnessed the greatest show ever held in Delhi. Native rulers pledged loyalty to the British royalty. The King announced that the seat of the Government would be transferred to Delhi. To lessen the blow, Bengal was united. Bihar, Chotta Nagpur and Orissa got a new Lt. Governor, and Assam was placed under a Chief Commissioner. Hardinge supervised the foundation laying ceremony of the new capital by the King Emperor. The King announced that he had done his job. It was now the job of Hardinge to build yet another Delhi, which should reflect the glory and magnificence of the British Empire.

The original site of new capital was at the north of the northern ridge where the foundation stone was laid. But the Town Planning Commission, consisting of G.S.C. Swinton,

Edwin Lutyens and J.A.Brodie, found the original site unsuitable. On their recommendation the location of the new capital was changed to the area around Raisina Hill. Two years later in 1913, one midnight, the foundation stone was quietly removed by a young Punjabi contractor, Sobha Singh, wrapped in a gunny bag and taken on a bullock cart to Raisina Hill. Thereafter, the intense planning of the new capital began . In the meantime a temporary capital was erected in the Civil Lines Area. Thomas designed the Government Secretariat and Council Chambers, along Alipur Road (now called Old Secretariat). Private houses and hotels were leased or acquired. Barracks in Kashmiri Gate were converted into police offices. The Director of Temporary Works, Lieutenant Colonel H.W.G. Cole boasted that he had constructed temporary Delhi at a cost of only six million rupees. He could see the old Fort and the sparkling waters of the Yamuna towards the east and the ridge on the north. From another angle he could see the Jama Masjid. He could also see the Safdar Jung Tomb and Qutub Minar down south.

Report of the
Delhi Town Planning Committee on the possibility of Building the imperial capital on the North side,

June 13, 1912

Chairman : Mr. George S.C. Swinton
Members : Mr. John A. Brodie; Mr. Edwin L. Lutyens.

Appointment

The Delhi Town Planning Committee was constituted by His Excellency the Viceroy and Governor-General of India on 13th June, 1912.

Terms of Reference

To choose a site for the New Imperial Capital on the north side at Delhi.

Contents

The previous consideration of the North Site by the Committee;

Revival of Interest in the North Site; Reason for Reconsideration of the North Site; The possibility of reducing the area required for the new city; The area available for the New City on the North Site (Area subject to flood; Area irrigated by the Western Jumna Canal; The Civil Lines; The Bela); Special Points in Connection with the North Site [Cost and result of purchase of Civil Lines; Difficulties about the treatment of areas west of the ridge (The Najafgarh Drain; low-lying land; sewage disposal)]; General points in connection with the North Site (The question of room for expansion more vital than ephemeral amenities; The initial cost of the ground; The provision for cantonments; The provision of land for recreation; The narrowing of ideals); Planning on the North Site (Scenic aspect from the North Ridge); Comparison of cost of a city on the North Site with a city on the South Site; A Brief Discussion of Sir Bradford Leslie's scheme; Conclusions in regard to the North Site; Appendices; Map.

Recommendations

The advantages and disadvantages of the north and south sites may now be finally considered. On the north site there are the associations of 1857, of the Durbars and of the Commemorative Stones laid by Their Imperial Majesties. Proximity to the river and the Ridge give certain scenic advantages. In the winter months the site is generally upwind of the present city. It is also up stream. There are the temporary amenities of proximity to a shopping area, a railway station and existing recreation grounds. It is apparently nearer to the present city of Delhi. It is at present used as a residence by an existing permanent population and by the camp officers of the Government of India in the cold weather; its adaptation to be the permanent seat of the Government of India is therefore not beyond the limits of possibility. There are some roads, bungalows and trees on the area already. The Committee freely admit the great architectural possibilities in the site provided the area required can be restricted to three square miles and there is no lack of money to be spent.

In the first place, in order to fit the city on to this area at all, the areas allotted by the Government of India for each item in the city have to be cut down, and certain items have to be excluded entirely. This is beginning town planning at the wrong end, when equally suitable sites are available elsewhere. The site should be chosen to fit the requirements, and not the requirements modified to suit the site. By adopting the south site, the heritage of the memories of 1857 and the Durbars are not lost to us. The new city on that site however goes back further and gathers the strands of many centuries and empires into the new imperial whole. The scenic effects of the Ridge and River can be secured on the south side also. The Ridge can be afforested there and a wild park made where the view will not be spoilt by the smoky vistas of Sabzi Mandi. A water effect can be afforded there at less cost and without sanitary drawbacks. It is to be remembered that all the fine monuments of the Delhi of the past are to be South. During the period of the residence of the Government of India the site to the south is sheltered from the cold weather winds and far enough from the Ridge in the warmer months to escape the radiation of heat. On the north, half the site is exposed to the north and north-west winds of the winter and the rest is too hear the Ridge for comfort in the heats of the autumn and spring. The remarks about sewage disposal on the north site show that the upstream position of the city is a positive disadvantage. The temporary amenities of the norther site would mostly disappear in the process of reconstruction. Better trees and better gardens can be made on the southern site. The work of construction on the southern site can proceed without disturbance to the present population of Civil Lines or the temporary residents from the Government of India. The Government House on the southern site may actually be nearer the Jama Masjid, which may be taken as the centre of Delhi, than when located on the north site. The distance of the nearest edge of new Delhi to old Delhi on either site will be the same. The southern is already healthy and has healthy surrounding. The northern site even after expenditure on sanitary requirements will never be satisfactory. If the northern site is to be made healthy, this involves going outside the site itself and making the neighbourhood healthy also. There is no really suitable healthy site for a cantonment in proximity to a city on the northern site. The exigencies of fitting in the requirements to the limited area of the northern site endanger the success of a layout as a whole and tend to make for cramping and bad arrangement. The result of placing a city on the northern site appears to the Committee to be the creation of a bad example in place of a good one.

On the north, once the overlaps a limited area, the land becomes more costly to buy or to treat, worse in soil and less healthy.

The northern site is too small and too cramped, and that a worthy city cannot be safely fitted upon it at all, far less provided with ground over which to expand, without including some land which will be very costly to buy and much land which will be very costly to make healthy, even if so sour and poor a soil can ever be made really healthy.

When there is a better, cheaper and healthier site conveniently at hand it is out of the question to advise the Government of India to select this northern area for the site of the Imperial Capital.

Source: Superintendent, Government Printing Press, Delhi, 1913, 199p.

The work of planning the new capital was entrusted mainly to Edwin Lutyens, an ambitious architect who had dreamt of constructing monumental buildings. He had got a rare opportunity, one of a lifetime, to build a new city, an "Anglo Indian Rome", which would reflect the might, glory and vastness of the British Empire. This mammoth task of planning and supervising the layout of a city which was to accommodate 65,000 persons and allow for unlimited growth in the future required Lutyens to get a great deal of assistance. He chose to work with Herbert Baker, already well known for his government buildings in Pretoria. The two divided their spheres: Lutyens retained the Viceroy's house with its fountains, the waterways and King's Way, the Record Office and the general layout of the city streets as his province and Baker undertook the Secretariats and the Council Chamber with the All India War Memorial, an archway at the end of King's Way, which was later assigned to Lutyens. The main buildings of New Delhi, as they stand today, are the work of two men united by a single scheme of conception and materials.

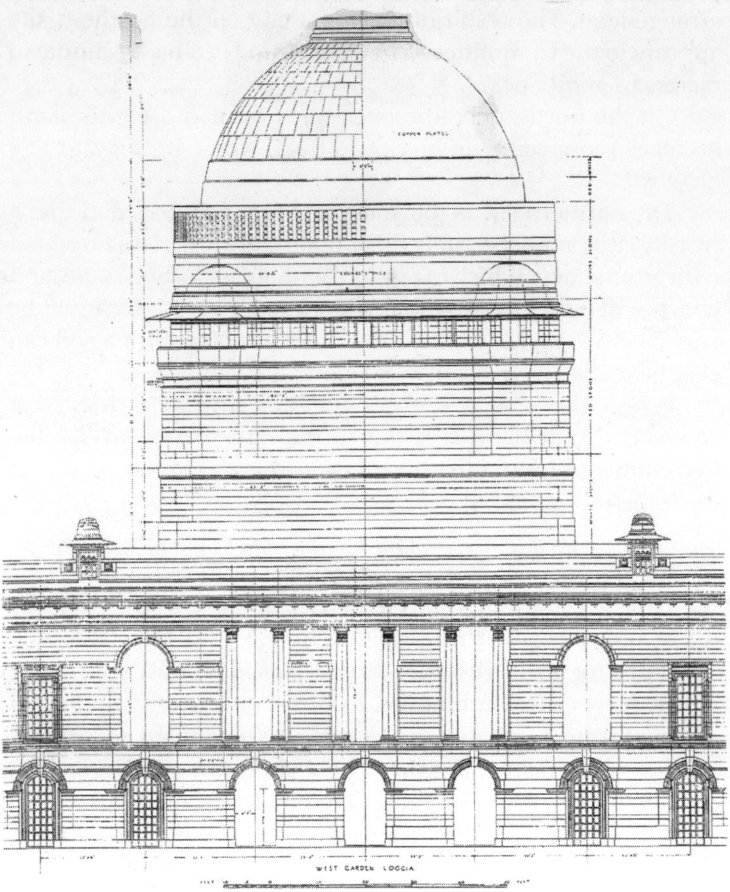

The Design of Viceroy House by Edwin Lutyens

Source: Buttler ASG, 1950

The Plan of New Delhi

The plan of New Delhi is geometrical in shape with hexagonal and triangular patterns. The plan can be viewed in 2 parts—a rectangular grid or main central axis that has the monumental government buildings and the hexagonal layout that focuses on the local and residential aspects of the city. The central axis, which was known as Kingsway (now called Rajpath) runs through the layout of the new city with several avenues and

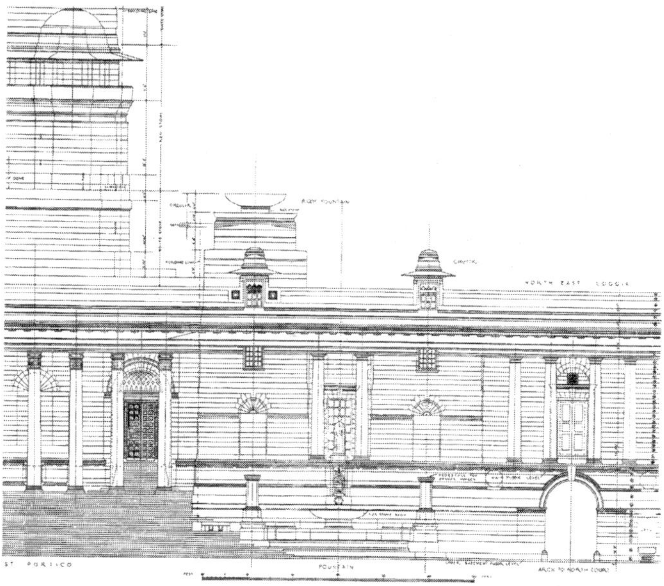

Imperial Delhi Viceroys House – Part of East Elevation

Source: Butter ASG, The Architecture for Sir Edwin Lutyens, 1950.

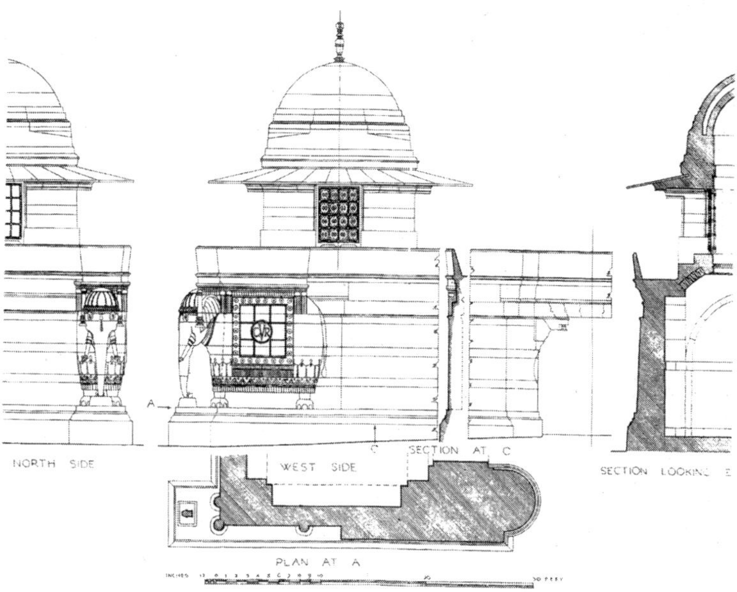

Imperial Delhi – Viceroy's Court – North-East Guardroom, C.S. Jagger, Sculptor

Source: Central PWD, New Delhi/Butter ASG, 1950.

streets radiating from it. It was designed by Lutyens as a processional path that linked the Viceroy's House (now the Rashtrapati Bhavan) at the west end to the war memorial arch or India Gate and the canopy of George the V at the east end. The central Vista is a picturesque, centre piece of new city with large, shady trees and ornamental ponds. The grand vista still functions as a ceremonial path during the celebrations of the Republic Day Parade held annually on the 26th of January. The Secretariats were planned in close proximity to the Viceroy House.

Lutyens enjoyed using geometrical shapes in his designs and architectural plans. In his plan for New Delhi, the triangle, hexagon and square are used frequently. These geometrical forms were also used by Lutyens' predecessors, the Mughals. The hexagon is commonly used in Mughal architecture, a perfect example of which can be seen in the inlay work in red sandstone and white marble at Humayun's Tomb.

The plan of New Delhi is a combination of two separate and distinct geometric systems. The monumental grid is comprised of the Central Vista; with recreational activities and the India Gate as a symbolic entry on the riverside, while the capital complex and Viceroy's Palace on the Raisina Hill. The capital complex is an architectural ensemble of unique value. Lutyens visualized that the Central Vista would have a grand vision, highlighting the supremacy of the British rule. The other geometric system comprised of a hexagonal pattern which linked the major activities of the triangular base, viz., governmental, commercial and recreational, flanked by the residential areas. The circulation network provided a visual continuity of the new city with the monuments of ancient capital, like the Purana Quila, Jama Masjid, Safdarjung Tomb, Ferozshah Kotla, Lodhi Tombs, etc. The city was nestled between two ecological features of the site, which were river Yamuna on the east and the Aravali ridge on the west. Lutyens' plan was to landscape a vast expanse joining the river Yamuna and the Ridge. The water pools of the India Gate were surrounded by a number of palaces and stadium. The hexagon was conceived as a vast park with buildings hidden by trees.

The Central Secretariat Complex was planned to dominate the skyline of New Delhi. The Viceroy's Palace with the two Secretariat buildings on either side occupied the highest land of the Raisina Hill. The Central Vista was laid out as a vast foreground to the imperial complex, which accentuated the grandeur and superiority of the new city. The panorama of monumental buildings enveloped within a rich landscape is unique. The central vista has become almost symbolic of New Delhi as a stage of the world's largest democracy.

The main feature of New Delhi's street pattern is a broad processional avenue, which was known as the King's Way and now called Rajpath, linking India Gate with the Viceroy's residence. Various roads cross this main avenue at right angles, but the general street pattern is diagonal to the main axis. The system of diagonal avenues provides directness of movement for vehicular traffic. Lutyens had a far sighted perspective and planned the roads with liberal widths. That is the reason that today while the population of Lutyens' Delhi has multiplied ten times that what it was planned for, still most of the roads have been able to bear the burden of multiplying traffic.

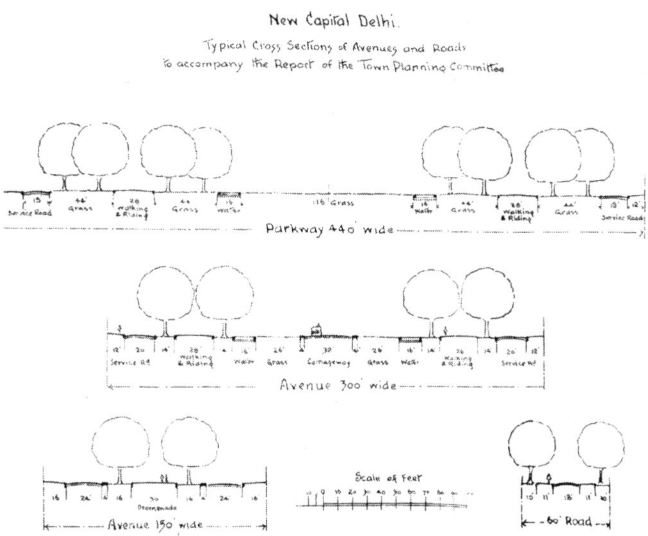

Delhi Town Planning Committee Proposals for Avenues (1913). For a common man, wide, comfortable and beautiful roads of New Delhi with overarching greenery make the image of the Capital. A common perception is that Edwin Lutyens had a long vision in providing liberal road widths 100 years ago when city had less than 1000 cars, which still cater to more than 7 million vehicles in Delhi (2013).

Source: Central PWD, New Delhi

In contrast to a compact and introvert Shahjahanabad, the new city was designed on an extrovert and low density pattern. With a maximum density of 25 persons per acre, no attempt was made to relate the new to the old city. The plan proposed large plots of 1 to 6 acres (with some plots even bigger) for residential development. However, the city remained deserted and looked barren for decades. In attempts to populate the deserted New Delhi, housing allowance given to government employees working in New Delhi was refused to those residing outside it. Businessmen were given incentives to open their shops in the Connaught Place. About Rs. 115 millions were spent on building the new city, which was completed in 1931. To service and maintain the new city, the New Delhi Municipal Committee was constituted in 1916, but it did not become effective until 1925. In 1927 the Imperial Delhi Municipal Committee renamed Imperial Delhi as New Delhi.

The planning and design of New Delhi have been the subjects of enormous discussions throughout the world. It certainly lent India a place among the countries with great capitals, like Washington, Pretoria, Paris and Canberra. Lutyens' efforts did achieve a grand capital for India. Sixteen years after the inauguration of New Delhi, political events precipitated the independence of the country and the native government of the new republic moved in to the abode of the British. People die and the governments change, but the cities and buildings survive. Perhaps with this in mind, Lutyens designed New Delhi as a tribute to India's greatness.

Bungalow for gazetted officers, class B

Copy of resolution No.2 of the 77th Meeting of the New Delhi Municipal Committee, held at New Delhi on Tuesday the 22nd February 1927.

----

2. Considered letter No.276/M dated the 19th January 1927 from the Deputy Commissioner, Delhi, enquiring whether the Imperial Delhi Municipal Committee desires to adopt the New name "New Delhi".

<u>Resolved</u> -

That the new name "New Delhi" be adopted and that this Committee be designated the "New Delhi Municipal Committee".

No.366/27 dated New Delhi the 3rd March 1927.

A copy (in duplicate) is forwarded to the Deputy Commissioner, Delhi, for information with reference to his letter No.276/M dated the 19th January 1927.

Secretary,
New Delhi Municipal Committee.

Decision to name the Imperial Delhi Municipal Committee as "New Delhi Municipal Committee"

C.W. Waddington visited New Delhi after its inauguration in 1931, and was a guest of Jaipur Maharaja. He wrote the following about the lands at Raisena, which belonged to the Maharaja and were ceded for the capital.

(i) The Jaipur Maharaja, received lands in Raisena near Shahjahanabad as a grant from the Moghul Emperor two hundred years ago, and built on it a palace and the remarkable Observatory, known as the Jantar Mantar, which still stand near the Viceroy's House. When the Raisena site was found to be the most suitable for New Delhi, His late Highness, the Maharaja Madhosingh of Jaipur, ceded his right to the land, in exchange for a corresponding revenue, and generously offered the Pillar, as a memorial of the lustre of his House in Moghul days, and a token on his abiding loyalty to the Crown. If the shade of the great Jaisingh should ever visit the spot, would he not smile with serene benevolence on the town-planners who have at last followed the lead he gave them two centuries back when he laid out his city of Jaipur on lines which seem modern even in our own day?

Below the Secretariat buildings is a great Place flanked on either hand by three splendid fountains, and rounded off by high stone railings of Buddhistic origin. This is the heart from which the arterial roads diverge. The great central avenue, or parkway, nearly 1200 feet broad, known as the King's Way, is lined by noble rows of tees and sheets of ornamental water, leading the eye to the War Memorial Arch and Indrapat beyond. Another vista is closed by the solid dome and graceful minerets of the great Mosque in the heart of the old city, another by the garish tomb of Safdar Jung; beyond this the splendid spire of the Qutb-Minar rises from the southern horizon. The nearby avenues are bordered by white houses in spacious compounds filled with trees, giving the aspect of a garden city."

C.W. Waddington (1933)

When the Imperial Delhi was formally inaugurated in 1931, it indeed was discerned to be an Anglo-Indian Rome. Lutyens, who was deeply influenced by the Greeco-Roman roots of city planning and architecture faithfully followed them in the design of New Delhi. In spite of the fact that in the West "modern architecture", with new materials, functional emphasis and changing concepts of structural engineering were raising a storm, Lutyens ignored them while planning and building the New Delhi.

Edwin Lutyens gave credit for the creation of Imperial Delhi to Lord Hardinge:

"The new city owes its being to Lord Hardinge, whose statue now stands surveying the length of the central vista (King's Way), and has inscribed upon its pedestal the right, proper, and proud word 'FOUNDER'. His patience and courage in times of great stress, personal and political, his even temper in the midst of diverse discussion remain in my memory as being parallel only with the greatness of his conception. His command that one avenue should lead to Purana Kila (Indrapat) and another to Jumma Masjid was the father of the equilateral and hexagonal plan. This was a sorry nuisance to all whose thoughts could not merge beyond the right angles of New York, nor embrace the intelligence of I'Enfant at Washington.

It was early in 1912 that Sir Richmond Ritchie, then Permanent Under-Secretary at the India Office, sent for me and asked if I could undertake the planning of the New Delhi. We went on to his club where in the guest book he wrote my name and gave my address as 'Delhi'. This was the first intimation I had of being selected for this momentous work. The last I heard of Sir Richmond Ritchie was from Lord Curzon, who told me he had just come from the funeral of one of his old secretaries. He spoke with great respect, affection, and praise; but it was a very dull affair—no horses, no plumes.

In April of that year, Mr. J.A. Brodie, the distinguished engineer of Liverpool fame, captain George Swinton (at that time chairman—bespoke of the London Country Council), and myself started on our great venture. We were three gay musketeers—luckily unarmed—and ignorant of all that India really was and meant, with the exception of Captain Swinton, who had served as an A.D.C. during Lord Landsdowne's Viceroyalty. Montmorency (now Sir Geoffrey, the Governor of the Punjab) was attached to us. We grew even more attached to him, and regretted—we really argued—the quick following promotions that were his due and which eventually separated us in the progress of the Delhi project. We had great and exciting disputations, and the outer world joined us.

In the following year the Government gave as a help Sir Herbert Baker, and all I can say is that I am a difficult person to work with. Each successive winter brought its annual flock of Cassandras flirting across the Indian skies, and self-constituted town planners; one of which was loquacious enough to be turned out and forbidden in the city."

—Edwin Lutyens

Lutyens revealed life in every rib and moulding and distilled essence of beauty. The Viceroy's house was the centre of his scheme, the pivot on which he lavished his thoughts; not only designing it, or overseeing the making of the furniture, but he even saw to the placing of the pansies in the garden! Lutyens' ambition was to create for the Viceroy of India, the most superb dwelling on earth.

Mustoe and Walter George were appointed the landscape architects for planting trees in the New Delhi area. Mustoe and Lutyens often discussed and agreed which trees were to be planted where. Mustoe raised them and planted them, while the job of spacing them was done by Walter George. From the Central Lutyens wanted the biggest tree available and for sometime *Imli,* Tamariscus Indica, was considered but it was finally turned down in favour of the Rai *Jaman*, Eugina Jambolina.

Climbing up the ramp, fixed in the alcoves of the two Secretariats, are slabs of sandstone inscribed with the names of the architects, engineers and builders of New Delhi: Sobha Singh, Dharam Singh, Basakha Singh, Seth Haroon and Nawab Ali. Thirty thousand unskilled workers came from various parts of Northern India and the largest single contingent was from Rajasthan. They were the Bagris, who were paid at the daily rate of eight annas for a male labourer and six annas for a female. There were also many skilled craftsmen who worked in marble and stone. The *sangtarash* or stone cutters came from Agra, Mirzapur and Bharatpur. Enormous sheds were constructed at the site of what is today Broadcasting House, where electrically driven saws and drills cut the stone into the required dimensions. The designs in stone were executed under the direction and supervision of a Scottish master-mason, Cairns.

A Sindhi builder, Seth Haroon, helped in building the Viceregal Lodge. Lachman Das was the main builder of Parliament House. Narain Singh from Sangrur in Sind, who was responsible for the arrangements during the Royal Durbar, constructed most of the roads and bungalows as well as the foundations of the Viceroy's House. Dharam Singh Sethi had a virtual monopoly on the supply of stone marble. He lived in a palatial house on Jantar Mantar Road which is now the office of the Indian Congress Committee. Basakha Singh of Mucchal village in the district of Amritsar, built the North Block of the Secretariat and many bungalows. Khan Bahadur Akbar Ali of Jhelum built the National Archives and Nawab Ali of Rohtak had a big share in laying out the Mughal Gardens.

Lutyens and his team of architects, engineers and contractors atop a scaffolding, hoisting the Union Jack in order to celebrate the completion of the central dome of the South Block.

One of the primary contractors was Sujan Singh his son, Sobha Singh. The family came to Delhi before World War I and after a few insignificant attempts in textile they went into buildings and construction in a big way. Thus the lion's share in the building of New Delhi was Sobha Singh's South Block, the Court of Viceregal Lodge, the War memorial Arch, Baroda Palace, Broadcasting Centre, the National Museum and innumerable bungalows, chummeries and living quarters were amongst his contributions. Sobha Singh had a vision of the

Lord and Lady Willington (centre) with some of the architects, engineers and contractors responsible for the building of New Delhi.

future. When Raisina was a jungle of barren rock and trees he bought large tracts of land at an open auction. The highest price he paid was a rupees per square yard for land he acquired in Connaught Circus. Later he became President of the New Delhi Municipal Committee and a member of the Council of States. Finally, he was knighted by the British Government.

The building of New Delhi was completed in 1931 for which about $ 15 million had been spent. These figures were not small but included the official buildings, all roads, water and lights, the planting of 10,000 trees, the cartage of stone from Dholpur as well as the enormous task of excavation and levelling of land. The Viceroy, seeing the mounting expense, began to curtail the original proposals which led to Lutyens' rueful remark, "the Viceroy thinks only of what the place would look like in three years time; three hundred years is what I think of". Lutyens was not a man to give up easily and cultivated Lady Hardinge, using her influence to get his schemes sanctioned.

The entire work of the actual construction was undertaken by the government of India's Central Public Works Department. Between this department, shivering in the blast of public economy and an artist concentrating on the realization of his aesthetic conception, occasional disagreement was inevitable. The final product, the capital complex, is seen as an architectural ensemble of unique aesthetic and functional value. Lutyens visualized that the Central Vista would have two distinct views.

From one end, there would be the grand vista, the large expanse of space orchestrated by trees, lagoons and fountains with the War memorial in the foreground and the horizon in the distance. From the other end one would see the gigantic scale of the buildings of the Secretariat and the Council Chamber, (now Parliament House,) with the Viceroy Palace (now the President's House), gradually coming into view completing the grand scene. Lutyens plan was to landscape the vast expanse that joins the river Yamuna with the Ridge, buildings being sculptural in their treatment. The water pools of the Central Vista were surrounded by a number of palaces and stadii. The buildings around the Hexagon were designed to give a feeling of vast park with mansions hidden by trees.

The Capital Complex was planned to emphasize the Imperial rule in India and the supremacy of the Viceroy. With the two Secretariat buildings on either side it occupies a very prominent position on an elevated platform. The Central Vista was laid out as an approach to this Imperial complex of power. Stretching from the Ridge on one side to the river on the other, the landscape flows into the heart of the city. In this vast expanse, the buildings of the Central Secretariat, the War Memorial Arch and Purana Qila assume monumental proportions and a sculptural quality. This panorama enveloped in a rich, lush landscape remains utterly splendid. It provides a classic example of a vista which integrates the river, ridge and the monumental buildings, such as the Viceroy's Palace. The result being that only the dome of this building, flanked by the imposing Secretariats can be seen as one moves away from it. However, it sinks out of sight halfway down King's Way. The conception and building of New Delhi is an architect's tribute to India's greatness. Lutyens scripted the following words to be inscribed on the Jaipur column at the Viceroy's Palace:

"Endow your thoughts with Faith
Your deeds with courage
Your life with sacrifice
So all men may know
the greatness of India."

The Revival of Indo-Roman Heritage

The new city was planned adjacent to Shahjahanabad yet separated from it by an open space buffer and railway embankment. This was accessible from the Walled City only through two underpasses, namely Minto and Lady Hardinge Bridges. Beyond this New Delhi was laid in a geometric pattern over a triangular based formed by Connaught Place, Government Complex and the India Gate. The centerpiece of the plan was the Central Vista. The residential areas were laid with lower and middle income employees to the north of the Vista and senior British officials to the south. To the north the fashionable shopping centre of Connaught Place and the New Delhi Railway Station were laid. This insulated the new capital from the old city.

Despite, Lutyens' own ignorance of Indian architecture, it is intriguing that the plan of New Delhi is not very alien to the principles of Vastu Shashtra. The location of the city, its zoning and functional classification coincide quite well with the Vedic principles. Its criticism by Indian and Western Scholars as a Western transplant is superficial and limited to its direct contrast and comparison with Shahjahanabad. It is quite amazing that the New Delhi by Lutyens' was located on the western bank of the River Yamuna, like Indraprastha. The Viceroy House had been sited on top of the Raisina hill, overlooking the river Yamuna. It is facing the east, so as to get cool breeze and morning glory of rising sun. Two major roads, namely Kingsway (Rajpath) and Queensway (Janpath), provide major linkages to various functions. At the crossing of these two roads, a socio-cultural institutional centre was planned. This is the place of Brahma in the Vastupurush Mandal. The planning establishes a monumental grid, comprising the city gate, institutional buildings and royal complex. The residential grid is distinct in scale. It is low rise and low profile in character. The Mitras (i.e. the Princely estates) in the East, around India Gate, Vivasvat, the business class in the South. Aryaka and Shudras towards the East and North. It may not be a surprise if the archaeological excavations at Raisina unearth the traces of a temple or a palace of Indraprastha era. Perhaps the Roman and Indian heritages derive from some common Indo-European culture. This interaction might have taken place perhaps during the time of Alexander, who came to India from Greece. The mythology and rituals of Greece and Rome suggest a deep influence of Vedic culture. It is believed that many of the epics and Shastras in India, including the Sathpatha Brahman were composed at a period contemporary with the rule of the Kings of Rome. These included many canonical books which dealt with the rules, rituals of buildings, proportions, and basic principles of settlement planning.

In the 'Politics', Aristotle makes explicit recommendations for a site:

> *"The land upon which a city is to be sited should be sloping that we must just hope to find, but we should keep four considerations in mind. First and most essential the situation must be a healthy one. A slope facing east, with winds blowing from the direction of sunrise, gives a healthy sites, rather better than the lee side or north, though this gives good weather. Next it should be well situated for carrying out all its civil and military activities."*

Vitruvius makes similar recommendations:

> *"The choice of a healthy site must come first. Such a site will be high, either misty nor frosty, the climate neither too hot nor too cold, but temperate. There should be no marshes in the neighborhood. If the town is on the coast and exposed either to the south or the west it will not be healthy... In founding towns, in short, beware of districts where hot wind can blow on the inhabitants."*

In the fifth century BC Hippocrates formulated the basic principles of city planning. These might have been a revolutionary period as earlier cities were more organically developed. It was after Hippocrates that the selection of site of a city, its orientation, topography and health aspects of ground became important considerations, besides its military necessities. Rome was founded on the Palatine hill, overlooking the valley of the forum. Street layout to the direction of the winds emerged an important facts of planning. Vitruvius, following his Greek preceptors, warns that "if the streets run straight in the direction of the winds then their constant blast rush in and...sweep the streets with great violence. The lines of houses must therefore be directed away from the quarters from which the winds blow, so that they may strike against the angles of the blocks and their force be broken up and dispersed."

Vitruvius described a sixteen rayed-tablet arrangement for orienting the main streets at an oblique angle in the strongest winds. 300 years after Vitruvius, Oribasius modified the principle of orientation and recommends the following:

> *"When streets are parallel in a town, some in length and some in breadth the first running from east to west, the others from south and north, so that they pierce the town through length and breadth without any obstacles, and none of the winds meets any building which might obstruct its course... (the town will be) well aired and sunlit, healthy and clear. For all the winds, Boreas and Notus, Eurus and Zephyrus, which are the dominant and most regular winds, sweep through the streets without meeting obstacles and pass freely without causing any disturbance. This kind of plan also makes the town a good suntrap because at sunrise and sunset and sun lights up the streets which run east-west, and at midday those run north south..."*

However, the logic continued to be interspersed with faith, rituals and symbolism. Fustel de Coulanges, wrote that, "the choice of a site is a serious matter on which the whole fate of the people depended...., was always left to the decision of the gods." Innumerable myths about the intervention of divinity in town foundation continued to prevail. The ritual of a sacrificial animal, for instance, were long continued. Complex principles were reduced to such rituals. These interventions were an integral part of the foundation laying and construction proceedings. Various rites which were not very different from Brahmanical Hindu rites, were always incorporated into the process of Roman cities and building process which reassured of good fortune and an auspicious place. A common sacrificial animal, such as a goat or a bird was slaughtered on the occasion. In later times even more complex methods of divination were employed. When the animal were sacrificed, the pieces of their meat were exposed for birds of prey. The site was fixed where the first bird dropped its find. Pious Aenas himself followed a pregnat sow to a place where it furrowed and founded Alba Longa on the spot. Romulus also followed this practice in founding of the Rome.

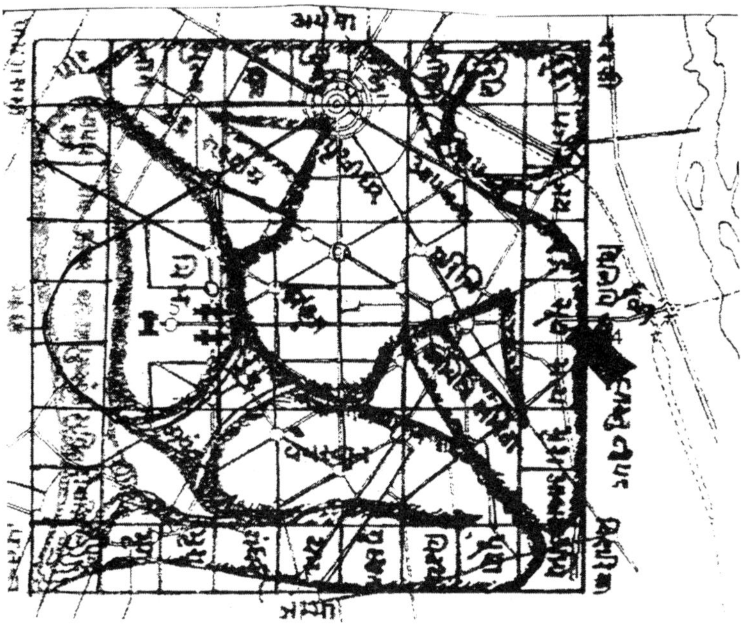

Superimposition of Vastu Purush Mandala on Imperial Delhi Plan

As in Mansara, town was perceived as a total cosmic symbol, Romans also curiously acquainted themselves with traditional cosmology. They inferred the 'templum' from the layout of the town. The city represented a complex structure of symbols, notions and patterns. The parallel between the 'garbha' and the 'mundus' is obvious. The templum, like the Mandala becomes a prophecy of a building or a town. At the same time, it guarantees its stability in the uncertain world. As a temple represents the application of the 'Vastupurush Mandala', in a similar way a Roman town identifies the 'templum'. Lutyens' New Delhi is perhaps an unintended revival and a tribute to the Indo-Roman heritage of city design.

The Mughal Garden

The splendid Mughal Garden of the Rashtrapati Bhavan is a geometrically laid out garden based on the char-bagh (four gardens) concept of the Mughals with water channels flowing out in the four cardinal directions from a central point. The complex consists of 12 gardens and a circular pool. Lutyens placed fountains with a hexagonal plan at the intersections of the central path of the garden. Lutyens travelled to Agra and Kashmir and became familiar with the gardens of the Mughal emperors, which he adopted for the Viceroy Palace. 600 varieties of trees were selected for the Mughal Garden at Viceroy Palace.

The Mughal Garden at Rashtrapati Bhawan

Source: Volwalisen, A., 2002

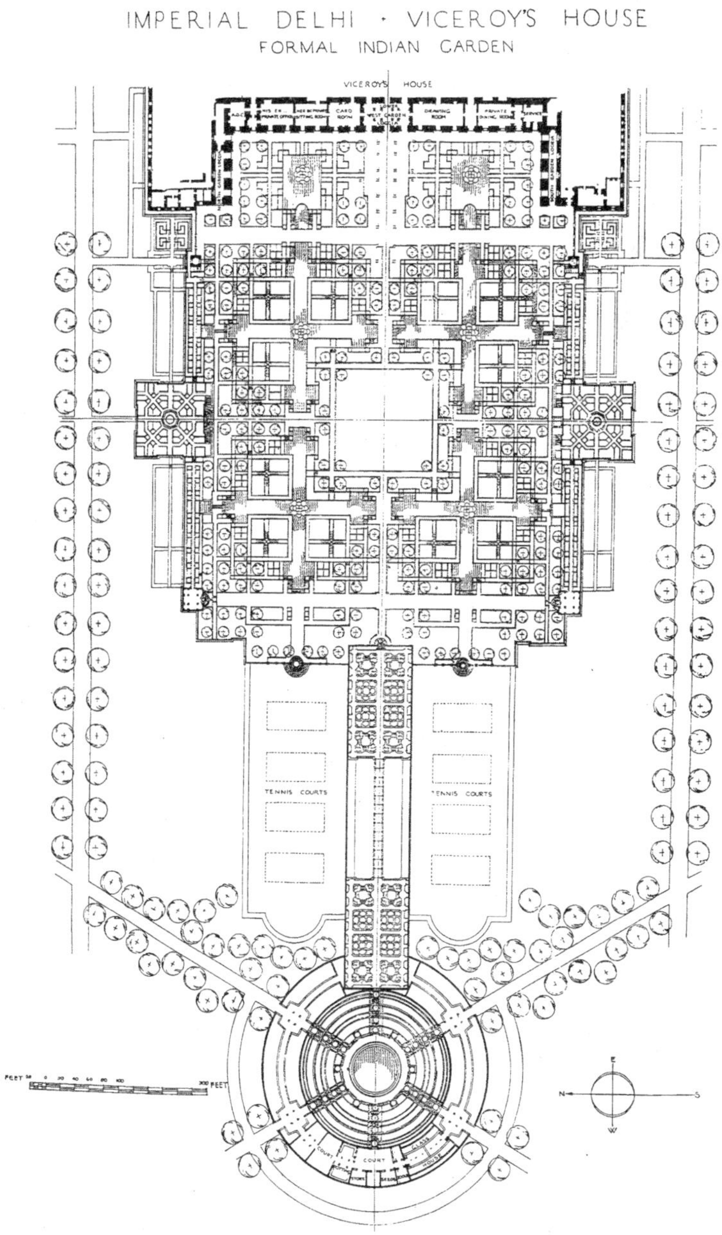

The Mughal garden of Viceroy's House

Source: Butter ASG, 1950

The Viceroy's House, now the Rastrapati Bhavan. Photo: G. Berengo Gardin

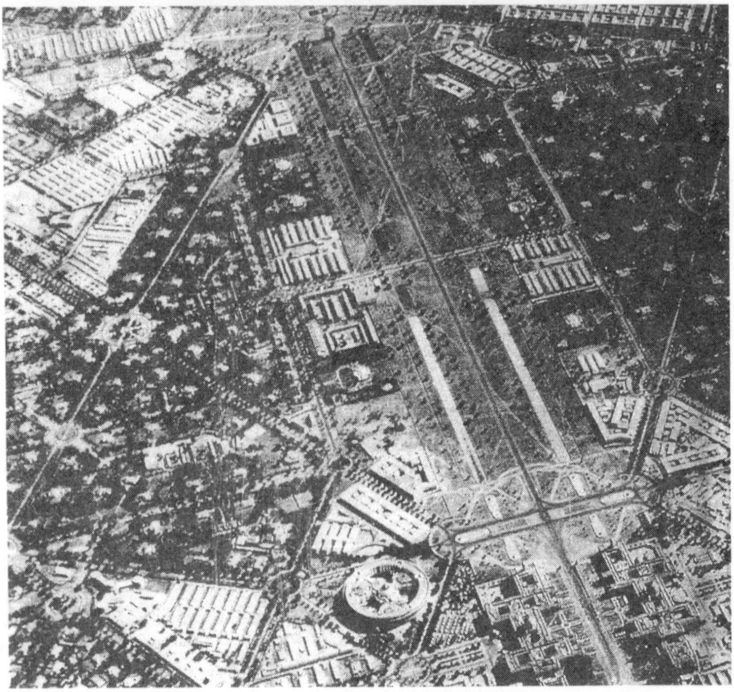

An aerial photograph of the1930s showing the Central Vista as the Centrepiece of Imperial Delhi

Source: Central PWD.

The Central Vista and Landscaped avenues from the centre piece of Imperial City as shown in this 1920s aerial vision.

Source: A. Volwahson, 2002/Centre of South Asian Studies, University of Cambridge, UK.

'The traveller drives out of Old Delhi, past the Jama Masjid and the Fort. A flat country-brown-scrubby and broken-lies on either side. This country has been compared with the Roman Campagna: at every hand, tombs and mosques from Mogul times and earlier, weathered to the colour of the earth, bear witness to former empires. The road descends a curve and embarks imperceptibly on a gradient. Suddenly, on the right, a skyline of towers and domes is lifted from the horizon, sunlit pink and cream dancing against the blue sky, fresh as a cup of milk, grand as Rome. Close at hand the foreground discloses a white arch. The motor turns off the arterial avenue, and skirting the low red base of the gigantic monument, comes to a stop. The traveller heaves a breath. Before his eyes, sloping gently upwards, runs a gravel way of such infinite perspective as to suggest the intervention of a diminishing glass; at whose end, reared above the green tree tops, glitters the seat of government, the eighth Delhi, four square upon an eminence–dome, tower, dome, red, pink, cream, and white washed gold and flashing in the morning sun.'

–R.Byron, 1931

The Jaipur Column

In 1915, Maharaja Sawai Madho Singh of Jaipur donated the sum of about 14,000 pounds to the British Government to build a column to commemorate the building of a new capital. The Maharaja of Jaipur, like other princely states were loyal to the Crown in order to protect their property from British occupation. The column was to be placed in a prominent location and Lutyens decided that the most suitable spot would be the forecourt of the Viceroy's house, known as Vijay Chowk today. The Jaipur Column is white sandstone that stands on a double base. On top of the column is an egg shaped pedestal, on which rests a bronze lotus flower. The flower balances a 6 pointed star of glass that was put in position in 1930. The plinth of the column has inscribed upon it the plan of Imperial Delhi.

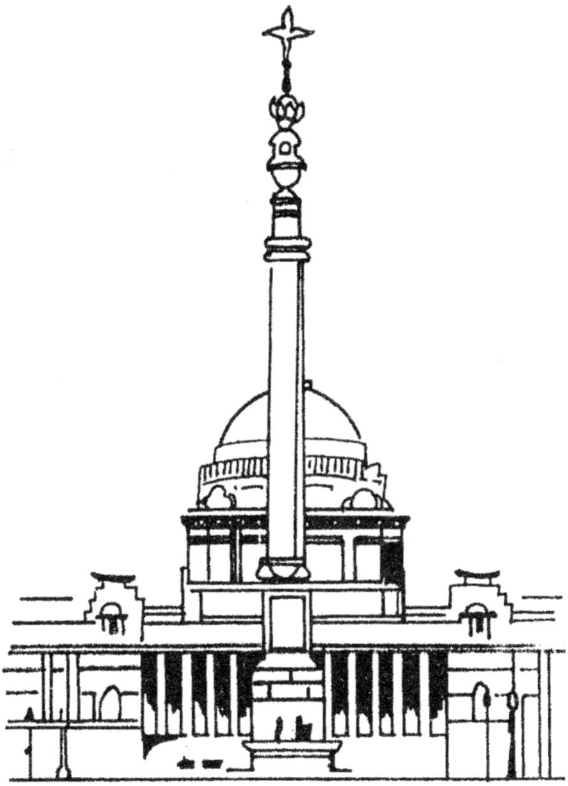

Jaipur Column in the forecourt of Viceroy House

The Secretariats

Two identical buildings, the Secretariats, designed by Herbert Baker and built from 1914 to 1927 were place close to the Viceroy Palace on either side of Kingsway or Rajpath. The Secretariats housed the government offices of the British Empire. Today, they house the administrative offices of The Government of India. The building complex is divided into the North Block and the South Block.

Baker gave in to the demands of the Viceroy Lord Hardinge of using Mughal architectural elements in the design of the Secretariats, some of which are easily visible. The buildings are constructed of red sandstone and elevated on a plinth, a common

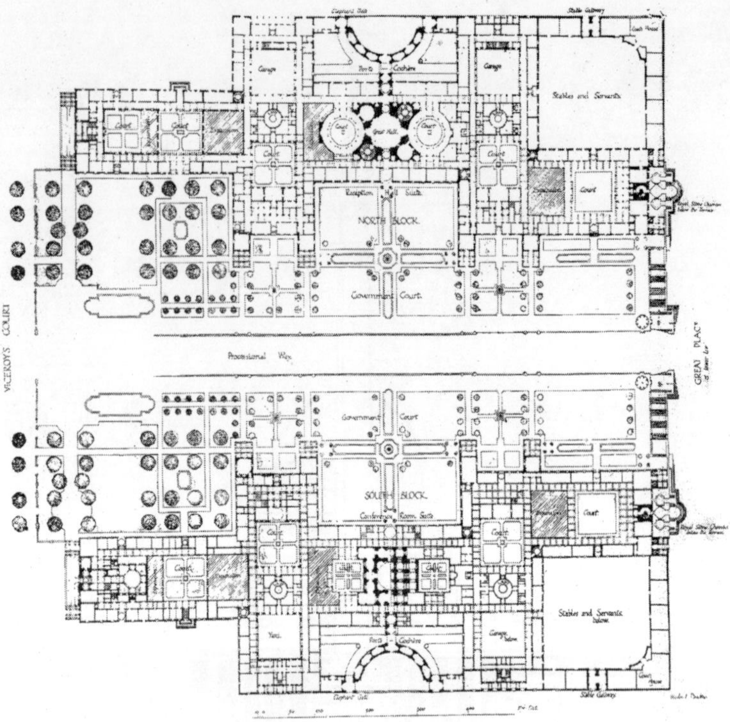

Ground Plan of Secretariats

Source: Central PWD, New Delhi.

feature seen in Mughal buildings and monuments. The entrances to the Secretariats are in the Mughal style. However, Baker did not use the Indian keel or pointed arch but the rounded arch of western architecture. The other indigenous elements used by Baker in the Secretariats are chajjas (overhanging cornices) and chattris (domed pavilions) which protect walls and windows from rain and sun and marble jali or lattice windows that admit air and not the severe afternoon sun. The Secretariats are 3-storeyed high and nearly a quarter a mile long. A striking feature of these buildings are the columned porticos with bells in stone added to the buildings on all sides. Baker termed these columned porticos as 'temples,' and inscribed the following inscription at the entrance arch of North Block.

"LIBERTY DOES NOT DESCEND TO A PEOPLE: A PEOPLE MUST RAISE THEMSELVES TO LIBERTY; IT IS A BLESSING, WHICH MUST BE EARNED BEFORE IT CAN BE ENJOYED."

The Persian words inscribed on the entrance archway of South Block read as under:

"Kimiya khwahi zaraat kun,
Khush guft aan ki guft;
Zaraa-e-sulusansh zar ast,
Sulus baqihun zar ast"

This translates as follows:

"If you want to convert brass into gold cultivate land.
This idea, propounded by whosoever, has been well said.
The two-thirds of agricultural product is like gold.
And the remaining one-thirds is also as precious as gold."
(Source: Dhirendra Singh and Mohan Joseph, 2011)

Parliament House

Parliament House was designed by Herbert Baker as the Council House, which housed the Chamber of Princes, the Council of State, and the Legislative Assembly. Work on the building began of 1921 and was completed six years later. The Viceroy of India, Lord Irwin inaugurated the Council House on January 18, 1927. Also known as Sansad Bhavan, the seat of Parliament is a

An aerial view of the Parliament House of New Delhi

circular structure, 171 metres in diameter and about one-third of a mile in circumference. It is raised on a red sandstone plinth that has niches that contain stone tablet commemorating those individuals who built the city. Two semicircular house chambers flank a Central Hall with a prominent dome. The building has a continuous open corridor on the first floor with a colonnade of sandstone pillars. Parliament House consists of three halls– the Lok Sabha (Council of the People), the Rajya Sabha (Council of the States) and the Central Hall.

Legislative Building, Cross Section (Parliament House)
Source: CPWD Archives, New Delhi

India Gate

India Gate, formerly known as the All India War Memorial Arch was designed by Edwin Lutyens. The foundation stone of this commemorative arch was laid in 1921 by the Duke of Connaught, the King's uncle and the structure was completed in 1931. This commemorative arch honours over 60,000 Indian soldiers who died in the First World War and other wars fought for the British. Also inscribed on the arch are the names of 13,516 British and Indian officers and soldiers who were missing in battle during the Afghan war of 1919. A symbol of Delhi, India Gate is located at one end of Rajpath.

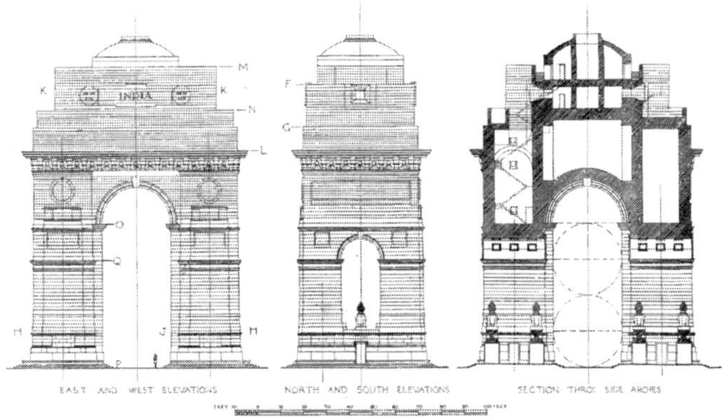

India Gate, Architect Edwin Lutyens

The Canopy of King George V

To commemorate King George V, Lutyens designed a 73 feet high canopy located east of India Gate. A white marble figure of the King was placed under a canopy facing westward. The canopy has a red sandstone roof and stands on a white marble pedestal. The monument is flanked by fountains on all sides. After independence the statue was removed and the canopy lies empty.

Canopy for King George Statue at India Gate: The inauguration of New Delhi was celebrated with the unveiling of the Dominion Columns and Ceremony of Commemoration on the completion of the Indian War Memoral Arch (India Gate) in February, 1931.

Hyderabad House designed by Edwin Lutyens

Hyderabad House (1926)

Lutyens was asked to design a palatial house for seventh Nizam of Hyderabad, one of the richest members of Indian royalty. Lutyens' built the largest and the most expensive residence for the Nizam costing 20,000 pounds. Hyderabad House has a dome, in the style of Viceroy Palace.

Baroda House

The Maharaja of Baroda commissioned Edwin Lutyens to build a palace in European style. Now it houses the Railways offices.

National Archives

At the intersection of Rajpath and Janpath, Lutyens had planned the cultural hub, one of which was the Imperial Records Department that later was known as National Archives.

National Archives Building

> "There are two ways to build in India. One is to parade your building in a fancy dress as at a fancy dress ball, so that the creation becomes something really funny; or to dress as an Englishman dresses for the climate, conscious only that your tailor is of Agra or Banaras, and not of Savitle Row or Petticoat Lane. It is the latter method I prefer and to be unconscious of all but the essentials and that without capitulation of our great traditions."
>
> *–Sir Edwin Lutyens*

Residence of the Commander-in-chief (Flagstaff House)

Robert T. Russel designed a palatial home for the Commander-in-Chief with enormous verandahs, pillars and open courts in stucco and stone. The residence was completed in 1930, and now houses the Nehru Memorial Museum and Library.

Flagstaff House

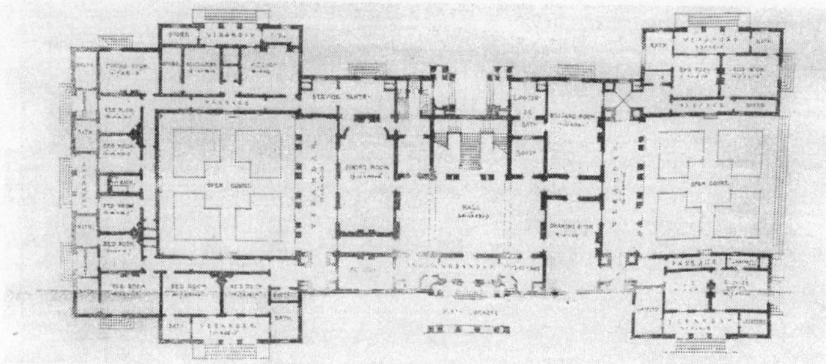

Commander-in-Chief's Residence, called Flagstaff House (Robert Tor Russel)
Source: Central PWD, New Delhi

Western Court and Eastern Court

Robert T. Russel was the architect for the Western and Eastern Courts on Queen's Way, now Janpath. These buildings today are guest houses for members of Parliament.

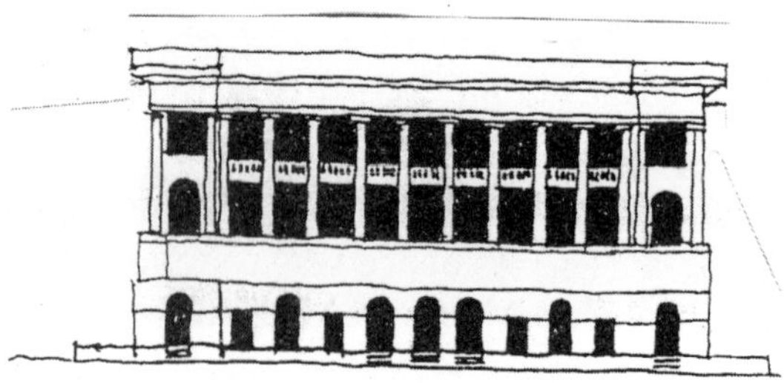

Western Court and Eastern Court

Connaught Place

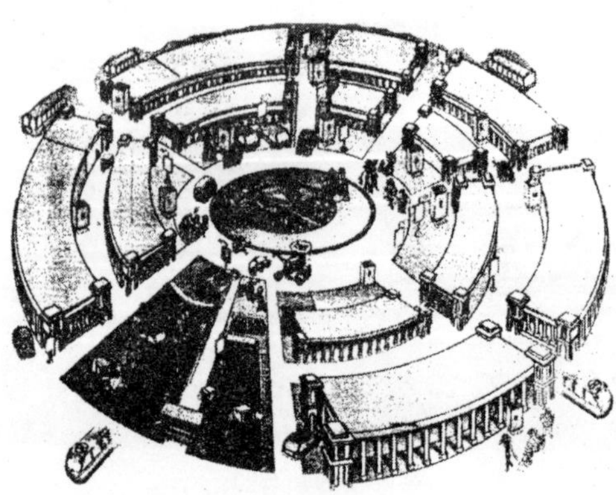

Connaught Place

An artist's impression of Connaught Place in the fifties

Robert T. Russel and his team planned the commercial centre at the heart of the new capital that was called Connaught Place, and is still one of the major business zone of the city. Russel designed 3 concentric circles of buildings with colonnades and wide archways built of stucco that today are burdened with an indiscriminate growth of shops, advertisement hoardings, etc.

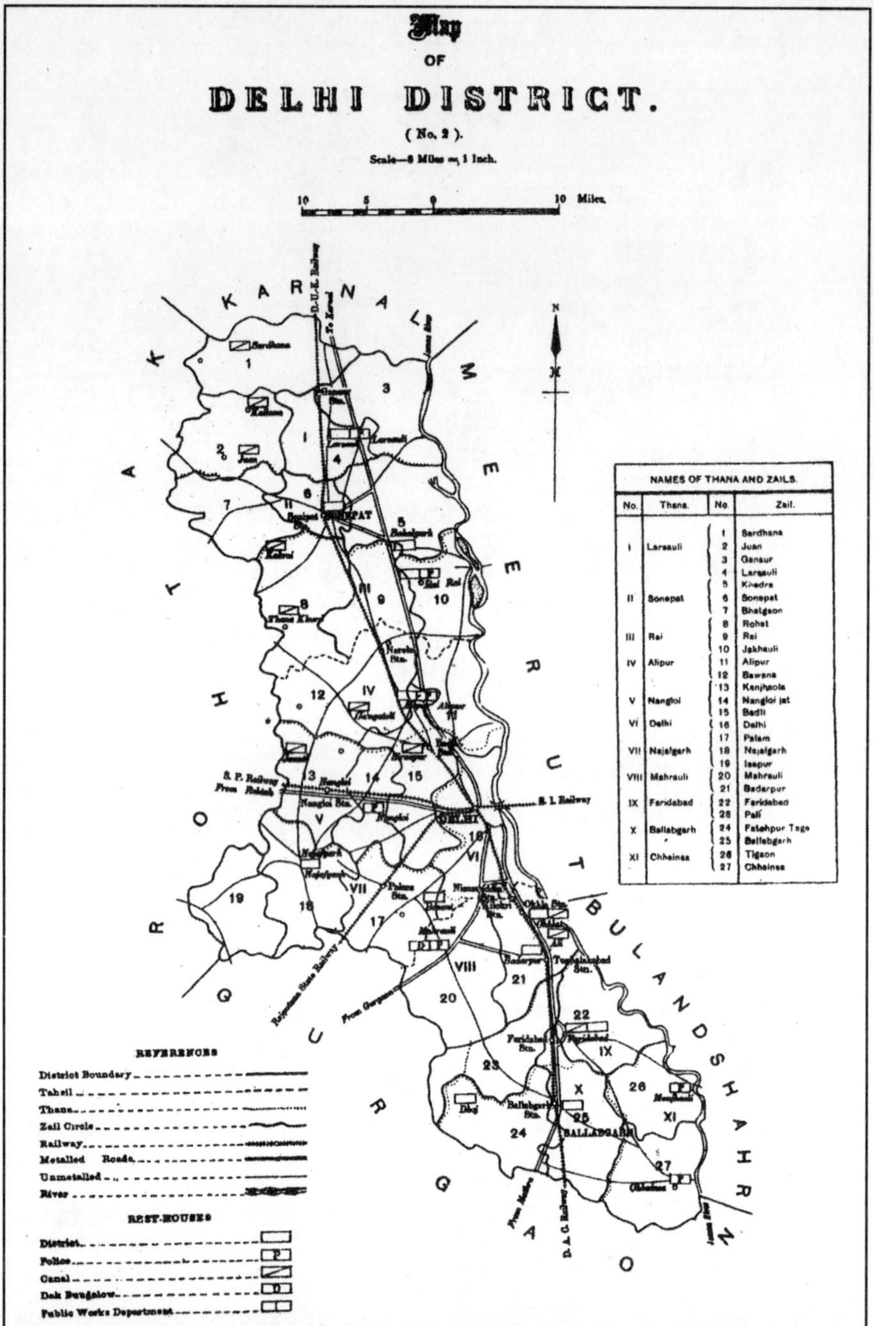

With Delhi becoming the capital of India, Delhi District was reorganised, which used to be a part of Punjab Province. While Shahdara Tehsil was added, Sonipat, Faridabad and Ballabhgarh were excluded from Delhi District.

Source: Government of India, 1913.

16. Transformation of the Old City

After the announcement of Delhi as the capital of India in 1911, the preparations for building a new city started with majesty, pomp and show. The British were determined to show their best skills in design, construction and city management. Shahjahanabad became 'old' and was rejected as a big slum. It was relegated as a potential area of danger, insanitation and crimes. Once termed as a most glorious and beautiful city in the Orient, Shahjahanabad was now often referred and devalued as a congested, dark and dirty hovel of overcrowded buildings. Of course, this was the perception of a foreign culture, which started with the hostilities of the war of 1857.

The British architect-town planner Lanchester, who was appointed by the Government to give a report on planning the new capital, also gave proposals for possible extensions to the existing Shahjahanabad. He recommended expansion to the west with a Karol Bagh-Jama Masjid Link Road. In 1915, Viceroy Hardinge's assassination attempt in Chandni Chowk resulted in furthering the devaluation of the Old City.

The administration of land in Delhi during the early twentieth century evolved through a period of last two hundred years of British authority. It was in the year 1803, when the British while setting the terms of protectorate, took under their control the lands, revenue and administration, although the revenue from the lands near the city was to be set aside for the emperor. After the arrival of the British, the demand for urban land increased manifolds and there had been a steady increase of land values. In the early days the settlements were ad hoc and crude. These started in 1817 with several summary settlements or in the form of a series of agreements. There were no regular records, surveys and maps. The Delhi Territory was first divided into districts in 1819. It consisted of two parganas, the 'Northern' and the 'Southern', which included Delhi, Sonepat, Gurgaon, Rohtak and Ballabhgarh. Besides acquiring and developing the lands for troops, camps, lines, magazines, churches, hospitals, clubs, race course, golf course, etc., several palaces and mansions were built by the British. Trevelyan, planned a suburban colony by the name of Trevelyanpore later known as Deputyganj, which was developed south of Pahari village and west of the Shahjahanabad. The urban structure of Delhi underwent basic changes, both in physical and socio-cultural terms. The cantonment occupied one-third of the area of Shahjahanabad i.e., 468 acres out of a total of 1437 acres.

The first regular settlement in the three tehsils of Delhi district was made during 1842–1844 to cover the estates belonging to the Raja of Ballabgarh, other Jagirdars and chiefs. Between 1848–53, 160 villages and an area of 193 square miles was added to Delhi from the districts of Meerut and Bulandshahar. This area is located towards the east of river Yamuna. During the Revolt of 1857, the revenue records were destroyed. By way of punishment, the estates of all rebels were escheated and were subjected to summary settlement. In 1858, Delhi was annexed to the newly constituted Lieutenant Governorship of Punjab. The assessments were framed under the North-West Provinces Rules based on Regulation IX of 1883.

The revision of the First Regular Settlement began in 1872 and was completed in 1880. Systematic record of rights and other statistical records were prepared in the form which did not much differ from the present form. This revision settlement had two remarkable features, namely introduction of fluctuating assessment in flood prone villages and dry assessment in the canal village. The Punjab Government sanctioned the revised settlement and Delhi was placed in the first class in the State.

In the view of the emerging importance of Delhi and need to exert more control on the land, the Third Regular Settlement was conducted during 1906–10. H.C. Beadon in 1906 undertook the work of revision Settlement (known as the Third Regular Settlement), which formed the basis of land administration in Delhi for rest of the century. In this operation, extensive surveys and measurements were made and the maps of 74 villages prepared in 1880 were revised. A Record of Rights was also prepared according to the Punjab Land Revenue Act, 1887. Assessment Circles were fixed for three Tehsils, viz., Sonepat, Delhi and Ballabhgarh. These circles were categorised on the basis of the character of land, i.e., Khadar (low, riverine tract), Bangar (Uplands), Dabar (hill areas) and Kohi area (area on sides of hills). The soils were classified into grade, chahi, nahri, sailab bhur and barani and the rates were fixed accordingly. The land revenue was regulated by the Punjab Land Revenue Act, 1887, and the United Provinces Land Revenue Act, 1901 in the constituent areas, which originally belonged to the States of Punjab and United Provinces.

According to the Delhi District Gazetteer (1912), there were 773 villages in the district. They were subsequently recognized as mauzas or revenue estates. Out of them 56 were classified as Zamindari, 321 pattidari and 396 bhaichara. An estate could from the beginning be either pattidari and bhaichara, but it was zamindari khalis, i.e., owned by a single proprietor. There were also the Crown lands which were acquired almost entirely through escheat after the Revolt. These were divided into two categories; viz.,

(i) the taiul land-lands which were originally owned by the King of Delhi, and,

(ii) the nazul land-other remaining Crown lands which might be rural or urban.

These Crown land were cultivated by tenants, who paid as rent the land revenue, cess and malikana. A part of the rural nazul land within the precincts of mauza Delhi was vested in the Municipal Committee for management. Urban nazul comprised town sites, building sites and non-agricultural lands in Delhi and its suburbs, which were vested in the Municipal Committee. Ground rents were realized from them.

Delhi, after becoming the capital of India in 1912, was detached from Punjab and Delhi Enclave covering an area of 1240 sq. miles was formed. New roads were constructed between the temporary Capital near the Civil Lines and Raisina. Geoffrey de Montmorency, who was in charge of the Capital transfer programme, on 19th March 1912, addressed the question of Delhi's expansion, mainly with the regard to protecting the government from charges that the Capital transfer checked the commercial expansion of Old Delhi. De Montmorency ordered the planning of a Western Extension for the city in March 1912. Viceroy Hardinge in April 1912 suggested that the Capital should comprise both New and Old Delhi and that one officer should rule them. Viceroy Hardinge outlined the burden that Old Delhi would bear in his address to the DMC on 23rd December 1912:

> *"You must become a Capital City, not only in name, but in fact; you must make your town a model of municipal administration; your institutions, your public buildings, your sanitation, must be an example to the rest of India, to attain these results will demand on your part much sustained effort, and the cultivation of a high sense of public duty. I can promise that the Government of India will be prepared to sustain you in those efforts by every means in its power. We shall not forget, when building a New Delhi outside our walls, that there exists an Old Delhi besides us which claims our interest and our assistance."*

Deputy Commissioner Lt. Col. H.C. Beadon wrote to the Chief Commissioner explaining the increasing pressure on Delhi's urban form. The letter, dated 1913, argued that an Improvement Trust must be created in Delhi 'before many years are passed', while the pressure on the city brought by the capital meant that it could legitimately claim aid, the city had been provided with no orderly expansion, people had been 'huddled into a totally insufficient area' leading to encroachments, slums and inflation that made building impossible. Census data showed the city expanding at between 20,000 and 24,000 people a decade, so a (constant) rate of 25,000 was assumed for the future (the actual increase between 1921 and 1931 was recorded in the later census as 1,00,605).

In 1913, land was acquired in Karol Bagh and Western Extension Area to resettle the displaced persons from Jaisinghpura. The workers were brought to Delhi to construct the new capital. The Municipal Committee undertook the development of Sadar Bazaar West and improvement of drains and sewers. It also passed new building byelaws and proposed Lahori and Kabul Gate Improvement Schemes. Circular roads along the Old City ditch with development of commercial plots were undertaken. These are the G.B. Road and B.B. Road schemes. In 1914, the famous British humanist-planner Patrick Geddes visited Delhi and gave a report on planning of the Walled City. The Burn Bastion (BB) Road Scheme at Kabul Gate was taken up to decongest the Khari Baoli. In 1915, Daryaganj Cantonment land was handed over to civil authorities and was used for residential purpose. Shahdara was also added to Delhi Province.

In 1916, butchers and tanners were removed from the area and resettled in Basti Reghar. At Qadam Sharif, a new slaughter house was planned in order to sanitize the old city. To discourage cattle in the city, milch cow tax was raised again. For garbage disposal in the walled city, in 1918 a system of dhalaos (garbage bins) was started.

In 1920, Daryaganj North was developed for residential plots while Daryaganj South plots were allotted to schools and charities. In 1922 the Punjab Town Improvement Act was passed and became a town planning legislation. In 1925 Delhi Municipal Committee demanded that Act be applied to Delhi. Expansion to the north was mainly in the Civil Lines area. To the north-east was valuable garden land and the poorly developed Sabzi Mandi suburbs, while to the west lay Sadar Bazaar suburb, to the south the new city, and the river to the east. New Delhi was directly administered by the Government of India and the rest of Delhi Province by a Chief Commissioner. Asaf Ali, a prominent public figure, wanted the formation of Delhi Improvement Trust. The Municipal Committee in 1926, proposed demolition of the city wall between Delhi and Ajmeri Gate. Lutyens opposed the idea to "protect the New Delhi from the rats of Old Delhi". However, due to heavy rains, part of the

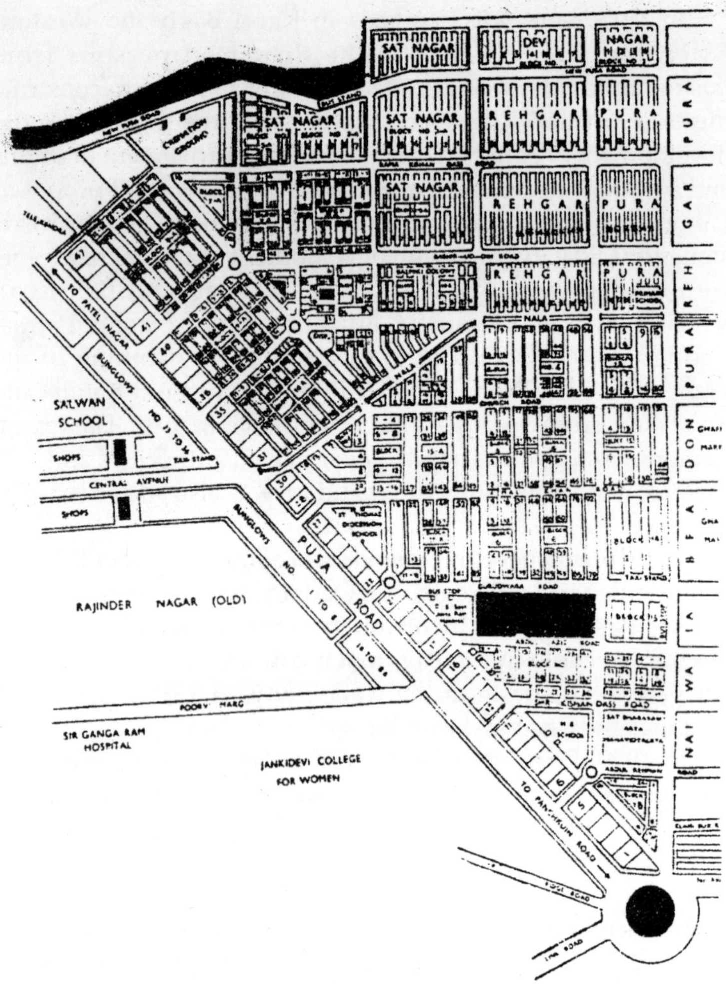

Western Extension Area: The development of Jhandewalan, Karol Bagh and Western Extension area took place with the building of the New Delhi. The Delhi Improvement Trust after its formation in 1937 took up these schemes to decongest the old city, Paharganj, etc. Delhi, which was confined between the river and the ridge so far, crossed the Aravali Ridge in Delhi.

city wall collapsed. The combination of urban congestion, deteriorating health and government inaction attracted criticism from various levels of society, the sum total of which represented a significant and increasingly widespread attack on the regulation of the capital.

In 1924, Muhammad Asaf Ali, who would later represent Delhi in the Legislative Assembly, persuaded the DMC to request the extension of the Town Improvement Act (IV 1922) to Delhi. The request was made by a resolution of 16 September 1925 to which Chief Commissioner Abott reacted enthusiastically. However, the response was delayed by 2 years before being rejected in 1927. In response, on 10 November 1927, the DMC put forward a resolution calling for proposals to combat tuberculosis. The extension of the Town Improvement Act to Delhi had been denied on the grounds of finance. So cheaper, less comprehensive, measures were decided upon. Stow made this decision following a letter from the Secretary of the Education, health and Lands Department of the central government, received in May 1926. This stated that, due to improved financial circumstances, the government would now consider funding public health initiatives in centrally funded areas like Delhi. In 1934, Delhi Municipal Committee acquired the Deputy Ganj area to relieve congestion in the Walled City. Land was transferred to the Delhi Municipal Committee near Jama Masjid to widen Jama Masjid Road. There were sparking rumours of British takeover of the mosque. The Jamuna Village (Bela) Improvement Scheme was proposed by the Delhi Municipal Committee. Motia Khan was planned for relocating industries and Kabari Market from Jama Masjid area.

The question on insanitation, congestion and slums in old city were raised in the Legislative Assembly on 12th September 1935. Muhammad Asaf Ali followed up on his tireless campaigning for an improvement trust. Asking when the government would hand over the Nazul land for development in order to aid congestion, the government replied that an officer had been placed on special duty to ascertain the degree and nature of congestion, the success so far achieved in tackling it, what should be done to remove congestion, and the way such a body establishment of the DIT. The Municipal Committee decided to pull down the rest of wall between Delhi and Ajmeri Gates in 1935 which invited strong objections from the residents of New Delhi against exposure of the "slums" to their views. The Government in 1936, appointed A.P. Hume as Officer on Special Duty to prepare a report on the "Relief of congestion in Delhi."

The report was finished on 5th May 1936 and highlighted the deadlock between the Government and the DMC over the improvement of Nazul lands. In assessing the nature of the congestion problems, Hume focused on population description, eschewing an emphasis on disease, economy or the cultural landscape. Chapter II of his report began by pointing out the rapid increase in population expansion in the 1930s. The 'patch-work policy of city development' had been unable to cope with this increase, although Hume renegaded on his direct criticism of the government by arguing that Old Delhi had been congested since the days of the Mughal time and thus the problem was also one of great antiquity. The problem was thus identified as one of the congestion of people in houses and houses on land within the walled city of Delhi and the surrounding suburbs.

The extent of the problem was supported by a statistical analysis of the 1931 census data. On the assumption that Old Delhi could support 200 people per acre, Hume calculated that Delhi Municipality had an over-population of 88, 169, which was rounded up to 1,00,000 for 1936–7. Hume went further and produced a map setting forth the geography of population congestion in the city. This map was deemed essential because it would allow people a concrete basis on which to estimate the nature of the problem.

Population in Delhi, 1881-1931

Year	*Population*	*Decadal increase*	*Percentage increase*
1881	173,393		
1891	192,579	19,186	11
1901	208,575	15,996	8
1911	232,837	24,262	12
1921	246,987	14,150	6
1931	347,592	100,605	40

The Viceroy issued a note on the 'Future Administration of Delhi' on 26th September 1936 that had far-reaching consequences for the Trust regarding Old Delhi. The Viceroy concentrated power in the hands of the new Chief Commissioner E.N. Jenkins, leaving the Deputy Commissioner to deal with law and order. Hume, was also named Chairman 'ex-officio of the New Delhi Municipality'. This placed Hume in charge of all matters of improvement between the two cities.

The DIT came into being in 1937 with the extension to Delhi the improvement Acts of the United Provinces Act VIII of 1919, the elements of the Rangoon Development Trust Act of 1920 and Section 78 of the Calcutta Improvement Act of 1911. The Government would determine the extent of the Trusts activities, but is could automatically work within the entire limits of the DMC. The basis of the Trust was the 'Government Estate; the 23 plots of Nazul land (the Nazul account) which, it was made clear, the Government could resume possession of at any time. The separately accounted 'Trust Estate' consisted of some small DMC lands given to the Trust, but was mostly constituted by privately acquired lands. As such, the Trust had to raise money to both purchase and develop its land.

The Delhi Improvement Trust was constituted under notification No. F. 23-10/37-H, dated the 2nd March 1937, of the Government of India in the Department of Education, Health and Lands. This notification extended to that part of Delhi Province which was described in the schedule to the notification, the United Provinces Town Improvement Act, 1919 (United Provinces Act VIII of 1919) with certain modification to make it applicable to the circumstances of Delhi Province. While deciding on the form of statute best suited to conditions in Delhi, a comparison was made of the provisions of the Punjab, United Provinces and Calcutta Improvement Trust Acts, Rangoon Development Trust Act, and the Colombo Ordinance of 1915. The officer on special duty had the opportunity to see the working of the United Provinces, Calcutta and Rangoon Acts. As a result, it was decided that conditions in Delhi approximate more nearly to those for which the United Provinces Town Improvement Act was framed, and although this Act was in many respects deficient, it was adopted as the basic law for Delhi, and extended to Delhi by virtue of section 7 of the Delhi Laws Act. Into this basic law were then grafted three sections from Rangoon Development Trust Act, 1920 (Burma Act V of 1920) and one section from the Calcutta Improvement Act, 1911 (Bengal Act V of 1911) with necessary modifications in each case to make the sections applicable to Delhi Province. The Trust Law consisted of the three notifications extending to the scheduled parts of Delhi Province the United Provinces Act and sections of the Calcutta and Rangoon Acts as noted above. The modified Act referred to as the "Trust Law". The three sections taken from the Rangoon Act were sections 32,59 and 86 of that Act, which appeared in the Trust Law as sections 22-A, 54-A and 54-B, and were extended to Delhi Province primarily on account of the extensive Nazul estates which the Delhi Trust had to administer. The administration of the Rangoon Development Trust was mainly concerned with Government estates. The section taken from the Calcutta Act was section 78 of that Act which appeared in the Trust Law as section 64-A, in order to permit abandonment of acquisition of land on certain conditions.

The Board of the Delhi Improvement Trust was incorporated under section 3 of United Provinces Town Improvement Act, 1919, as extended to the Province of Delhi, and consisted of seven trustees of whom one was an officer of the Central Public Works Department, one Assistant Director of Public Health, Delhi (redesignated as Chief Health Officer, Delhi Province), and one financial adviser. The Chairman and the three officers named above, and one other person were appointed by the Chief Commissioner by notification. The two remaining trustees were the members of the Delhi Municipal Committee and were elected by that committee.

The jurisdiction of the Trust extended to the areas in the schedule to notification No. F.23-10-37-II, dated the 2nd March 1937, extending the modified United Provinces Town Improvement Act, 1919, to the Province of Delhi. In fixing the jurisdiction, the various spheres of responsibility under the Trust law covered the following:

1. The Nazul estates;
2. The local bodies, within the limits of any of which the Trust might be called upon to take action under the Act;
3. The areas for control of malaria;
4. The areas affected by the sewage disposal scheme, and
5. Such other areas not included in the above as may reasonably be affected by urban expansion.

The Nazul estates contained considerable areas of vacant land which were to be used to relieve overcrowding, and city improvement. It also contained some of the worst slums in the city. On the financial side the agreement stipulated that net profits from the Nazul estates shall be utilized to finance (a) the development of these estates, (b) in part, a scheme for the disposal of sewage, and (c) a scheme for the control of malaria. By net profits it was meant that the sum which was at the disposal of the Trust annually after paying to Government each year a sum of Rs. 2 lakhs. The other essential and more onerous side was the task of relieving congestion and improving conditions of life in privately owned areas of Delhi city, of providing new areas for extension and of controlling haphazard and unserviced suburban development.

The DIT had to mould its activities around the fragmented Nazul sovereign land rights of the Government of India in Old Delhi. These lands had been violently appropriated from the previous Mughal sovereignty regime after the 1857 uprising and were used to orchestrate the improvement of the old city. The Trust was granted the Nazul land and had to pay Rs.200,000 per year for the privilege, positioning the central government as landlord and executor. Just a week after accepting his post as special officer, Hume realized that 'It is so largely a technical job for which I have no technical qualifications and I shall have to get much estimating and details done by the PWD (Public Works Department), screwing the work out often by tact and guile.'

On 5th May 1938, the Viceroy's Private Secretary wrote to the Chief Commissioner, following His Excellency's tour of some of the Trust's early schemes. Information was requested regarding the steps taken to preserve the vistas and approaches to historical monuments, to protect tombs and the city wall and to protect open spaces around objects of historical interest. It was the Viceroy's opinion that the Government's actions should be reproached for being 'actuated solely by hygienic or commercial considerations' and asked that Jenkins 'ensure that the artistic and aesthetic considerations involved are not lost sight of in planning and reconstruction schemes.'

An area could be announced in need of improvement should it be 'too badly arranged' or have 'any other sanitary defects', in line with the byelaws. The techniques combined into different assemblages to tackle specific cases of improvement. When such a case was decided upon, occupants on land required by the DIT were given 60 days to lodge an appeal, while the Trust could enter any land to measure, survey, assess or 'to do another thing'. However, these policing powers were checked by certain provisions; all such entries would be in sunlight hours, having given 24 hours notice in which females could be removed to an area of which were referred to as either Nazul (N) or Trust (T).

The DIT cast individual area as congested on the intensity map of population that demanded levelling technologies to secure even distribution and circulation. The main town expansion schemes were those of the Western Section (N7) Extension (T1) and the Northern City Extension (T2) to the north of Old Delhi. The development scheme were mostly run on Nazul land, in order to make it more profitable. They consisted of the housing estates of Daryaganj South (N1), Ramnagar (N2) and Mundewalan (N5), and the commercial areas of Garstin Bastion Road (N9) and Sabzi Mandi Fruit and Vegetable Market (N13). Deferred street development also took place on land already owned by the Government, such as Paharganj market (N3), estate (N12) and circus (T6). Besides town expansion, the Trust account was focused on the re-housing projects of the Delhi-Ajmeri Gate Scheme (DAGS) (T3) and Hathi Khana Slum Clearance (T7), while the Nazul account funded similar Schemes, such as that at Ahata Kidara (N11).

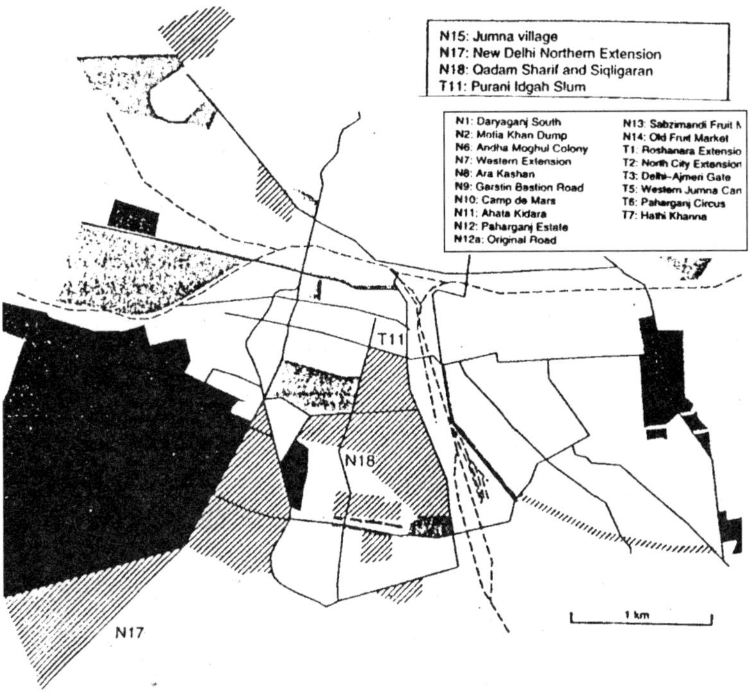

Delhi Improvement Trust Schemes, 1939-41.
Source: Legg, S., Spaces of Colonialism, Delhi's Urban Governmentalities, 2007

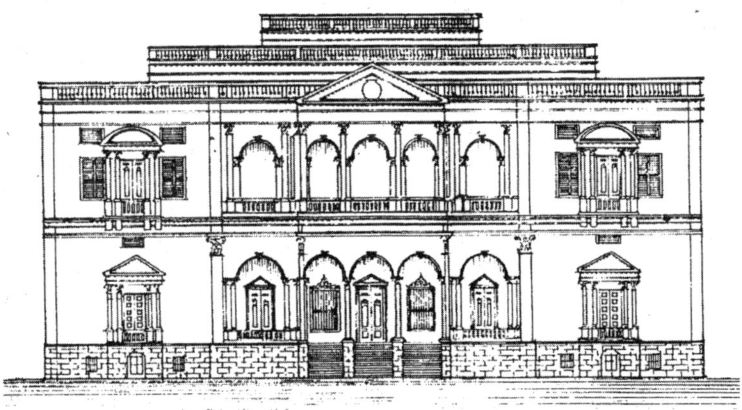

A Daryaganj Bungalow

In 1938 Muhammad Asaf Ali also wrote to the government reviewing the attempts to relieve congestion that had been made since he first suggested a Trust 14 years earlier. The Trust and the DMC were equally denounced, although the Government was also criticized, who in '... their preoccupation with the development of New Delhi and the strict observance of a policy of isolation of the old town...did not even so much as take themselves keenly felt by 1923'. New Delhi's retention of sovereign land rights with regard to the DIT also attracted criticism. It was accused of failing, as a landlord, to govern its territory, but also of failing in its task of knowing its people and its land. Hume, unearthed the reason for this in his continual exposition of the tensions between the biopolitical and financial domains. However, the Chairman of Delhi Improvement Trust, J.S. Hardiman, showed that the schemes had been built to budget and had not proved unpopular with their targeted populations.

In 1939 Government set up the Delhi Development Committee to study the existing situation and to make suitable recommendation so as to guide the future development of the capital. The Committee recommended that "No single authority had a complete picture of any general or overall plan for the capital, and therefore while there was no conscious intent to work at cross purposes, this appeared inevitable because of the working of so many agencies involved in planning and development". The Committee therefore recommended that an advisory body be formed at the technical level to coordinate the activities and programmes of the various government agencies involved.

The Advisory Committee had hardly been constituted when the Second World War broke out. This had its own effect on the entire pattern of the city, and the Advisory Committee could not function. Industry grew wherever it could find place to locate itself. Delhi was no more only a capital city or the major commercial centre for distribution and shipment of goods to the north and the north-west. Industry had started taking its requisite place in the economy of the city. This sporadic industrial growth and increase in commercial activities attracted more and more people from the neighbouring areas. During

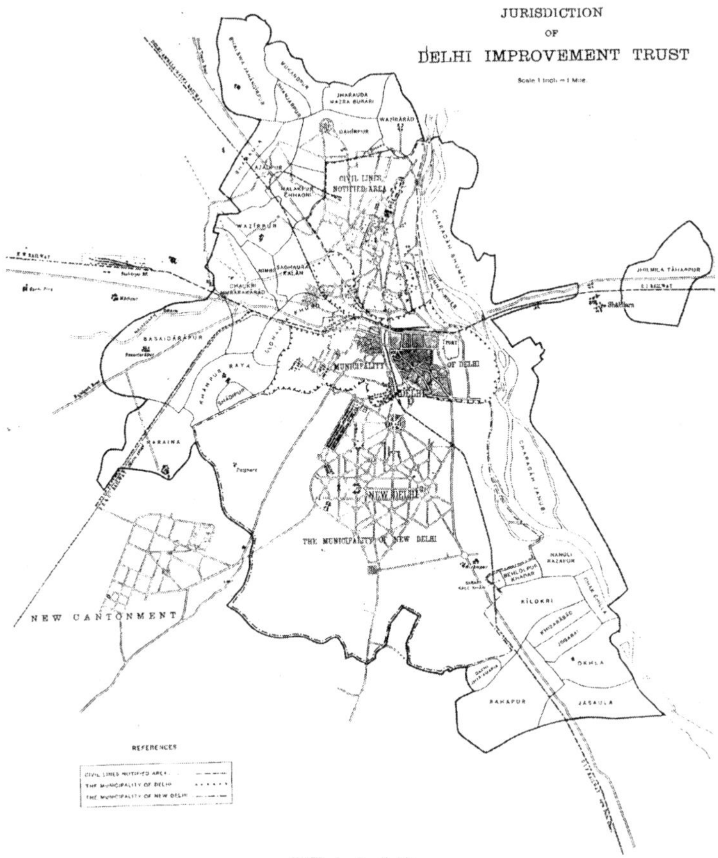

DIT Jurisdiction

Source: DIT Annual Report 1940

the war years substantial migration took place from the adjoining villages and the towns to meet the increasing labour requirements. Population grew very rapidly and assumed enormous proportions. The large influx of people who migrated from the neighbouring areas increased the total population of Delhi from 348,000 in 1931 to 522,000 in 1941.

As a result government activities increased rapidly. New areas had to be developed to house the additional population. Lodi Colony with two-storeyed apartments on grid iron pattern was developed during this period. The Lodi estate bungalows, west of the golf course and partly wedged on the east side of the Lodi Gardens, were built for senior officials. For military personnel additional accommodation was built in the new cantonment to the south-east of the new city.

Hundreds of single and two-storeyed temporary hutments were built around the Secretariat blocks to provide additional office accommodation to meet the war needs. In addition to these Barracks were built in the vacant plots around the India Gate Hexagon, which had originally been allotted to the princely states (Gwalior House, Jodhpur House, Bundi House, Bikaner House, etc.)

In 1943, Delhi Rent Control Ordinance was passed. Delhi Planning and Siting Committee was established for a better coordination of planning. In 1945, Chief Commissioner, W.H. Christie made proposals on Post War Reconstruction and Slum Clearance. In 1946, the Delhi-Ajmeri Gate Scheme was finally sanctioned. The demolition of wall was undertaken. In early 1947, with the pressure of population and the independence of the country in sight, the Delhi Improvement Trust proposed development of satellite towns in South Delhi. However, the partition of country halted most of its schemes.

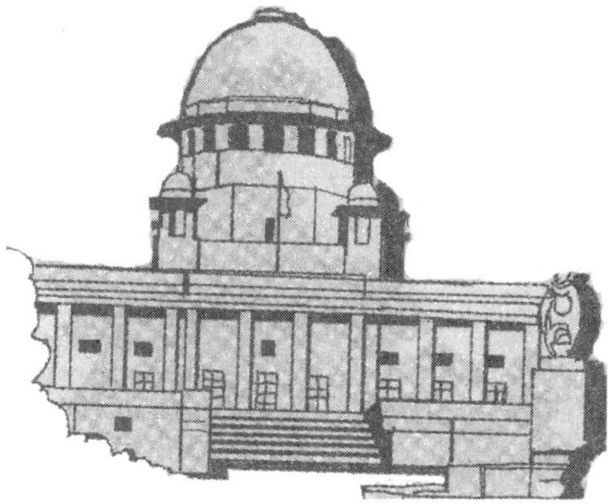

17. Partition, Independence and Rehabilitation

Empires, like people, have their ups and downs. They have the weaknesses of their strengths and the strength of their weaknesses. As soon as the British empire felt its weak feet on the soil, the whole edifice began to crumble. The nationalists, like Gandhi, Nehru and others brilliantly exploited the fundamental conflict between the concepts of the British empire—one of dominion and the other of freedom. The result was that the Britishers had to leave India. However, before they left in 1947, they divided the country. The partition brought its own problems. With the partition and independence of India, Delhi witnessed one of the largest immigration in the human history. Approximately half a million sought refuge in Delhi. Delhi was not prepared for doubling of its population in just two months. Tents were pitched to shelter the helpless, hungry and harassed people, uprooted from their homelands. Rudimentary services, mainly water, ration, fuel, clothing and medicines were provided by the newly born government. A national emergency was met with immediate action

1947 – Partition of India brought a stream of migrants to Delhi. The influx of refugees after the partition of the country and their settlement in New Delhi were to be dealt on an emergency basis; the physical change of New Delhi became fast apparent. It gained momentum after independence with the expansion of the national government, trade, industry and education.

Gandhi Smriti (Birla House) is an important place where on January 30, 1948 Bapu fell to the bullets of Nathuram Godse. It was at Birla House that many decisions pertaining to the freedom struggle were taken.

bequeathing large areas having camped townships with deficient development. A separate Ministry of Relief was created by the central government. New townships in the urban fringe of Delhi were planned during 1948–52 by the Delhi Improvement Trust and the Central Public Works Department for the Ministry of Relief (later Ministry of Rehabilitation). These Schemes housed the refugee population who were living in miserable conditions in the camps scattered all over.

The rehabilitation townships were planned and developed on all the four sides of Delhi. Starting with Sheikh Sarai and Kalkaji in the South and Tihar in the West, 36 rehabilitation townships were developed. These included Nizamuddin, Lajpat Nagar, Jangpura Extension, Malviya Nagar, Rajinder Nagars (East and West), Patel Nagars (East, West and South), Moti Nagar, Ramesh Nagar, Kingsway Camp and Gandhi Nagar (across Yamuna). These townships were generally planned on the basis of 80 sq. yd. plots for each family, and many of them were built up with modest single story asbestos cement sheet roofed houses. The plots and houses were offered at a subsidized price of Rs. 2,000 to Rs, 10,000 with the facility of long term installment payments.

In hastily acquired lands, schools, dispensaries, parks and shopping of marginal standards were provided. These were emergency projects and no time was available for immaculate planning. A national emergency was met with immediate action.

For government employees, who were multiplying with the fast growing central government, five townships, viz., Vinaynagar, Shan Nagar, Kaka Nagar, Man Nagar and Moti Bagh were developed by the Central Public Works Department. To meet the needs of the rich and the business class, Sunder Nagar, Jor Bagh and Golf Link were developed.

In 1949, a Central Coordination Committee for the Development of Greater Delhi was established as a part of the Central Public Works Department. Through years of improvisation, adjustment and resettlement, the refugees were resettled into 36 rehabilitation colonies.

The population of Delhi recorded in 1951 had been 1.764 million, almost double of 1941 population of 0.91 million. With

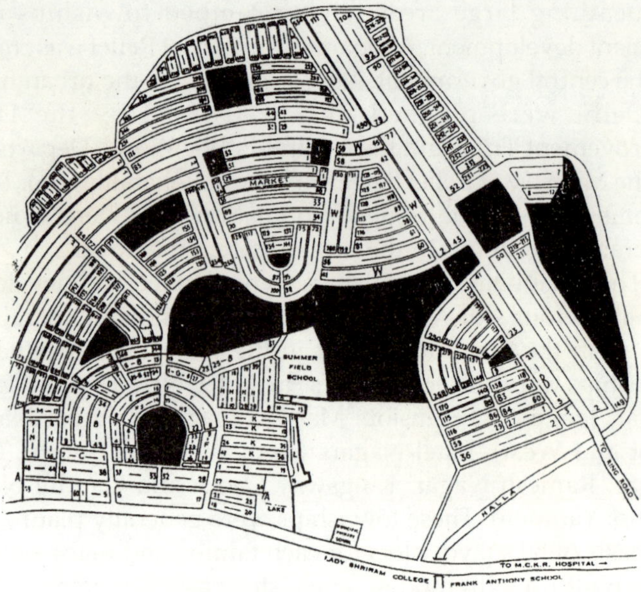

Kailash Colony & Greater Kailash

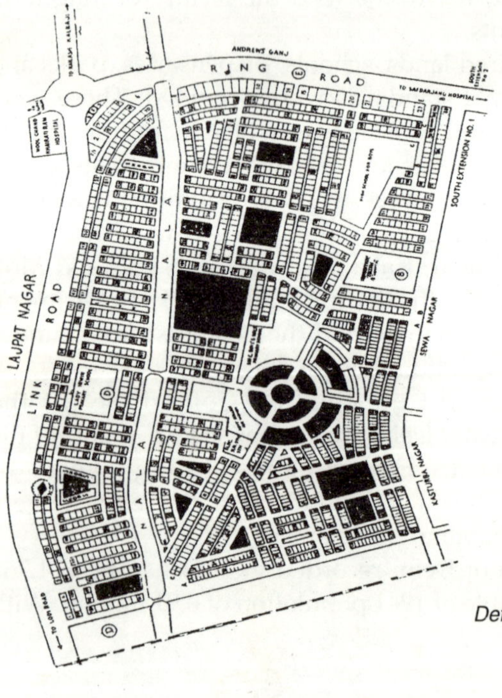

Defence Colony

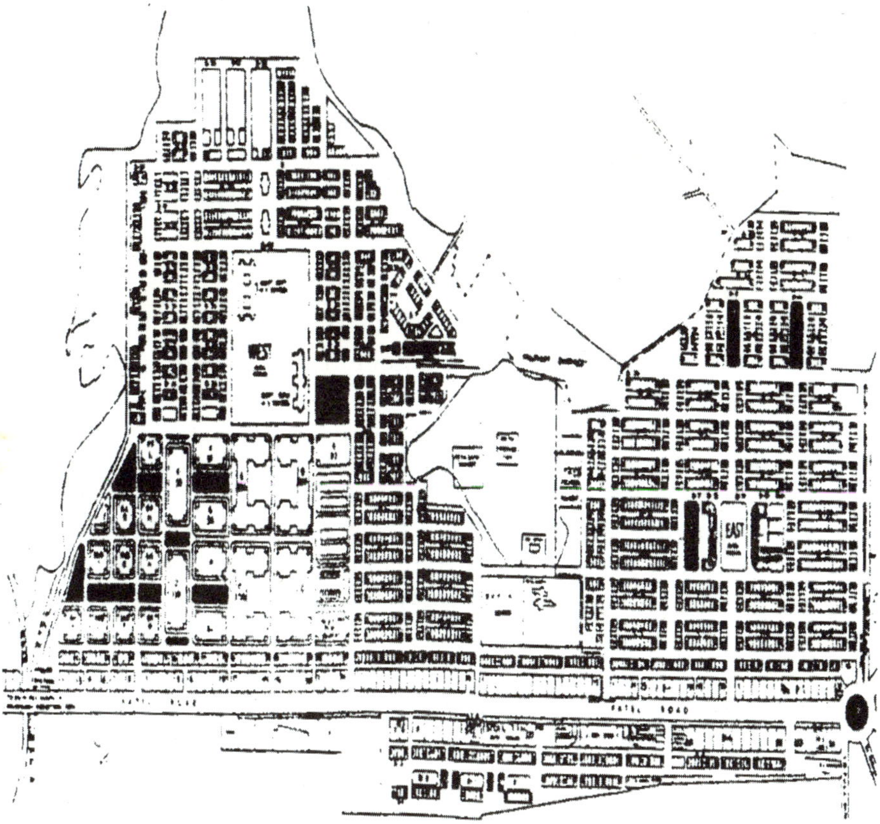

PATEL NAGAR

To meet with the increasing demand for housing the private developers. Ministry of Rehabilitation and Delhi Improvement Trust undertook several development schemes, such as Greater Kailash, Defence Colony and Shakti Nagar.

the growth of population and enlargement of government and various other activities, new colonies, markets, office blocks, power houses, etc. sprang up in various parts of the city. Delhi started expanding in all directions but without any overall plan. Private colonisers started their activities in transaction of land, without any development plan, services, amenities or controls. There were multiple agencies to run the city and the Delhi Improvement Trust was too preoccupied with its old schemes and property disputes. The congestion continued and the city grew haphazardly, with the lands passing into the hands of the speculators.

The Improvement Trust had not succeeded in its efforts in urban development and the Government in 1951 appointed the Birla Committee, also known as Delhi improvement Trust Enquiry Committee. The report focused on rehousing problem and need for rapid expansion. For this the Committee suggested setting up a single planning and controlling authority for the development of the whole of the urban Delhi. It also suggested to develop the city under the frame of a master plan. The Government of India in November, 1955, set up "Delhi Development (provisional) Authority". It was charged with the responsibility of preventing "bad" laying out of land, haphazard erection of buildings or growth of sub-standard colonies and "ensuring development and expansion of Delhi according to proper planning." With the help of Town Planning Organisation an interim General Plan for Greater Delhi was issued in September 1956. Simultaneously there were pronounced concern for slum clearance. Prime Minister Jawaharlal Nehru held meetings on the issue and the Parliament enacted the "Slum Area (Improvement and Clearance) Act" in 1956.

In December 1957, the government replaced the Delhi Development (provisional) Authority and the Delhi Improvement trust by passing the Delhi Development Act, 1957. The slum clearance and improvement work was transferred to the Municipal Corporation.

The Delhi Development Authority had been set up with the wide mandate and functions for the planned development of Delhi, the basic objective being "to promote and secure the development of Delhi according to plan." As a result, a new phase of development began which snowballed Delhi into a super-metro.

18. Delhi—the Future of its Past

The historiography of Delhi reveals a complex socio-political process of urban growth, its cultural diversity and artistic richness. Delhi's strategic location and growth indicates its relative importance in its regional context. Security from the invaders had been an important consideration in locating this capital city. From the ancient times, trade with the North-West Frontier states governed the Indian economy. Situated on the perennial Yamuna, in the fertile Doab region and along the trading route, Delhi was centrally located. It grew as a prosperous market and trading centre.

Delhi through the history had been one of the most beautiful cities. Political attitudes and historical changes during last two centuries, have gradually reoriented the perceptions regarding traditional cities, which are sweepingly seen as the slums.

The old Delhi, the medieval capital, built by Shahjahan in 1648, remained one of the most beautiful and graceful cities in the Orient, till 1803, when the British arrived in Delhi. The British and the natives lived side by side within the walled city. After the war of 1857, the British attitude had been hostile and over one-third of the city was razed to ground. The city came to be seen as dark, unhealthy and congested. It was perceived as a 'useless maze' and its surroundings as "heterogeneous patches of dirty hovels."

The transfer of imperial capital from Calcutta to Delhi in 1912 furthered the process of devaluation of Shahjahanabad. The New Capital's Hausmannian vistas and imperial scale dwarfed the walled city and brought immediate and direct comparison. During 1920s, the concept of 'congestion' crystallised into 'slums'. After the independence (1947), the slum clearance remained a pipe dream of the policy-makers and politicians.

With the formation of the Delhi Development (Provisional) Authority in November 1955, the Delhi Improvement Trust moved on its death bed. In December 1957, with the enactment of the Delhi Development Act, the Delhi Development Authority became the successor of the Delhi Improvement Trust. It was a tiny organisation of 40 workers and with a budget of less than Rs. one crore. It was entrusted with the enormous functions of planning and development of the national capital. A Town Planning organisation was created under the Ministry of Health, which was assisted by the town planners from the United States of America and Europe, sponsored by the Ford Foundation. It undertook the preparation of a Master Plan for Delhi on behalf of the DDA. An interim General Plan was prepared and published in 1956. Simultaneously in 1957, by an Act of the Parliament, the Municipal Corporation of Delhi was organised as an apex servicing and maintenance body by merging several local bodies. A 20 year Master Plan was finally approved by the Parliament on September 1, 1962. It assessed the deficiencies in housing, community facilities, services etc. and projected requirements of 4.6 million (revised to 5.3 million) population in 1981. From the urbanised area of 18000 Ha in 1958–59, it was proposed to enlarge the urban area to 44736 Ha. All operating agencies were brought within the overall framework of the plan. From a modest annual budget of about a crore, the Delhi Development Authority budget has multiplied to about Rs. 4000 crores and it is now one of the largest urban development and housing agency in the world.

Perpetuating colonial attitudes, Delhi Master Plan described the walled city as "slum, congested, filthy and obsolete". It proposed shifting out of about 45 per cent of its population to decongest the old city. However, no significant realization of the Master Plan proposals in this regard could be achieved. Whatsoever plans were implemented, the experience indicates that the proposals have worked at cross-purpose and became counter-productive.

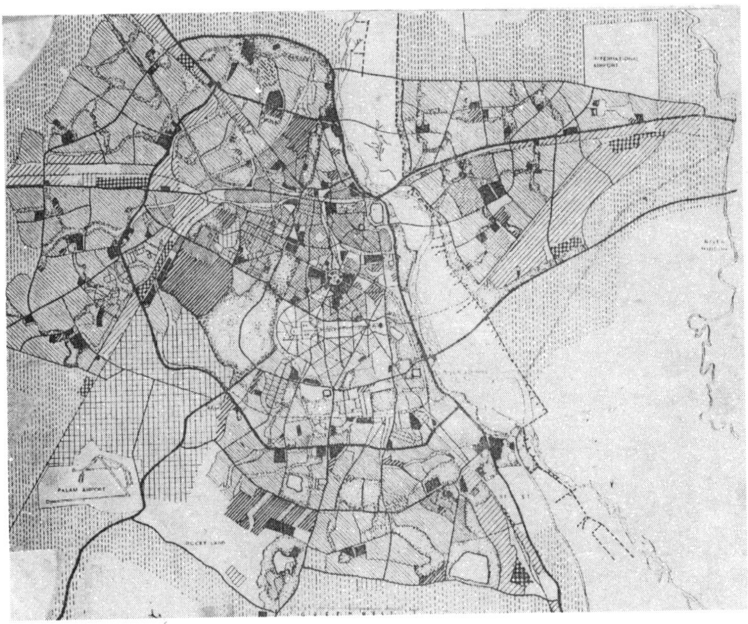

Delhi Master Plan (1962–81)

Source: Delhi Development Authority

The proposals, like the clearance, rehabilitation of slums, proved to be a case where the cure is worse than the disease. The replacement of traditional, organic and indigenious form of high density housing in the Old City by formal, planned, modern apartment blocks stands as its testimony. It is a mute edifice which reminds that the plans were wrong and the people were right. The concerns of externals for improving the living conditions of the traditional settlements had been pigeonholed under the physical manifestations, like slums, overcrowding, blight and sub-standard. The evaluation by the borrowed perceptions had been contradictory with the rich heritage and the reality.

None of the priorities of official agencies, such as

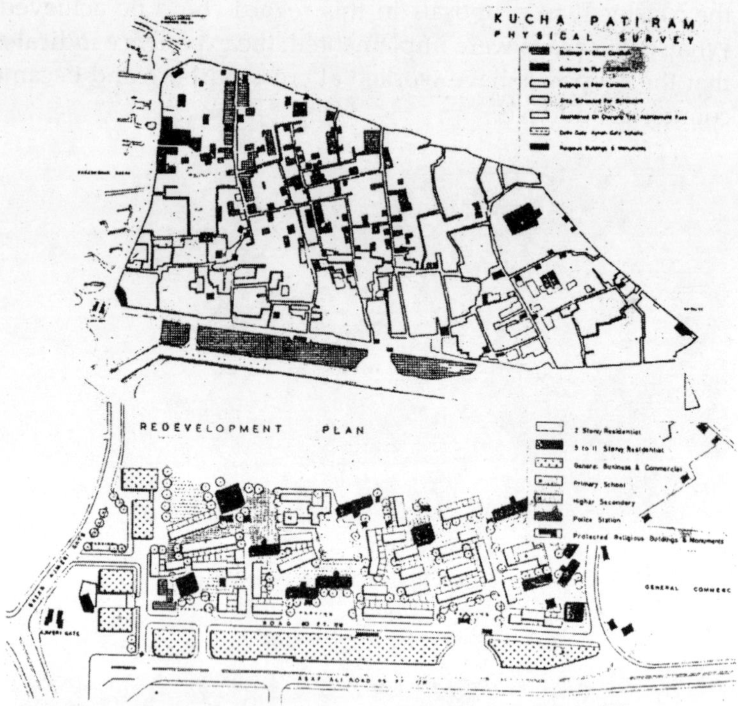

Delhi Master (1962) Plan proposed large scale redevelopment of the walled city bringing the densities of 600 to 1000 person per acre down to a maximum of 250 persons per acre. It envisaged to replace to the "disorganized congestion" by new multi-storeyed housing.

decongestion, open space, aesthetics, land use zoning, building byelaws and physical accessibility figure among the main issues of the community. This is a clear expression of separation of planning programmes from cultural roots, social needs and realistic considerations. There is a need to abandon such concepts and to evolve the plans based on a deeper understanding of historical, social and cultural heritage of the city.

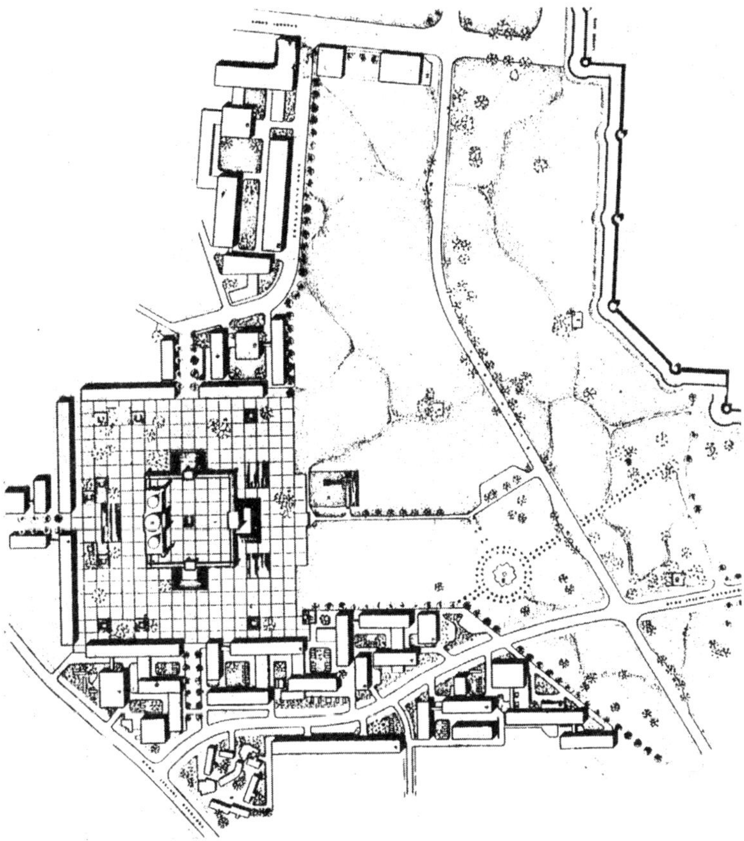

Delhi Master Plan (1962) proposal for redevelopment of area around Jama Masjid.

Delhi Metro

Sanctioned by the Union Cabinet in September 1996, work on Delhi Metro (Phase I) commenced in April 1998, after the setting up of the Delhi Metro Rail Corporation Ltd. the implementing agency for the project. The Metro Rail network for the entire city has been identified in four phases, which comprise of under-ground, elevated and surface corridors aggregating to approximately 415 km., and is expected to carry 3-4 million daily passengers with an average trip length of 15 km by 2021 :

Phase one (65 km) is already in operation since 2002.

Phase two (2006-11) covering 121km is in operation.

Contd...

Phase three (2011-16) will cover 120km, and

Phase four (2016-21) will cover 108.8 km length, which is to be completed by the year 2021.

It is expected that about 60% of Delhi will be walkable, within 15-minute from the MRTS stations. Additional areas could come within easy access and connectivity with the Metro Rail through inter-linkages with other transport modes. About 15% of urban area of Delhi is likely to be directly affected, undergoing a dramatic impact and change. Due to the development of economic activities along the Metro Corridors and optimization of connectivity provided by it, the ridership on the Metro has been growing rapidly. It is expected that vehicular trips may progressively shift from road-based transport to Metro Rail Transport Systems, particularly, with reference to the longer trip lenghts (greater than 10km) within the city. About one-fifth of the capital costs of Delhi Metro project have been met by the Central and State Governments each. Japan International Co-operation Agency (JICA) and other subordinate soft loans contributed about half of the capital cost and the remaining costs are covered through fare box collection/integral resources and by property development (6 to 7%). Given that about 43% of women commuters in Delhi face sexual harassment while using public transport, Delhi Metro has reserved a coach for women passengers, besides installing CCTV and women marshalls.

Table: Delhi Metro vis-a-vis global systems

City	*Opened*	*Length 2012*	*No. of Stations*	*Daily ridership (millions)*
London	1890	402	270	2.74
Paris	1900	199	368	6.00
New York	1904	368	468	4.27
Moscow	1935	292	177	9.00
Delhi	2002	186	130	2.00

Sources: Delhi Metro Rail Corporation, 2012; JAGORI and GNCTD.

The Future Delhi: During 1981–2001, three sub-cities covering about 18,000 Ha, namely Rohini, Dwarka and Narela were planned to accommodate a population of about 40 lakhs.

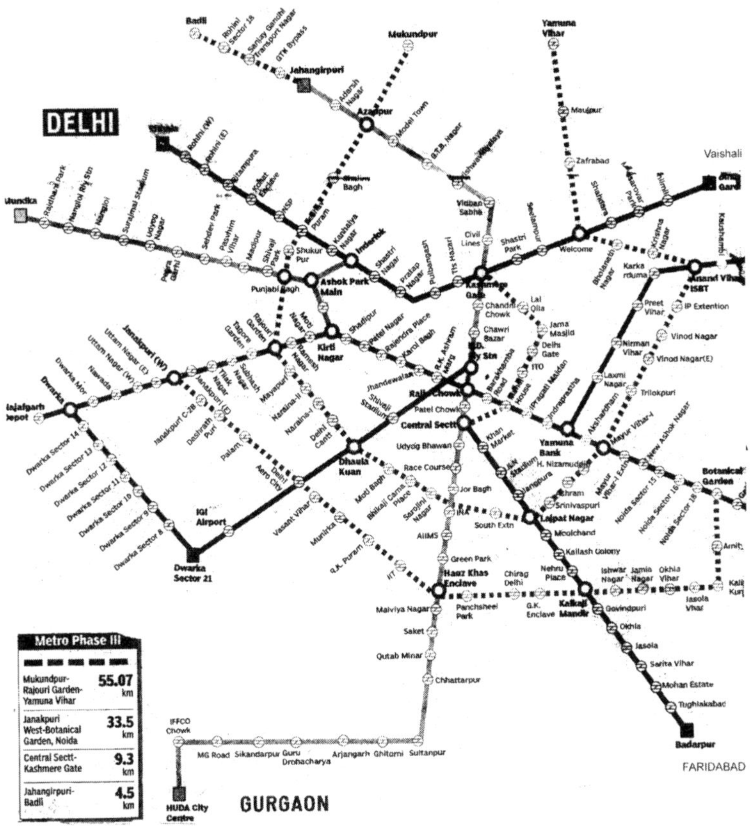

Delhi Metro Network, 2012

As per the Master Plan for Delhi-2021 (MPD-2021), the projected population of Delhi is estimated to be 230 lakh and almost the whole of Delhi (except agricultural green belt, reserved forests, ridge, River Zone and water bodies) will be urbanized by the year 2021. It stipulates the development of 5 new sub-cities as given below :

Delhi Metro is largely elevated which is inviting criticism from the heritage activists.

Table : Five Sub-cities for Delhi-2021

Zone/ Sub-city	*Zonal Area*	*Urban Area*	*Proposed Population (Lakh)*	*Existing Population (Lakh)*
Zone J (South Delhi-II)	15178 Ha	8268 Ha	20	8
Zone K-1 (Nangloi Area)	6515 Ha	6515Ha	12	5
Zone L (West Delhi-III-Najafgarh Area)	22840 Ha	11611 Ha	20	9
Zone N (NW Delhi-III)Khanjawala	13975 Ha	9670 Ha	24	6
Zone P-II (North Delhi)	8149 Ha	6270 Ha	19	5
Total	**66,657 Ha**	**42,334 Ha**	**95**	**33**

These sub-cities would accommodate a total population of 95 lakh which includes about 33 lakh existing population. The total area under 5 sub-cities (66,657 Ha) includes regional park/forests/water bodies, mandatory agricultural green belt (54 border villages measuring about 11,000 Ha), existing built-up areas/villages/unauthorised colonies, etc. (about 7681 Ha) and land reservations for power plants, services, utilities, solid waste, sewerage, etc. This is a unique opportunity to plan in the context of local culture, traditions and heritage. It should manifest a vision, that as New Delhi has celebrated 100 years of its founding in 2011, the new sub-cities should be so designed and developed that the people are proud of them and celebrate their century in the year 2121 or so.

Conservation of Heritage

Delhi had the distinction of imagery city design as evident in the classical Shahjahanabad and the Imperial Delhi. Today the process of city planning has become compartmentalised and the urban extensions planned for millions remain anonymous—without a face. However, during the last decade, there has been an awakening towards conservation of the heritage of the city with stringent mandatory guidelines. According to Master Plan for Delhi-2021, 1208 historical monuments, 6 heritage zones and 3 archaeological parks have been listed for conservation and protection. The conservation of the Natural and Built Heritage is now a madatory requirement.

Shahjahanabad has been designated as the Conservation Area, for which Special Area Conservation Plans are to be developed, based on a study of the heritage typologies, resources, built form, culture and issues related to services, land uses and the community. The work on redevelopment of Jama Masjid area and the preparation the local area plans of Sahajahanabad and its extensions (Special Area) has been initiated. The conservation of heritage is linked with urban design, redevelopment strategy and development controls. This needs participation of the local community, property owners and the private sector. The incentive of additional Floor Area Ratio (FAR) alongwith other measures, like mixed land use, time bound approval, etc. can motivate the owners and residents to take up conservation and urban renewal

Lutyens Bungalow Zone comprises large bungalows and is a pleasant garden city. Its wide avenues, large plots, landscape, low rise development have a heritage value which are to be conserved. New Delhi has been acknowledged as the 'most beautifully designed urban form in India'. Conserving this unique legacy becomes an important agenda for the national capital, which cannot be treated as 'property', but is a source of national pride.

The built heritage of Delhi is an irreplaceable and non-renewable cultural resource. Besides being part of life for many, it has educational, recreational and tourism potential. The heritage resources include symbols of successive civilizations and cities that came up over the millennia, historic buildings and complexes, historical gardens, water engineering structures and their catchments, the remains of fortified citadels, places for worship and for the deceased, historic cities and villages, unearthed heritage and their components.

In Delhi the Archaeological Survey of India has declared 174 monuments (Annex. 2) as protected. Built heritage of Delhi needs to be protected, nourished and nurtured by all citizens and passed on to the coming generations. The following steps are necessary for a systematic heritage management :

i. Maintain and update the database.
ii. Develop organizational capacity for heritage management.
iii. Define all the applicable terms.
iv. Listing of Heritage Buildings based on the following criteria:
   (a) The age of the building:
   (b) Its special value for architectural or cultural reasons or historical periods;
   (c) Its relevance to history;
   (d) Its association with a well-known character or event
   (e) Its value as part of a group of buildings;
   (f) The uniqueness of the building or any object or structures fixed to the building or forming part of the land and comprised within the curtilage of the building.
v. Prepare guidelines for development, redevelopment, additions alterations, repairs, renovation and reuse of the heritage buildings.
vi. Implementing programmes for education and awareness.

In Delhi the following areas have been identified as Heritage Zones:

i. Heritage complexes within Shahjahanabad
ii. Heritage complexes within Lutyens' Bungalow Zone
iii. Specific heritage complexes within Nizamuddin and Humayun's Tomb.
iv. Heritage complex at Mehrauli.
v. Heritage complex of Vijay Mandal - Begumpur - Sarai Shahji - Lal Gumbad.
vi. Heritage complex within Chiragh Delhi.

The following areas have been designated as Archaeological Parks :

i. Mehrauli Archaeological Park
ii. Tughlaqabad Archaeological Park
iii. Sultan Garhi Archaeological Park

The plans of built heritage and Archaeological Park should be based on evaluation of the pertinent aspects like form and design, materials and substance, use and function, traditions and techniques, location and setting, spirit and feeling and other internal and external factors. "Special Development Plans" for the conservation and improvement of listed heritage complexes and their appurtenant areas are necessary.

Delhi as a World Heritage City

UNESCO has 226 cities inscribed on its list of World Heritage Cities, but not a single Indian city. Given its historicity and international importance, Delhi qualifies to be designated a World Heritage City. For nominating Delhi as a World Heritage City, INTACH, Delhi Chapter prepared a Nomination Dossier (2011-12) of the historic 'capital cities' of Delhi. Some of these have disappeared completely leaving no trace of their urban morphology yet others have their urban form and streetscape almost intact with only the buildings having been replaced with newer construction over the last decades. Delhi's unique historic urbanscape comprise the area of Mehrauli, Nizamuddin, Shahjahanabad and Lutyens Delhi (Imperial Delhi).

The normination aims to :

— Make citizens aware of the incredible richness of their

cultural patrimony.

— Change the cognitive image of the city—at the local, national and international level.
— Boost tourism by encouraging visitors to experience the city as a destination.
— Inculcate pride and ownership amongh its citizens and thereby create a more inclusive city.
— Provide a catalyst to spur decision makers to conserve Delhi's heritage.
— Provide a platform for visionary strategies for city planning.

The main components for the revitalisation of historic urban areas are the following:

- To prepare comprehensive heritage management plans, regulations, specifications and Detailed Project Reports (DPR).
- To replace incompatible activities, such as the godowns/ warehouses, with activities that are more appropriate to the environment of the traditional city;
- To link the historic areas with the adjoining nodes and tourist hub
- To conserve existing old and dilapidated buildings with appropriate infrastructure
- To revitalize indigenous handicrafts and promote local artisans.
- To improve infrastructure sevices, health, education and community development of historic areas and villages.

The first step would be a systematic survey of each and every structure in terms of its stability, heritage value, usage and occupation. Once the data is collected, a practical revitalisation plan can be prepared, in the light of the heritage management guidelines through a participatory process whereby the concerns of the stakeholders are duly addressed.

Natural Heritage

Delhi has been classified into seven land forms. Each of these have different geological characteristics, of which Delhi Older Alluvial Plain is recognized as the most suitable site for the development of city on account of advantageous geomorphic setting. This north-south range forms triangular plain with the River Yamuna in the East and Badarpur-Mehrauli Range of the Aravali as the base. It is this triangle that has been the cradle of many ruling dynasties in the Indian subcontinent. Conservation of Delhi's biodiversity and natural heritage is of utmost importance for its eco-system.

River Yamuna is the lifeline of Delhi. It is a source of water supply for Delhi and acts as a drainage and flood channel. It is also a major lung space between urban mass on two sides. However, indiscriminate urban growth and damming the river for water supply have disrupted environmental balance. River Yamuna is polluted by continuous discharge of effluents, waste water and sullage from surrounding urbanization and storm water drains. Besides augmenting the water supply, it is necessary to control the pollution and dumping of sewage and waste water in the River. As the population trend indicates, Delhi will not need to import water from the proposed Kishau dam in Himachal Pradesh, but its water demand can be met locally from River Yamuna, besides recycling of treated wastewater and reducing the leakages. It is necessary to build a public interest by linking the population with the river and by creating public spaces along the river front. For a sustainable river regime an eco-sensitive approach is to be adopted by mapping its hydrology, respecting the terrain, the river front, water courses, channels and lakes.

Natural ecology of the river and streams requires eco-sensitive land use and pollution control for the protection of their biotic character. The river front needs to be carefully landscaped with the species that improve quality of aquatic environment, and soil and micro-climate. Eco-sensitive landscape based planning can strike a balance between development and environment. The landscape can reduce soil erosion, groundwater depletion, and conserve the bio-diversity.

Ecology, besides bio-diversity and greens, is related with water systems, energy, industry, transport, drainage, water, sanitation and other services, which need to be given ecological orientation.

The built heritage of Delhi has a uterine relationship with the natural heritage. Delhi Ridge covering 7777 Ha of area is characterized by bio-tropical thorny secondary forest. The topography of the ridge is undulating with a large natural drainage network. The ridge has number of perennial tanks and pits which act as groundwater recharge points. Delhi Master Plan and Zonal Plan for Zone 'O' (River Yamuna) notified by the DDA (August 2010) give a comprehensive strategy for a clean river regime and green river front. A major component of riverfront would be to enhance the walkability, so that the public would approach, view and enjoy it. This can showcase the river and generate public participation and pressure to make the river clean and sacred, rather than a sewer that it has become.

Canals/ Drains as Green Corridors: Delhi has a network of canals and major drains which are about 350 km kong. These include Gazipur Drain, Hindon Cut, Eastern Yamuna Canal, Western Yamuna Canal, Najafgarh, Barapula, Kushak, Wazirabad, etc. Some of the drains are over 700 years old and were built to provide water to Delhi. Many of Capital's archaeological sites are situated along the drain network. These are valuable ecological resources, however due to neglect these have become the corridors of filth, garbage, squatting, insanitation and spines of mosquitoes, vermins, stray and dead animals. These canals and drains could be developed as green corridors with jogging tracks, pedestrian and cyclist pathways, interconnecting paths, monuments, art galleries, etc. Besides their development as landscape stretch, treating sewerage in micro STPs and local plants, balancing ponds for rainwater surplus, porous paving and slow surface run off to recharge the water table are necessary, using the system of organic reedbeds and aerators to clean the sewage entering drains, will improve public health as well as help replenish aquifers. This will also help cleaning of the river Yamuna which carries the sullage of 22 major drains. The improved drainage system will help prevent flooding of urban areas and significantly reduce risk of water-borne diseases.

Drains with interconnected walkways/cycle tracks can make the city more lively, healthy and sustainable. Apart from pollution control, primary treatment and removal of encroachments, boating, maritine sports, aquatic sports, aquariums and development of pedestrian boulevards, landscape trails along the drains/canals and bridges on Yamuna will be integral part of the development.

Rejuvenation of Water Bodies: Out of 600 odd water bodies, the following are to the taken up on priority :

a. Najafgarh Lake
b. Mayur Vihar
c. Shahdara Lake
d. Neela Hauz
e. Hauz Khas
f. Hauz Rani

For integrated rejuvenation and beautification, the water bodies need to be linked with natural drainage channels, rain-water storage and primary treatment. Delhi also has about 60 baolis (stepwells) and 300 wells which have historic significance and need to be revived and conserved.

Regeneration of River Yamuna in Delhi

The basic goal is to rejuvenate river Yamuna as a 'City Lifeline' by striking a balance between development parameters and ecological aspects to achieve sustainable development. This needs a multi-pronged strategy comprising the following:

Water supply augmentation

(i) Availability of water in the river throughout the year
- Capacity Augmentation of the existing barrages.
- Planning and Development of "regulated flood plain reservoirs" in low lying areas.
- Construction of storage rseservoir upstream, to collect the monsoon excess flow and regulate the flow.

(ii) Up-gradation of river water quality to prescribed standards through:

- Innovative technologies for better standards for treated effluents.
- Effective and air-depth monitoring by concerned agencies to take action and reduce impacts of waste and strict enforcement of Water Pollution Control Act.
- Installation of treatment facilities by polluting units, through regime of control and command industry and ensure efficient and effective functioning of the STPs and ETPs.
- Removing non-compatible and pollution generating land uses from the river bed.

(iii) Increased accessibility to the river—physical, functional and visual, e.g. in the basin areas lying behind Raj Ghat, Gandhi Nagar, between Wazirabad and ITO, etc.

(iv) Development with suitable land forms/landscape is recommended based on certain environmental and technical limitations. This will make land available for recreational, development remunerative purposes and improve the aesthetics of the river front.

(v) Identification of developable, un-developable and degraded land based on the following environmental parameters:

- Conceptualize the river development in terraces and utilize the high land areas by identifying the various inundation levels.
- Removal of non-conforming and polluting land uses, e.g. Jhuggi Jhompri (JJ) clusters and unauthorised colonies.
- Adopting suitable, positive, compatible and conforming land uses.

(vi) Better co-ordination among different agencies involved in the management of the Yamuna, its drains, canals and water treatment works in Delhi.

(vii) Adopting special zoning controls for a regulated, three dimensional comprehensive development.

(viii) Strengthening commitments of various stakeholders by addressing the issues and implementing mitigation measures. Prompting community awareness and participation, conduct surveys, workshops, etc. to expand citizen participation in the planning and design of the river front.

The river front development will be the lifeline for the community and a mark of distinction and pride for generations to come.

Reclaiming the River Front

(i) Preventing dumping of urban wastes, untreated sewage, etc.

(ii) Compatible and conforming landuses along the basin.

(iii) Use of infiltration beds, buffer strips, along the river to absorb and filter contaminants and sediment in runoff from paved surfaces.

(iv) Utilising vegetation to stabilize banks from erosion.

(v) Designing with porous paving material that allows rain to be absorbed rather than running off the trails, parking lots, etc. carrying sediment and other urban pollutants into river/streams.

(vi) Adding natural in-stream elements, e.g. root wads of downed trees that provide essential slow-water habitat for young fish and insects and replanting native wetland and upland plants and trees that will provide ambient growth environment for fish, migratory birds and wildlife.

(vii) Providing wildlife observation areas, theme parks and interpretive nature/historical trails that explain river ecology and the historical significance.

Strategies for riverfront development

(i) To establish riverfront walkways, trails, parks, etc.

(ii) To create visually pleasing order to the river's edge.

(iii) To attract people and investment to the riverfront.

(iv) To develop an arts/entertainment/cultural district.

(v) To expand leisure, recreational use, and boating in the river.

Reclaiming the riverfront ensures not only its environmental integrity but also stimulates the economy. The aim is to achieve maximum economic benefit with minimum public investment to ensure a self-sustaining set up. Thus, the riverfront development will be based on environmental aspects, for an economically viable and healthier riverfront. This healthier vision is critical for new, long-term ecological conservation. Improved transport and physical infrastructure will service the riverfront and provide easy access to several recreational and development sites.

Ensure availability of sufficient quantity of water in river

- By using "regulated flood plain reservoirs", in identified low lying areas in the river basin, for water retention during dry seasons. These reservoirs can be created at the existing barrages, e.g. North of Wazirabad, at Okhla, etc. or by utilizing the existing embankments.
- A survey of water bodies, catchment area, feeder channels and water retention capacity is required to be undertaken to improve storage of water.
- State Govt. and city authority may take action for implementing programme for renovation of water bodies.
- Central Water Commission (CWC) and the CPCB may estimate maximum flow requirement at different points of River Yamuna. CWC to prepare schemes for release of minimum flow in the Yamuna in Delhi based on fresh water saved and availability of water from lakes and ponds.

Capacity augmentation of the existing barrages can be done by desilting and increasing the existing pondage areas. As per the orders of the Supreme Court, minimum 10 cumecs of water is to be let downstream into the river to ensure water in the river throughout. Construction of Dams (micro) upstream can help in collecting the monsoon excess flow and regulate the flow.

Strategy of Pollution Abatement: The strategy involves improving the quality of water in the drains (especially the major ones, such as Najafgarh, etc.), ban on dumping of untreated sewage into the river. This can be achieved by steps such as bio-remediation, using alternative technologies, such as oxidation ponds, aeration, etc.

There is a need to adopt innovative technologies which can treat sewage to such output standards so that the treated waste water can be used for non-potable purposes thereby reducing demand of fresh water.

Cleaning the drains

Delhi's drains can be cleaned by tapping and connecting them to existing STPs. Laying of interceptor sewers in a 59 km length along the three major drains (Najafgarh, Supplementary and Shahdara) to intercept sewage flowing from subsidiary small drains and convey it to the nearest Sewage Treatment Plants (STPs) will ensure that only treated sewage is discharged. There is a need to augment the existing capacity of STPs, besides other measures, such as given below:

(i) Interception of 13 small drains falling into Bela Road and Ring Road Trunk sewers.
(ii) Construction of additional STPs after utilization of full capacity of existing plants.
(iii) All waste generated in the catchment area is trapped and treated.
(iv) Augment and optimize waste treatment facilities, for which appropriate technologies should be adopted.
(v) Treated effluent to be reused and not mixed with untreated effluent before it flows into river.
(vi) Trapping the residual waste of the drains before it outflows into river, thereby treating it at the nearest sewage treatment plant.
(vii) Regular and accurate monitoring of flow and pollution in drains. Monitor pollution at outlet points.

To clean the Yamuna, unsewered areas must be provided with sewerage. According to estimates, 50% of Delhi is unsewered. There are five types of unsewered areas : unauthorised and unregularised, unauhoised and regularized, resettlement, urban villages and rural villages.

Some Key Proposals

All power plants located in River Zone "O" are proposed to be shifted or gradually converted to gas based power plants. Thus the existing fly ash brick plants located in this zone will not be required and thus to be closed. The area under the plants will be developed for green/recreational areas/part of comprehensive scheme.

The area under water course is part of the river hydrology. The area between water course and embankment is to be conserved as flood plain. Any development in this area should be taken up only after the detailed hydrological studies and with approval of Yamuna Standing Committee/Central Water Commission. The area outside the flood plain, i.e. outside embankments (River front) should be conserved and developed considering the eco-sensitive nature of the river zone and based on comprehensive scheme.

Yamuna Bio-diversity Park

Source: DDA

Yamuna Bio-diversity Park

Source: Delhi Development Authority.

At present width of the river bed varies between 1.5 kms to 3.0 kms and at most sections neither the water course nor the opposite banks are visible. In order to integrate the river within the larger framework of the city and to bring the river closer to the citizens, at certain stretches, "aesthetic" and "active" river front development may comprise of the following activities/ uses:

The Akshardham Temple in Delhi on the banks of the Yamuna.

(a) Bathing Ghats
(b) Pedestrian Boulevards
(c) Landscaped avenues
(d) Sports activities, play fields, etc.

Revival of water reservoir at Hauz Khas

Hauz Khas lake was built by Allaudin Khalji in 1305. The lake, filled by rainwater during the monsoon season, provided water for the whole population for an entire year. Hauz Khas is now in the midst of of South Delhi. The lake had been dry for almost fifty years due to the diversion and decline of storm water inflow, due to the construction of buildings and roads. In 2004, the Delhi Development Authority (DDA) and INTACH took up the revival of Hauz Khas Lake project. It took treated water from a sewage treatment plant, cleaned it by biological processes and diverted it into the dry lake.

The recycled water from Vasant Kunj is treated in two ponds with aquatic plants, such as water hyacinth and duckweed, which absorb the organic matter. The quality of water improves as the water moves from one pond to the other. In order to avoid contamination, the water is channelled back to Hauz Khas Lake through a pipeline. Fish species feeding on mosquito larvae and organic matter have been introduced in the lake and floating fountains prevent water stagnation. Many birds have started repopulating the area.

Planning and Legal Framework

The conservation process under the Archaeological Survey of India (ASI) is governed by the Ancient Monuments and Archaeological Sites and Remains Act, 1958. It physically protects the ancient monuments identified to be of national importance, as a preventive measure. The Act does not cover the heritage zones, precincts and districts.

The 1959 Ancient Monuments and Archaeological Sites and Remains Rules further protect the ancient monuments by creating zones around the historic structures. According to these Rules, areas up to 100 metres from the protected limits of a monument is declared as a 'prohibited' area and further 200 m

Delhi Tourism (DTTDC Ltd.) proposals for River Yamuna in Delhi: The Plan proposed reclaiming river front for urban development, which invited criticism

from the monument as 'regulated' area in which construction is only allowed after permission from the ASI.

Town planning legislation in India requires that Master plans and other supporting plans (like Zonal and Local Area Plans) are drawn up for all major cities and towns. A Master Plan is a long term perspective plan for guiding the planned development of a city. This document lays down the planning guidelines, policies, development code and space requirements for various socio-economic activities supporting the city population. It is also the basis for all infrastructure requirements

The Delhi Master Plan 2021 includes the conservation of heritage as an important task to be undertaken and identifies heritage zones and archaeological parks. It defines a Heritage Zone as an area which has strong concentration, linkage, or continuity of buildings, structures, groups or complex united historically or aesthetically by plan or physical development, while the archaeological park is an area distinguishable by heritage resources and land related to such resources, which has the potential to become an interpretive and educational resource for the public in addition to the value as a tourist attraction. The Master Plan promotes the preparation of *Special Heritage Management Plans* for the conservation and improvement of listed heritage complexes and zone.

The Master Plan divides the city into different zones, and the detailed planning of these areas is done through the Zonal Development Plans. These outline the land-use, public and semi-public facilities, utilities and services, roads, housing, standards of population and densities, etc. and other components of development in that particular zone. The Delhi Master Plan is supported by 15 Zonal Plans, including one of the Walled City (Shahjahanabad), giving importance to its historic character. It highlights its historical characteristics, and recommends measures for urban renewal along with building controls and regulations.

There are various other legislations which relate to conservation of heritage, as given below:

List of Acts relating to preservation of Ancient Monuments and Archaeological Sites and Remains in the Country.

1. The Ancient Monuments and Archaeological Sites and Remains Act, 1958 and 2010 (Amendment) of Rules, 1959.
2. The Ancient Monuments and Archaeological Sites and Remains Rules 1959 (of Central Govt.)
3. The Antiquities and Art Treasures Act. 1972.
4. A. P. Ancient and Historical Monuments and Archaeological Sites and Remains Act, 1960.
5. Assam Ancient Monuments and Archaeological Sites and Remains Act, 1959.
6. Gujarat Ancient Monuments and Archaeological Sites and Remains Act, 1965.
7. Jammu and Kashmir Monuments Preservation Act, 1977.
8. Jallianwalla Bagh National Memorial Act, 1951.
9. Madras Ancient and Historical Monuments and Archaeological Sites and Remains Act, 1966.
10. M.P. Ancient Monuments and Archaeological Sites and Remains Act, 1964.
11. Maharashtra Monuments and Archaeological Sites and Remains Act, 1961.
12. Mysore Ancient and Historical Monuments and Archaeological Sites and Remains Act, 1962.
13. Orissa Ancient Monuments and Preservation Act, 1956.
14. Punjab Ancient and Historical Monuments and Archaeological Sites and Remains Act, 1964.
15. Rajasthan Monuments and Archaeological Sites and Antiquities Act, 1961.
16. Rajghat Samadhi Act, 1951 (of Central Govt.)
17. U.P. Ancient and Historical Monuments and Archaeological Sites and Preservation Act, 1957.
18. Victoria Memorical Act, 1903.
19. West Bengal Preservation of Historical Monuments and Objects and Excavation of Archaeological Sites Act, 1957.
20. Museums Act, 1961.
21. Salar Jung Museum Act, 1961.
22. ASI notification date 16-6-1992 regarding prohibited and regulated zone around protected monuments.

Source: A.I.R. Manual

Process of Conservation of Urban Heritage

The process of urban heritage conservation is essentially area based. It identifies a historic zone, district, settlement for conservation as a whole and not just archaeological monuments. Against the conventional understanding of heritage representing monuments and antiquities, awareness has grown to understand that heritage includes many more aspects which are witness to our past, and cultural traditions. Heritage, in the context of cities, needs to be defined in an encompassing way to include all aspects that have made the city what it is.

The 1976 UNESCO Recommendations on Safeguarding and Contemporary Role of Historic Areas, refer to ensembles of any group of buildings, structures and open spaces, in their natural and ecological context, including archaeological and palaeontological sites, constituting human settlements in an urban environment over a relevant period of time, the cohesion and value of which are recognized from the archaeological, architectural, prehistoric, historic, scientific, aesthetic, socio-cultural or ecological point of view.

The 2005 Vienna Memorandum introduces the term 'historic urban landscape' and explains further how the historic urban landscape is embedded with current and past social expressions and developments that are place-based. It is composed of character-defining elements that include land uses and patterns, spatial organization, visual relationships, topography and soils, vegetation, and all elements of the technical infrastructure, including small scale objects and details of construction (curbs, paving, drain gutters, lights, etc). The historic urban landscape acquires its exceptional and universal significance from a gradual, evolutionary, as well as planned territorial development over a relevant period of time through processes of urbanization, incorporating environmental and topographic conditions and expressing economic and socio-cultural values. As such, protection and conservation of the historic urban landscape comprises the individual monuments and their surroundings, ecology connections, physical, functional and visual, materials and association, with the historic typologies and morphologies.

Heritage has mythological, iconic and symbolic values, which are manifested in cultural and structural pluralism, arts and literature, music and performing arts, crafts and industry and customs and festivals. The following matrix gives a broad idea of various constituents and components of heritage, which are related to the dimension of time.

Urban Heritage Components

Urban Heritage	*Components/Dimensions*
1. Physical/Environmental	
a. Natural	Geographical, Geological, Morphological, River, water bodies, Flora and Fauna, Ridge, Forests, etc.
b. Man-Made	Built Form/Settlements, canals, drains, Archaeological, Architectural, Engineering structures, etc.
2. Socio-Cultural	People/Tribes/Community/Language, Literature, Arts, Sculpture, Painting and Crafts, Music and Performing Arts, Festivals, Faiths, Archives, Records, Artefacts, etc.
3. Heritage Resources	Crafts and Industry, Tools and Technology, Natural and Man-made Resources, Transport, Communications, Tourism, etc.

Conservation of heritage as a holistic process needs a sequential study, development of a strategic heritage management plan, projects and programmes and their implementation, monitoring and evaluation.

Conservation Management

1. ***Situation analysis and inventory***

- Comprehensive assessment of the historic district in relation to its position and role in the city at large, including demographics, socio-economic profile, housing, infrastructure and services, informal sector assessment, environmental profile;
- SWOT (Strengths - Weaknesses-Opportunities-Threats) analysis;
- Inventory of all resources in and around the historic

district like cultural, environmental (potential greening of the district), human and socio-economic (potential economic redevelopment linked to traditional know-how), available and potential resources for the districts economic redevelopment;

- Listing of prominent heritage structures;
- Identification of key stakeholders and preliminary consultations on situation analysis.

2. ***Development of a vision and strategy***

- Stakeholder consultations on concerns, aspirations and fears: develop a collective vision for revitalisation of the historic district;
- Identification of project objectives and strategic areas for intervention: concentrating on "what", "how" and "for whom".
- Prioritisation of interventions, focusing on cross-cutting requirements.

3. ***Development and implementation of action plans, projects and programmes***

- Development of action plan(s) for priority strategies, linked with broader development programmes
- Integration of short and long-term plans;
- Feasibility assessment, establishment of time frame and resources required;
- Impact studies of priority projects in close cooperation with all stakeholders;
- Identification and mitigation of risks;
- Resource mobilisation (physical, financial, human, technical) for action plan implementation;
- Development and negotiation of public-private-community partnerships;
- Establishment of flexible and transparent procedures;
- Ensuring involvement of beneficiaries in all stages of implementation.

4. ***Monitoring and Evaluation (M & E)***

- Development of clear indicators for monitoring and evaluation, including quantitative and qualitative indicators;

- Establishment of M & E procedures;
- Involvement of all major stakeholders in monitoring and evaluation;
- M & E as a learning and training exercise.

5. ***Learning from the experience***

- Identification of lessons that can be applied to other districts in the same city of other cities;
- Integration of new individual and community practices into established procedures;
- Promotion of lessons learnt for and by inhabitants to value their participation to the process and create a sense of belonging.

Source: UNESEO, 2010, Historic Districts for All.

Conservation Guidelines

The objectives of conservation should be clear and candid. The INTACH Charter for the Conservation of Unprotected Architectural Heritage Sites (2004) gives the following comprehensive guidelines:

1. Retain visual identify

In a globalising world, where visual spaces are rapidly becoming homogenised, it is necessary to retain the specific visual identity of a place created by the presence of unprotected architectural heritage and sites. Yet, this image should not be preserved in the manner of legally protected monuments, but must accommodate the imperatives of change in making the heritage relevant in contemporary society. The objective must be to integrate unprotected heritage and sites into daily life by balancing their needs so that neither overshadows the other.

The visual cacophony created by advertisement boards, signage, hanging electric cables, air conditioning units, dish antennas, etc. must be carefully controlled to enhance the visual character of the architectural heritage and site. Additions of street furniture, pavement material, lighting, signage, etc. can add to the experience and appreciation of the heritage.

In this respect the objectives of conservation can mediate

even new buildings or neighbourhoods by requiring them to make reference to the old by employing elements, methods and devices characterising the architectural heritage of the area so that the new is linked with the old.

2. *Adaptive re-use*

The re-use of historic buildings and neighbourhoods is economically sensible. It is an effective strategy to conserve architectural heritage, particularly by using traditional craftspeople in the process. Such re-use distinguishes between preservation as an ideal on the one hand and , on the other, the goal to prolong the useful life of architectural heritage by retaining as much (and not necessarily all) of the surviving building.

Priority must be accorded to retaining the continuity of original functions. Any new use must be introduces only after studying its effect on the local context, and must conform to the carrying capacity and vulnerability of the architectural heritage.

All changes to the original fabric should be preceded and followed by comprehensive documentation. Additions and alterations must respect the coherence of the whole, and must, to the extent possible, engage traditional materials, skills and knowledge in the process.

When it becomes necessary to modernise and comprehensively alter the original internal functional characteristics of the building or site, its external image must be retained.

At the outset, the local community must be made aware of the changes envisaged and explained the benefits to be derived.

3. *Restoration/Replication/Rebuilding*

Restoration is an appropriate conservation strategy to reinstate the integrity or complete the fractured whole of the architectural heritage/site. It must aim to convey the meaning of the heritage in the most effective manner. It may include reassembling of displaced and dismembered components of the structure and conjectural building or replacement of missing or severely deteriorated parts of the fabric. Invariably, restoration work must be preceded and followed by comprehensive documentation in order to base interventions on informed understanding of the resource and its context, and in conformity with contemporary practices of local craftspeople.

In consonance with traditional ideals, replication can be accepted as an appropriate strategy not only to conserve unprotected historic buildings, but especially if such replication encourages historic ways of building.

At the urban level, the objective of rebuilding historic structures should be to enhance the visual and experiential quality of the built environment, thereby providing a local distinctiveness to contest the homogenising influence of globlalisation.

In addition, reconstruction/rebuilding can provide the impetus to develop a parallel market for local buildings materials and new opportunities for the use of alternative systems of building.

Reconstruction based on minimal physical evidence is appropriate where it is supported by the knowledge of local craftspeople, including folklore, beliefs, myths and legends, rituals, customs, oral traditions, etc. The objective of this practice must be to interpret the original meanings of the resource in the contemporary context and reinforce its bond with society.

4. *Employment generation*

Conservation strategy must focus on the potential for employing *raj mistris*, labour and materials because this will prolong the economic viability of traditional ways of building. In conditions of resource scarcity, the use of architecture heritage can provide and alternative and more economic strategy to meet contemporary needs as well.

5. *Local materials and traditional technology*

The use of local materials and traditional technologies must invariably be preferred. Their choice must be based on the availability of traditional knowledge systems. Modern substitutes should be considered only after their use is proven efficient and judicious, and must not compromise the integrity and continuity of local building traditions.

6. *Integrated Conservation*

Conservation of architectural heritage and sites must be integrated with the social and economic aspirations of society conservation-oriented development must be the preferred strategy for social and economic progress. This necessitates the formation of multi-disciplinary teams to undertake integrated conservation projects. Since social aspirations are diverse and often at odds with each other, the conservation team must include social workers to facilitate dialogue and decision-making.

7. *Sustainability*

The objective of conservation should be to sustain the building and/or the traditional skill and knowledge system of building. In this context, continuity must be seen as evolving over time. The test of its validity must be the positive contribution it makes to the quality of life of the local community.

Heritage Management Plan

Emerging from the objectives and broad guidelines, the Heritage Management Plan is evolved. For a Heritage Management Plan the participation of the local community is crucial. As such the process has to be participatory.

A heritage conservation zone has a range of heritage components, which include the buildings (mosques, dargahs, sarais, tombs, etc.), open space, and natural features/heritage. The identification of ownership is necessary to identify the stakeholders.

Traditional Housing Stock

The housing component has to be dealt separately. The proposals should include policies for maintenance, additions and alterations, new construction, etc. Rent, taxation and loans are important instruments to achieve the aims of conservation.

The housing inventory forms the basis of conserving the housing stock. The development norms for historic housing areas have to consider controls on Floor Area Ratio (FAR) and height, bulk, materials, finishes, elevations, openings, etc.

Land Use Policy

The proposed land use should conform to the original land uses as a drastic change in land use alters the character of the area not only in spatial sense but also in terms of economy, traffic, pollution, etc.

Physical Infrastructure

Provision of basic infrastructure is a necessity. Many times poor or partial waste management, lack of water, power, etc. lead to degradation of the old areas. Most of the visible problems of the old city are problems of urban management. Provision of services in old areas has to be done sensitively, keeping in mind its historic fabric. It is clear that unless the basic needs of people are fulfilled there can be no conservation.

Traffic and Transportation

Most of the heritage zones face chronic traffic problems. Some of the approaches towards these problems are:

- Rerouting through traffic
- Restricting vehicular movement
- Efficient public transport system to discourage use of private vehicles
- Pedestrianization of certain areas.

Road widening is not a solution for traffic problems, which may lead to destruction of the old fabric and the relief in traffic congestion is very short lived.

Information Management

Information is the basis of a Heritage Conservation and Management Plan. Information collected from inventories and secondary sources has to be compiled in a database. This needs to be comprehensive, open ended' geo-referenced and be searchable through complex query formulations, for example, list of residences with locations of a particular conservation zone giving their ownership status, various heritage values and structural condition.

To achieve this goals the people's participation, education and awareness are necessary. Heritage management plan and the regulations will be effective only with public awareness and participation.

Tourism

The tourism policy and heritage management go hand in hand. The tourism policy should aim at utilizing the heritage resources while not compromising with their pristine quality.

Financial

The financial policies are to be based on a long term investment and incentives for the structures to be protected. For private properties various instruments like soft loans, tax relief and tax concessions can be worked out. Direct financial assistance has to be avoided as far as possible. In case of public properties allocation of funds and the possibility of reuse have to be considered.

Technical

Structural conservation is a technical subject and in absence of dedicated specifications for conservation processes and materials, general specifications are often adopted for heritage conservation. There is a need to work out specific BSR for conservation of heritage structures. Regular maintenance is also crucial for the heritage building. At building level following plans and documents need to be prepared :

- Specifications for conservation works, materials and crafts
- Manuals on structures and materials
- Manuals for housekeeping and maintenance
- Architectural control guidelines and building bye laws for heritage zones/structures.

Knowledge Management

Heritage is a vast source of learning and education. Awareness about heritage is very crucial for conservation. The heritage database can be synthesized to feed into the awareness programs, heritage walks, web site, publications, etc.

Monitoring and Review

Monitoring and review are important for the implementation heritage policies and plans. Preparing an action plan with prioritisation and based on long and short-term objectives are important in this regard.

It is necessery to undertake field surves to identify heritage resources of cultural significance and categorise them to help in formulating conservation plans. Each typology will have a set of guiding policies.

Outline of a Heritage Management Plan

- Topographical documentation and analysis
- Layered digitised maps of historic evolution
- Heritage maps of villages and historic cities, heritage canals, water bodies, streams, river, forests, etc.
- Hierarchical organisation of heritage components:

  1st Level : Historic cities and villages

  2nd Level : Neighbourhoods (*Mohalla, katra*), Clusters, Bungalows, administrative buildings, urban elements.

  3rd Level: Fort, Major Religious structures, Mosques, Sarais, Tombs, Walls and Gates, Hunting Lodges, Gardens, Water Structures, archaeological mounds, water bodies, natural features, etc.
- Delineation of zones on maps (based on the study of secondary sources, preliminary analysis and inventory), styles, typologies, particular aspects of crafts, etc.
- Integrated heritage management plan,

  Guidelines for overall conservation and management, Urban Conservation Management, architectural, development and building controls, natural heritage conservation, Environment Management Plan, Infrastructure Management Plan, Mobility Plan.

- Technical and Working Plans, Specifications, Guidelines, Controls, Manuals, etc.
- Legislation/rules and regulations
- Financial Plan and Programme
- Documentation and Knowledge Management
- Monitoring, Evaluation and Feedback.

Listing and Grading

The ASI protects monuments of national importance which are more than 100 years old. However, besides 174 such monuments (Annexure 2), Delhi has about 1025 historic, listed properties (Annexure 3) which need to be conserved. These have been categorised as given below:

1. Barbicans/Bastions
2. Bridges
3. Chattris/Cupolas/Colonnades/Pavilions
4. Churches/Chapels
5. Cinemas/Clubs/Community Centres
6. Commercial
7. Dalans/Baradari/Chaupal
8. Dargah/Mazar
9. Dharamshsala/Sarai
10. Embankment/Tanks/Baolis/Hauz
11. Gardens/Parks
12. Gateways
13. Graveyards/Cemeteries
14. Gurudwaras
15. Forts and Fortifications

16. Hospitals/Aushadhalayas
17. Hostels
18. Idgah/Mosque
19. Madarsas
20. Mahals/Palaces
21. Memorials/Commemorative Columns
22. Milestones/Kos Minar/Minars
23. Miscellaneous
24. Museums
25. Official Building
26. Police Station
27. Post Offices
28. Residences/Havelis
29. Rest Houses/Hotels
30. Schools and Colleges
31. Stadiums
32. Streets and Areas
33. Temples/Shivalayas
34. Tombs
35. Walls/Enclosures etc.

Source: INTACH, Delhi Chapter

After listing of the heritage properties (including buildings, structures, zones, area, precincts, parks, water bodies, canals, roads, etc.) and ownership details, zonewise maps and digitised location plans are put for public objections and suggestions. Thereafter the 'list' is notified in the gazette/newspapers by the concerned local authority. These are usually graded into 3 groups for a differentiated approach.

Table: Grading of Heritage Building/Precincts

Grade-I	Grade-II	Grade-III
(A)Definition: Heritage Grade-I comprises buildings and precincts of national or historic importance, embodying excellence in architectural style, design, technology and material usage and/or aesthetics; they may be associated with a great historic event, personality, movement or institution. They have been and are the prime landmarks of the region. All natural sites shall fall within Grade-I.	Heritage Grade-II (A&B) comprises of buildings and precincts of regional or local importance possessing special architectural or aesthetic merit, or cultural or historical significance though of a lower scale in Heritage Grade. They are local landmarks, which contribute to the image and identity of the region. They may be the work of master craftsmen or may be models of proportion and ornamentation or designed to suit a particular climate.	Heritage Grade-III comprises building and precincts of importance for townscape; that evoke architectural, aesthetic, or sociological interest through not as much as in Heritage Grade-II. These contribute to determine the character of the locality and can be representative of lifestyle of a particular community or region and may also be distinguished by setting, or special character of the facade and uniformity or height, width and scale.
(B) Objective: Heritage Grade-I richly deserves careful preservation.	Heritage Grade- II deserves intelligent conservation.	Heritage Grade-III deserves intelligent conservation (though on a lesser scale than Grade-II and special protection to unique features and attributes).
(C) Scope for Changes: No interventions be permitted either on exterior or interior of the heritage building or natural features unless it is necessary in the interest of strengthening and prolonging, the life of	*Grade-II (A) :* Internal changes and adaptive re-use may by and large be allowed but subject to strict scrutiny. Care would be taken to ensure the conservation of all special aspects for which it is included in	Internal changes and adaptive re-use may by and large be allowed. Changes can include extensions and additional buildings in the same plot or compound. However, any changes should be such that they are in

the buildings/or precincts or any part of features thereof. For this purpose, absolutely essential and minimum changes would be allowed and they must be in conformity with the original.	Heritage Grade-II. *Grade-II (B):* In addition to the above, extension or additional building in the same plot or compound could in certain circumstances, be allowed provided that the extension/additional building is in harmony with (and does not detract from) the existing heritage buildings (s) or precincts especially in terms of height and facade.	harmony with and should be such that they do not detract from the existing heritage building/precinct.
(D) Procedure : Development permission for the changes would be given on the advice of the Heritage Conservation Committee.	Development permission for the changes would be given on the advice of the Heritage Conservation Committee.	Development permission for changes would be given on the advice of the Heritage Conservation Committee.
(E) Vistas/Surrounding Development : All development in areas surrounding Heritage Grade-I shall be regulated and controlled, ensuring that it does not mar the grandeur of, or view from Heritage Grade- I.	All development in areas surrounding Heritage Grade-II shall be regulated and controlled, ensuring that it does not mar the grandeur of, or view from Heritage Grade-II.	All development in areas surrounding Heritage Grade-III shall be regulated and controlled, ensuring that it does not mar the grandeur of, or view from Heritage Grade-III.

Source: MoUD Gazette Notification dated 9-2-2004

Conservation

The term conservation encompasses the following:

- **Preservation** places a high premium on the retention of all historic fabric through conservation, maintenance and repair. It reflects a building's continuum over time, through successive occupancies, and the respectful changes and alterations that are made.

- **Rehabilitation** emphasizes the retention and repair of historic materials, but more latitude is provided for replacement because it is assumed the property is more deteriorated prior to work. (Both Preservation and Rehabilitation standards focus attention on the prevention of those materials, features, finishes, spaces, and spatial relationships that, together, give a property its historic character.
- **Restoration** focuses on the retention of materials from the most significant time in a property's history, while permitting the removal of materials from other periods.
- **Reconstruction**, establishes limited opportunities to re-create a non-surviving site, landscape, building, structure, or object in all new materials.

Preservation

As a broad concept, the approach towards conservation should emerge from the historic importance, age and context. All grade I buildings/precincts shall be preserved and protected with absolutely minimum changes and strictly in conformity with the original.

- A property will be used as it was historically, or be given a new use that maximizes the retention of distinctive materials, features, spaces and spatial relationships. Where a treatment and use have not been identified, a property will be protected and if necessary stabilized until additional work may be undertaken.
- The historic character of a property will be retained and preserved. The replacement of intact or repairable historic material or alteration of features, spaces and spatial relationships that characterize a property will be avoided.
- Each property will be recognized as a physical record of its time, place and use. Work needed to stabilize, consolidate and conserve existing historic materials and

features will be physically and visually compatible, identifiable upon close inspection and properly documented for future research.

- Changes to a property that have acquired historic significance in their own right will be retained and preserved.
- Distinctive materials, features, finishes, and construction techniques or examples of craftsmanship a property will be preserved.
- The existing conditioning of historic features will be evaluated to determine the appropriate level of intervention needed. Where the severity of deterioration requires repair or limited replacement of a distinctive feature, the new material will match the old in composition, design, colour and texture.
- Chemical or physical treatments, if appropriate, will be undertaken using the gentlest means possible. Treatments that cause damage to historic materials will not be used.

Rehabilitation

All grade II buildings/precincts shall be rehabilitated and used as it was historically or be given a new use that requires minimal changes to its distinctive materials, features, and spatial relationship.

- The historic character of a property will be retained and preserved. The removal of distinctive materials or alterations of features, spaces, and spatial relationships that characterize a property will be avoided.
- Each property will be recognized as a physical record of its time, place and use. Changes that create a false sense of historical development such as adding conjectural features or elements from other historic properties will not be undertaken.
- Changes to a property that have acquired historic significance in their own right will be retained and preserved.

- Distinctive materials, features, finishes and construction conservation techniques or examples of craftsmanship that characterize a property will be preserved.
- Deteriorated historic features will be repaired rather than replaced. Where the severity of deterioration requires replacement of a distinctive feature, the new feature will match the old in design, colour, texture and where possible materials. Replacement of missing features will be substantiated by documentary and physical evidence.
- Chemical or physical treatments if appropriate will be undertaken using the gentlest means possible. Treatments that cause damage to historic materials will not be used.
- Archaeological resources will be protected and preserved in place. If such resources must be disturbed, mitigation measures will be undertaken.
- New additions, exterior alterations or related new construction will not destroy historic materials, features and spatial relationships that characterize the property. The new work shall be differentiated from the old and will be compatible with the historic materials, features, size, scale and proportion and massing to protect the integrity of the property and its environment.
- New additions and adjacent or related new construction will be undertaken in such a manner that if removed in the future the essential form and integrity of the historic property and its enviroment would be unimpaired.

Restoration

All grade III heritage buildings/precints shall be restored as it was historically or be given a new use that reflects the property's restoration period.

- Materials and features from the restoration period will be retained and preserved. The removal of materials or alterations of features spaces and spatial relationships that characterize the period will not be undertaken.
- Each property will be recognized as a physical record

of its time, place and use. Work needed to stabilize, consolidate and conserve materials and features from the restoration period will be physically and visually compatible, identifiable upon close inspection and properly documented for future research.

- Materials, features, spaces and finishes that characterize other historical periods will be documented prior to their attention or removal.
- Distinctive materials features, finishes and construction techniques or examples of craftsmanship that characterize the restoration period will be preserved.
- Deteriorated features from the restoration period will be repaired rather than replaced. Where the severity of deterioration requires replacement of a distinctive feature, the new feature will match the old in design, colour, texture and where possible materials.
- Replacement of missing features from the restoration period will be substantiated by documentary and physical evidence. A false sense of history will not be created by adding conjectural features, features from other properties or by combining features that never existed together historically.
- Chemical or physical treatments, if appropriate, will be undertaken using the gentlest means possible. Treatments that cause damage to historic materials will not be used.

Reconstruction

All grade III heritage buildings/precints (also grade I and II in exeptional cases) facing extinction shall be taken up for reconstruction.

- Reconstruction will be used to depict vanished or non-surviving portions of a property when documentary and physical evidence is available to permit accurate reconstruction with minimal conjectures and such reconstruction is essential to the public understanding of the property.
- Reconstruction of a landscape building structure or

object in its historic location will be preceded by a thorough archaeological investigation to identify and evaluate those features and artefacts which are essential to an accurate reconstruction. If such resources must be disturbed, mitigation measures will be undertaken.

- Reconstruction will include measures to preserve any remaining historic materials, features and spatial relationships.
- Reconstruction will be based on the accurate duplication of historic features and elements substantiated by documentary or physical evidence rather than on conjectural designs or the availability of different features from other historic properties. A reconstructed property will re-create the appearance of the non-surviving historic property in materials, design, colour and texture.

The Future of Delhi's Past

Delhi treasures a most beautiful collection of culture and antiquity in form of its several cities, which are scattered, lost or lie buried. Its monuments provide only a partial glimpse of cotemporary cultural scenario. A discovery of its cities not only throws the light on the art of city building, but also reveals the panorama of social, economic, religious and political situation prevailing at that time. It reflects the ideals of rulers and the cohesion of the diverse ideologies of the people of Delhi. These cities represent the realm of the ethereal, exotic subcontinent. As Jawaharlal Nehru said, "Delhi is a symbol of old India and the new," its future lies in its past and its conservation.

ANNEXURE 1

Chronology of Delhi's Growth

PREHISTORIC		
About 1,00,000 B.C.	:	Prehistoric settlements near Suraj Kund, Anangpur, Narela and Purana Qila
INDRAPRASTHA		
15th century B.C.	:	Purana Qila, Indraprastha, the Capital of Pandavas built by Maya Danav and named after God Indra located at Purana Qila.
DILLI		
328 B.C.	:	Raja Dhulloo's Dilli
269–43		Reign of Ashoka and Chandragupta II, set up Iron Pillar at Mehrauli
LAL KOT		
972–1020 A.D.		Anangpal-Anangpur Palace Complex at Mehrauli, Sun Temple, (Suraj Kund)
MEHRAULI		
1191	:	Death of Prithviraj, Capture of Delhi by Mohammad Ghori, beginning of Delhi Sultanate (Mehrauli)
1206	:	Qutabuddin Aibak, First Sultan of Delhi, Iltutmish, Quwwat-ul-Islam mosque, Sultan Ghori, Qutab Minar
1236–1240	:	Sultan Razia: Tomb at Turkman Gate, Iltutmish Tomb - Mehrauli
1286	:	Muizzuddin Kaiqubad (Kilokari)

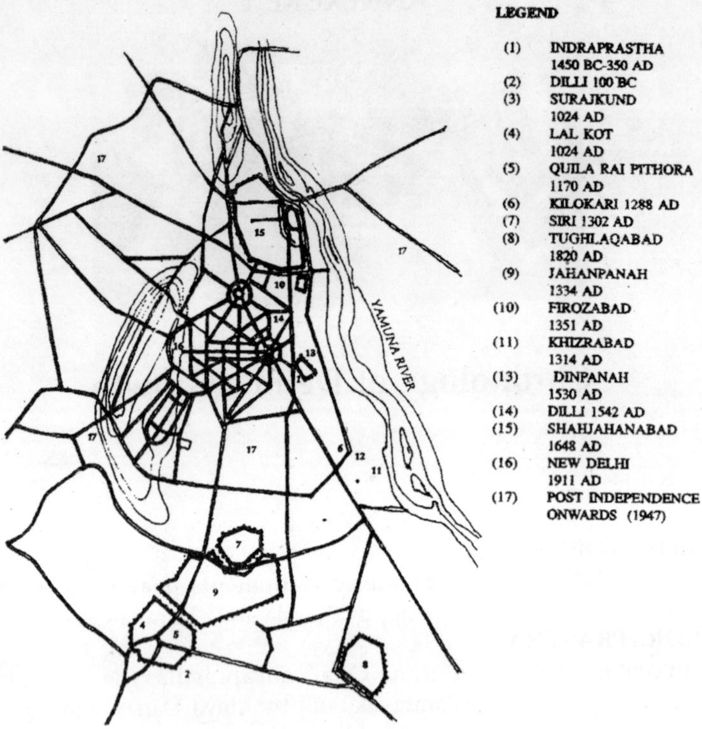

Cities of Delhi in Chronological Order

1290 : Jalaluddin Khijli

SIRI Alauddin Khijli: Massacre of Mongols at Chor Minar (Hauz Khas),

1296 : Siri Fort Palace and Hall of 1,000 Pillars, Alai Darwaja at Mehrauli, went to Chittor and Ranthambor for war and then to Madurai, Era of Hazarat Amir Khusro and Hazrat Nizammuddin Aulia Saint, Unifinished Minar at Mehrauli.

TUGHALAQABAD Tughlaq Dynasty

1321–25

1325–51 : Ghyasuddin (Tughlaqabad, Mohammad Tughlaq, Adilabad)

1327 : Deserted Tughlaqabad after 7 years of reign and shifted capital to Daulatabad towards South India.

	Ordered Delhi population to move to Daulatabad, Ghyasuddin Tomb built in 1325.
JAHANPANAH 1334–1351	Mohammad Tughlaq: Jahanpanah, Revolt in Deccan, Death in Gujarat
FEROZABAD 1351–1388	: Ferozshah Khirkee Masjid, Tomb and Madarsa at Hauz Khas, Ferozshah Kotla, Kalan Masjid, Chusanth Khamba, repaired Qutab, Ashoka pillars brought from Meerut and Ambala and placed at Ridge (Jahanuma) and Ferozabad, Karnal, Hansi-Delhi Canal (Western Yamuna), Nizamuddin.
SAIYYADS AND LODHIS	
12-12-1398	Taimoor Lang occupied Delhi (stayed for 2 weeks) and went to Meerut on 1st January, 1399.
1414	: Saiyyad Kings: Tombs, and Mausoleums raised
1433	: Mubarak Shah (Kotla Mubarakpur)
1451–1526	: Buhul Lodhi-Lodhi Tombs, Sikandar Lodhi-Masjid Moth and shifted capital to Sikandrabad (Agra), Lodhi Garden 1516–17, Tomb of Sikandar Lodhi.
1526	: Babar Killed
DINPANAH 1530–40	Humayun Dinpanah, Humayun Tomb (built during 1564-1565), Mirak Mirza Ghias architect.
SHERGARH 1540–56	: Sher Shah Suri, Capital shifted to Shergarh (Purana Qila), Sher Mandal, Shershah Mosque built.
1550–1555	: Salimshah (Salimgarh near Red Fort)
1556–1564	: Capital shifted to Agra by Akbar, Mughal buildings built in Delhi. Adam Khan Tomb : Mehrauli, (1562), Bhool Bhulaiyan, Atgah Khan Tomb (Nizamuddin), Mirza Aziz Tomb, (Nizamuddin)-1566-67 (Chausanth khamba) Maham Anka Madarsa
1603–1627	: Jahangir shifted capital to Lahore
1627	: Shahjahan as the emperor
SHAHJAHANABAD	
1638–48	: Capital shifted to Delhi (Shahjahanabad), built Red Fort, Jama Masjid Bhojla Pahadi, Nahar-i-Bisht (Canal to Red Fort)

1707–12	:	Bahadur Shah (Lahore as capital)
1714–17	:	Embassy of East India Company
1713–37	:	Emperor Farrukhsiyar and Bahadur Shah Zafar
1724	:	Jantar Mantar built by Maharaja Jai Singh
9.4.1737	:	Baji Rao, defeated at Kalka Devi Temple
9.4.1739	:	Nadir Shah defeats Mohammad Shah at Panipat and enters Delhi. Terror at Sunehri Majid
1754	:	Safdarjung (Safdarjung Tomb)
1782	:	Famine in Delhi
1786–88	:	Nazaf Khan, as the ruler
1793–1803	:	Gulam Kadir Rohila, Chief of Marathas (Scindias)

EAST INDIA COMPANY/BRITISH INDIA

11.9.1803	:	Scindias and East India Company, (General Lake) war at Patparganj
147.9.1803	:	East India Company defeated Marathas near Humayun Tomb
1806	:	Shah Alam died
1820	:	Canal of Ali Mardan Khan cleared
1824	:	First improvement and Development anency set up as the Town Duty Committee.
1828	:	European troops move to new Cantonment beyond the Ridge.
1830s	:	Development of suburbs Sadar Bazar, Kishanganj and Deputyganj.
1829–35	:	St. James Church built
1832	:	Delhi included in North-West province
1835	:	Sir Thomas Metcalfe's House built
1845	:	Metcalfe appointed Resident of Delhi
1848	:	Part of land on east bank of river included in Delhi Territory(Shahdara, Loni, Patparganj, etc.)
1853	:	Delhi population 1,51,000
11.5.1857	:	First War of Independence (Mutiny)
21.9.1857	:	Surrender of Bahadur Shah to East India Company
1857	:	East India Railways
6.2.1858	:	Delhi transferred from North-West province to Punjab, Delhi District formed

1.11.1858	:	The British Crown assumes the Governance of India
1863	:	First Municipal Committee for Delhi constituted under Act XXVI of 1850
1864	:	Town Hall built
1866	:	Railways come to Delhi
1865–67	:	St. Stephen's Church built
1.1.1867	:	Delhi linked with Railways
1869	:	Poet Ghalib dies
1870	:	Mutiny memorial at Ridge
1873	:	Rajputana State Railway (Delhi Bombay)
1876	:	Prince of Wales visited Delhi
1877	:	Durbar north of Delhi in which Queen Victoria is proclaimed Empress of India.
1881	:	Municipal Committee passed Building Bye Laws
1891	:	Delhi-Ambala-Kalka Railway opened
1892	:	Introduction of piped water supply
1895	:	Construction of Sewer in Chandni Chowck
1897	:	Karachi-Delhi Railway link
1900	:	Ghaziabad-Moradabad Railway link
1901	:	First notified Area Committee for Mehrauli formed
1905	:	Delhi-Agra Railway link
1907	:	Lord, Curzon-Delhi Durbar, Delhi Railway Station, two lakh population.
1910	:	Survey of city carried out on behalf of the Municipal Committee which brought out detailed maps of the city (Wilson Survey)

IMPERIAL DELHI

1911	:	Delhi Durbar, Delhi declared as capital of India, Population 2.30 lakh
1911	:	Punjab Municipal Act passed
1912	:	Seat of British India Government
1912	:	Bomb thrown at Viceroy Lord Hardinge. Raisina finally selected for new capital.
1913	:	Notified Area Committee for Civil Station formed.
1913	:	Land acquired in Karol Bagh
1915	:	Delhi District reconstituted, exclusion of

		Sonipat, Faridabad and Ballabhgarh and inclusion of Shahdara Tehsil.
1915	:	Daryaganj Cantonment land used for civil purpose
1916	:	Establishment of New Delhi Municipal Committee. Notified area Committee for Shahdara formed. Butchers and chamars removed from Paharganj to Rehgarpura.
1922	:	Punjab Town Improvement Act passed
1924	:	Notified Area Committee for Red Fort formed
1925	:	Delhi Joint Water and Sewerage Board constituted
1931	:	New Capital Committee acquired Deputyganj
1936	:	A.P. Hume appointed to prepare report on relief of congestion in Delhi.

DELHI IMPROVEMENT TRUST

1937	:	Delhi Improvement Trust constituted
1938	:	Cantonment Board constituted
1943	:	Delhi Rent Control Ordinance passed
1946	:	Delhi-Ajmeri Gate Scheme sanctioned

POST INDEPENDENCE

1947	:	Independence and partition of the country. Inmigration of half million population in Delhi.
1948	:	Ministry of Relief created
1948–52	:	Rehabilitation Townships in the urban fringes planned
1949	:	Central Coordination Committee for Development of Greater Delhi
1950	:	Delhi Road Transport Authority set up
1951	:	Delhi State Electricity Board Constituted
1957	:	Delhi Municipal Corporation and Delhi Development Authority created under Acts of Parliament
1962	:	Delhi Master Plan (1962-1981) notified, population 23 lakh (1961)
1973	:	DUAC Act 1973 passed by the Parliament, Delhi Urban Art Commission constituted in 1975.
1985	:	NCR Planning Board Act passed by the

		Parliament, National Capital Region Planning Board established
1985	:	Environment (Pollution Control) Act passed by Parliament
1988		Lutyens Bungalow Zone (LBZ) guidelines issued by the Government of India.
1990	:	Master Plan for Delhi-2001 notified
1992	:	Delhi Administration (Amendment) Act.
1992	:	Archaeological Survey of India Notification for Prohibited and Regulated areas around protected monuments.
1999	:	Delhi-The Built Heritage—A Listing published by the DDA and INTACH
2004	:	Delhi Heritage Conservation Regulations notified as part of Building Bye-laws, and Heritage Conservation Committee constituted by the MOUD.
2007	:	Master Plan for Delhi 2021 notified.
2011	:	New Delhi celebrates a century of its founding, Delhi Municipal Corporation split into 3 Municipal Corporations.
2011-12	:	INTACH prepares dossier for Delhi's nomination as a World Heritage City by the UNESCO.

ANNEXURE - 2

Monuments, Sites & Heritage Buildings in Delhi Protected by the Archaeological Survey of India

Old/ New no.	*Name of Monument*	*Location*
1/43	Bastion, where a wall of Jahanpanah meets the wall of Rai Pithora fort.	Adchini
2/2/44	Ramp and gateway of Rai Pithora's Fort	Adchini
3/45	Marble Tomb reputed to be that of Nawab Bahadur Jawid Khan	Aliganj
4/12	Lal Bangla	Babarpur (Kaka Nagar)
5/10	Khair-ul-Manzil	Babarpur Bazipur (Kaka Nagar)
6/11	Kos Minar or Mughal Mile stone	Babarpur Bazipur (Kakanagar)
7/00	The Moti Gate of Sher Shah, Delhi	Babarpur Bazipur (Kakanagar)
8/47	Begampuri Masjid	Begampur
9/00	Phool Chadar aqueduct near Najafgarh Jhil aqueduct	Chauki Mubaraka-bad

10/48	Lal Gumbad	Chiragh Delhi
11/49	Tomb of Bahlol Lodi	-do-
12/01	Ajmeri Gate	Bazar Ajmeri Gate
13/13/00	Alipur Cemetery	Delhi-Alipur Camping group.
14/02	Ashoka Pillar	Ferozabad (Feroz Shah Qila or Vikram Nagar Colony)
15/00	Bara Khamba Cemetery	Imperial City
16/19	Chauburji	Ridge near Hindu Rao Hospital
17/20	Eremo Cemetery	Kishanganj Railway Station
18/03	Delhi Fort or Lal Qila, Naubat Khana, Diwan-i-aam, Mumtaz Mahal' Rang Mahal, Baithak, Maseu Burj, Diwan-i-Khas' Moti Masjid, Sawan Bhadon, Shad Burj, Hamam with all surrounding gardens, paths, terraces and water courses.	Red Fort
19/04	Delhi Gate	Daryaganj
20/21	Enclosure containing the grave of Lt. Edwards and others, murdered in 1857	North Ridge near flag staff tower, Civil Lines.
21/50	Enclosure wall with Tomb of Najaf Khan	Safdarjung Fly-over,
22/22	Flag Staff Tower	400 yards North of Cheburji Mosque
23/13	Jantar Mantar	Connaught Place
24/37	Kashmiri Gate and portion of the City Wall, on either side of the Kashmiri Gate and on the other upto and including the water bastions at the northern corner of the wall and also the ditch outside the City Wall where this is exposed.	Kashmiri Gate

25/05	Kotla Ferozabad with the remaining walls, bastions and gateways and gardens, the old Mosque, well and all other ruins, buildings it contains.	Two furlongs east of jail and three furlongs due south of S.E. corner of Shahjahanabad, Delhi.
26/06	Lal Darwaza, the northern gate of the outer walls of the Delhi of Shershah.	Three furlongs due south of Delhi Gate,
27/23	Lothian Road Cemetery	Kashmere Gate
28/24	The Mosque	Qudsia Garden
29/25	Mutiny Telegraph Memorial	In front of Old Telegraph Building Kashmere Gate
30/26	Nicholson (or Kashmere Gate) Cemetry	Kashmere Gate
31/00	Nicholson statue and its platform and the surrounding gardens, paths and enclosure wall.	Outside Kashmere Gate
32/27	Old Baoli immediately to the west of Hindu Rao's House.	On the ridge, Delhi
33/28	The Old Entrance Gateway of the Garden.	Qudsia Garden Delhi
34/29	The Pirgaib to the north and near Hindu Rao's House	On the ridge, Delhi
35/30	Portion of City wall near which John Nicholson was mortally wounded on 14th Sept., 1857	On the ridge, Delhi
36/31	The Punjabi Gate in the Roshanara Bagh	Opposite Municipal Board School, Subji Mandi
37/51	Purana Quila (Inderpat) with all its walls, arcades, gateways and bastions, gardens, the mosque of Sher Shah (Quila-i-Kuhran Masjid). The Sher Mandal and entrance to subterranean passages.	Two miles south of the Delhi Gate of Shahjahanabad, Delhi

38/32	Rajpur (Mutiny cemetery)	Old Rajpur Cantonment, North Distt.
39/33	The remaining gateways of the Old Magazine with their adjoining buildings.	The Post Office, Delhi
40/14	Sher Shah's gate with the adjoining curon walls and Bastions and the remains of the double line of structures to its front	Opposite Purana Qila immediately north-east of the Khairul Manzil Mosque.
41/34	Site of Siege Battery known as Sammy House Battery bearing the following inscriptions Battery, Sammy house, Major Remington Tank, RA Commanding armament 89 pounds to command ground near Mori Bastion.	300 yards east of mutiny memorial
42/34	Site of Siege Battery with inscription.	East of the hospital in Police Lines.
43/34	Site of Siege Battery with inscription	Compound of Curzon House
44/34	Site of Siege Battery with inscription	In the garden near south west entrance to Delhi Club Ground
45/07	Sunehri Masjid near Delhi Fort	Delhi Fort
46/00	Tomb of Capt. Mac Barnatt & others who fell in an attack on Kishanganj.	Kishan Ganj.
47/08	Tomb of Ghyasuddin Khan,	Tughlaqabad
48/35	Tomb of Roshanara & Baradari	Sabzi Mandi
49/09	Tomb of Razia Begum in Mohalla Bulbuli Khana	Shahjahanabad
50/15	Tomb of Safdarjang (Mirza Muqim Mansur Ali Khan) with all the enclosure walls, gateways, gardens and the mosque on the eastern side of the garden.	Lodhi Road, New Delhi

51/36	Tripolia Gateways	Delhi-Karnal Road
52/16	Uggar Sen's Baoli	Near Jantar Mantar
53/52	Tomb of Darya Khan	Kidwai Nagar East
54/53	Baoli at Ghiaspur	Nizamuddin
55/54	Tomb of Mirza Muzaffar, Chota Batasha no. 153. Ghiaspur	Nizamuddin
56/55	Tomb of Amir Khusro, Ghiaspur	Nizamuddin
57/56	Tomb of Mirza Muzaffar, Bara Batasha no. 151 Ghiaspur	Nizamuddin
58/57	Tomb of Nizamuddin Aulia, Ghiaspur, 197	Nizamuddin
59/58	Unknown tomb Ghiaspur, 153	Nizamuddin
60/59	i. The tomb of Ferozshah ii. Domed building to the west of no. 1 iii. Dalan between 1&2 iv. Domed building & its court to the south of no. 3 v. Dalans and all ruined building to the north of no.1 and existing upto no.10 vi. Five Chhatris to the east of no. 1&5 vii. Old Gate to the north of no. 6 viii. Three Chhatris to the north-west of no. 7 ix. Ruined courtyard and its Dalans with the domed building to the north-west to the no. 8 x. Old wall running east from no. 4 xi. 2.23 Acres of land surrounding the above monuments and bouded on the north by house of Change and Mehra Chand sons of Hansram and house of Uderam, son of Kusha, South Gairmunkin Rasta, East by village site belonging to village community house of Nots Zadar	Hauz Khas

	sons of Jai Singh Chhamar and fields nos.338& 331 belonging to Naider and others West By field no, 185 belonging to Udaram, son of Kusal Jat and field no. 186 belonging to Jagins and Sajawal Rajput, no.195 Gairmunkin Johar, common of Jats and Musalmans and field no.196, Gairmunkin Pall.	
61/60	Bag-i-Alam Gumbad with a Mosque	Humayunpur
62/61	Kali Gumti	Humayunpur (Hauz Khas)
63/62	Tofewala Gumbad	Humayunpur Deer Park (Hauz Khas)
64	Arab Sarai	Patti, Ghiapur in Hauz Inderpat
65/114	The Gateway of Arab Sarai facing North towards Purana Qila	Near Arab Sarai
66/113	The Gateway of Arab Sarai facing East towards the tomb of Humayun	Near Arab Sarai
67/115	Remaining Gateways of Arab Sarai and of Abadi-Bagh-Buhalima	Near Arab Sarai
68/64	Lakhar Wala Gumbad (Tomb)	Inderpat Estate (Sunder Nursery), near Delhi Public School, Mathura Road, Nizamuddin
69/65	Sunderwala Burj	Inderpat Estate (Sunder Nursery)
70/66	Sunderwala Mahal	Inderpat Estate (Sunder Nursery)
71	Bijay Mandal, neighbouring domes, buildings and dalan to north of Begumpur	In village Kalu Sarai (Sarvapriya Vihar)
72/68	Old Lodi Bridge with approaches	Near tomb of Sikandar Lodhi, Khairpur

73/69	Mosque with the dalans and courtyard and the Bara Gumbaj (the domed entrance to the mosque)	Khairpur
74/70	The tomb of Mohammad Shah known as Mubarak Khan-ka-Gumbaz	Khairpur
75/71	Tomb of Sikandar Lodi with its enclosure wall and bastions, gates & compound	Khairpur
76/72	Unknown tomb with blue tiles decoration known as Shisha Gumbad	Khairpur
77/73	Bandi or Poti ka Gumbad III-280	Kharera Village between Hauz Khas and Qutab Road
78/75	Biran-Ka-Gumbad-282	Kharera village between Hauz Khas and Qutab Road
79/76	Biwi or Dadi-ka-Gumbad-281	Kharera village between Hauz Khas and Qutab Road
80/77	Chor Minar, No. 289, Vol. III	Kharera (Hauz Khas Enclave)
81/78	Choti Gumti	Kharera village Green Park
82/79	Idgah of Kharera, no.287, Vol III	Kharera village, Hauz Khas Enclave
83/80	Nili Mosque	Kharera village, Hauz Khas Enclave
84/81	Sakri Gumti-284	Kharera village Green Park
85/82	Khirkee Masjid	Village Khirkee
86/83	Satpula-III-216	Village Khirkee
87/84	Tomb of Yusuf Quttal	At Khirkee in field no.81 min,property of Shamlat deh

88/96	Jahaz Mahal	Mehrauli
89/94	Shamsi Talab together with platform, entrance gates	Mehrauli
90/97	Moti Masjid	Mehrauli
91/98	Old Palace of Bahadur Shah II alias Lal Mahal	Mehrauli
92/74	Bara Khamba-285	Kherera village
93/99	The Qutab Archaeological area as fenced, including the Mosque, Iron Pillar, Minar of Qutabuddin, unfinished Minar, all colonnades, screen arches, tomb of Altmash, college, buildings of Alauddin, Tomb of Iman Zamin and all carved stones in the above area with gardens, paths, water channels, and all gateways, including the Alai-Darwaza, also all graves in the above area.	Mehrauli
94/101	Tomb of Adam Khan (Rest House)	Mehrauli
95/100	Tomb and Mosque of Maulana Jamali Kamali	Mehrauli
96/102	Wall mosque	Mehrauli
97/104	Walls of Lal Kot and Rai Pithora fort from Sohan Gate of Adam Khan's tomb, including the ditch where there is an outer wall	Mehrauli kh. no. 1783, 1765,1766, 1767, 1770, 1772, 1773, 1798 & 1764
98/103	Walls of Lal Kot and Rai Pithora fort at the point where they meet together	Near Jamali Kamali's mosque Mehrauli kh. no. 1754, Ladho Sarai kh. no. 86, 87
99/105	Walls of Rai Pithora's fort including gateways and bastions	Mehrauli
100/107	Gates and walls of Mubarakpur, Kotla	Village Mubarak-pur Kotla
101/106	Moth-ki-Masjid	Behind South Extension Part II.
102/00	Inchla Wali Gumti	Mubarakpur Kotla
103/108	Kala Gumbad	Mubarakpur Kotla

104/112	Tombs of Bade-Khan and Mubarkpur Kotla, Kotla	Mubarakpur Kotla
105/112	Tombs of Chote Khan,	Mubarakpur Kotla
106/111	Tomb of Mubarak in Mubarkpur, Kotla	Mubarakpur Kotla
107/109	Mosque attached to Mubarak Shah Tomb	Mubarakpur Kotla
108/110	Tomb of Bhura Khan	Mubarakpur Kotla
109/141	Tin Burji Wala Gumbad	Mohammadpur village, II, 304
110/142	Unnamed Tomb	Mohammadpur village, 305
111/143	Baoli	Munirka, II, 318
112/144	Munda Gumbad	Munirka, 302
113/145	Unnamed Mosque	Munirka, 314
114/146	Unnamed Tomb	Munirka, 313
115/147	Unnamed Tomb	Munirka, 315
116/148	Unnamed Tomb	Munirka, 316
117/149	Unnamed Tomb	Munirka, 317
118/00	Unnamed Mosque Unnamed Tomb	Munirka, 321 & 322
119/150	Wajir pur-ki-Gumbad	Munirka, 312
120/116	The Afsah-wala-ki-Masjid situated outside the west gate of Humayun's Tomb with its dalans and paved court bounded on the east by Humayun's Tomb on the west by abadi Arab-ki-Sarai on the north by road and Khasra no 252 and on the south by abadi Arab-ki-Sarai	Nizamuddin
121/117	Bara Khamba outside north entrance to shrine	Nizamuddin
122/118	Bara Pulah bridge near Nizamuddin	South of Nizamuddin
123/119	Chausath Khamba and tomb of Mirza Nizamuddin Aziz-ka-Kokaltash	Nizamuddin

124/120	Grave of Jahanara Begum	Nizamuddin
125/122	Grave of Mohammad Shah	Nizamuddin
126/121	Grave of Mirza Jahangir	Nizamuddin
127/123	Humayun's Tomb, its platforms, garden, enclosure walls and gateways, khasra no. 258 bounded on the east by khasra no. 180, 181 & 244 of Miri Singh and on west by kh. no. 268 & 253 on the north by Khasra no. 266, on the south by kh no. 245 of Miri Singh & Khasra no. 248 & 249 of Sayyad Mohammad	Nizamuddin
128/124	Nila Gumbad outside the south corner of the enclosure of Humayun's Tomb (kh. no 243) bounded on the east by kh no. 182, on the west by Humayun's Tomb, on the north by kh no. 181 & on the south by kh. no. 244 of Miri Singh	Nizamuddin
129/125	Nili Chhatri or Subz Burz	Nizamuddin East
130/126	Tomb of Afsar-wala immediately near to the South of Afsar-wala-ki-Masjid	Nizamuddin
131/127	Tomb of Atgah Khan	Nizamuddin
132/128	The tomb of Isa Khan with its surrounding enclosure walls and garden gateways and mosque (kh. no.281) bounded on the east by Arab Sarai kh. no. 236 on the west by kh no 283 graveyard of Piare Lal and kh. no. 283 of Badon on the north by kh, no, 236 of Pandit Brij Vallabh and on the south by Arab Sarai, kh. no. 238	Nizamuddin
133/129	Tomb of Khan-i-Khanam	Nizamuddin
134/00	Tomb with three domes near Rly. Station	Nizamuddin
135/17	Sikargah Kushak-II-327	Old Kushak Village
136/38	Gateways of Badli-ki-Sarai	Village Pipalthala

137/131	Tomb of Sheikh Kaburuddin also know as Rakabwala Gumbad in field no. 84 min. situated at Sarai Shah 31 property of Thoks Shahpur and Adhchini	Malviyanagar
138/133	Ruined line of walls, bastions & gateways of Siri Kh. no. 88, 265 & 447 at village Shahpur Jat	Shahpur Jat
139/132	Internal buildings of Siri Mehammadi wali-kh. no. 14 Shahpur Jat, Bul-Bul-Ki-Kh. no. 256 Shahpur Jat, Makhdum ki kh. no. 255 Shapur Jat, Baradari Sahpur Jat, Motiyanwala dome Thana wala	Shahpur Jat
140/134	Nai-ka-kot	Tughlaqabad
141/135	Tomb of Ghyasuddin Tughlaq, walls and bastions, gates and cause way, including the tomb of Dad Khan	Tughlaqabad
142/136	Tomb of Mohammad Tughlaq Badshah	Badarpur Jail
143/139	Walls of old city of Tughlaqabad.	Badarpur Jail
144/138	Walls, gateways, bastions and internal buildings of both inner and outer citadels of Tughlaqabad Fort	Tughlaqabad
145/137	Walls, gate and bastions of Adilabad (Mohammadbad) and causeway leading thereto Tughlaqabad.	Tughlaqabad
146/42	The Tomb	Wazirabad
147/41	The Mosque	Wazirabad
148/40	Neighbouring Bridge	Wazirabad
149	Mound known as Joga Bai in part of survey plot no. 167	Jamia Nagar
150/46	Ashoka Rock Edict	East of Kailash
151/85	Mandi Mosque	Ladho Sarai
152/86	Rajon-ki-Bain with Mosque and Chhatri	Ladho Sarai
153/87	Badun Gate	Ladho Sarai

154/88	Gateway of Lal Kot	Ladho Sarai
155/89	Gateway of Rai Pithora fort	Ladho Sarai
156/91	Walls of Rai Pithora fort and Jahan Panah at the point where they meet together	Hauz Rani and Ladho Sarai
157/140	Tomb of Sultan Ghori	Malikpur Kohi
158/97	Baoli known as Ghandak-ki-baoli	Mehrauli
159/93	Enclosure containing the tomb of Shah Alam Bahadur Shah, Shah Alam II and Akbar Shah II	Mehrauli
160/94	Hauz Shamsi with Central Red stone Pavilion situated at Mehrauli in field no. 157-81, 1586-97, 1614 & 1624	Mehrauli
161/95	Iron Pillar Hindu	Mehrauli
162/151	Ancient Mosque	Palam
163/39	Sheesh Mahal	Shalimar Garden Village Hyderpur
164/18	Ashokan Pillar	On the Ridge between Hindu Rao Hospital
165/130	Sarai Shahji	Malviya Nagar
166/90,	Azim Khan Tomb	Ladho Sarai
167/154	Mazar of Sheikh Muhammad Ibrahim Zauq	Chand Bagh, Qadam Sharif, Paharganj, Delhi
168/035	Fortification Wall Asad Burj, Water Gate, Delhi Gate, Lahori Gate, Jahangiri Gate, Chhatta Bazar, Baoli	Red Fort, Delhi
169/152	Fortification walls, gates, bastions and ancient buildings of Salimgarh Fort	Bela Road
170/153	Portion of the City Wall of Shahjahanabad	Ansari road
171	Sat Narain Bhawan	Delhi Sahora Khurd, Dina Nath Marg, Roshanara Road, New Delhi.

172/100	Balban Khan's Tomb & Jamli Kamali	Lado Sarai, Mehrauli, Delhi
173	Unknown Tomb in the vicinity of Jawaharlal Nehru Stadium	Pragati Vihar, New Delhi
174	Mazar of Mirza Ghalib	Nizamuddin

List of Additional Monuments Notified by the GNCTD, Department of Archaeology

No.	*Name of Monument*	*Location*
1	Mutiny Memorial	Northern Ridge
2	Maqbara	G T K Depot
3	Dara Shikoh Library	Kashmere Gate
4	Turkman Gate	
5	Baradari	Sadhana Enclave
6	Tomb	Near Lodhi Road Flyover
7	Jail	Bawana
8	Lodhi period Tomb	Katwaria Sarai
9	Monuments	Delhi Golf Club, DDA Golf Club
10	Haveli of Mirza Ghalib	Gali Qasim Jan, Ballimaran.

ANNEXURE - 3

Listed Heritage Buildings in Delhi

(*Source:* INTACH, DDA, MCD, NDMC and Govt. of Delhi)

Zone - A, ShahJahanabad (Walled City)

S.No	*Buildings*	*Location*
1.	Idgah	West of Paharganj
2.	Lady Reading School	Sadar Bazaar
3.	Dispensary Lady Reading Health School	Sadar Bazaar
4.	Outer Gateway Qila Qadam Sharif	Nabi Karim
5.	Inner gateway Qila Qadam Sharif	Nabi Karim
6.	Mosque Qila Qadam Sharif	Qila Qadam Sharif
7.	Gateway of Qadam Sharif Shrine	Nabi Karim
8.	Qadam Sharif Shrine	Nabi Karim
9.	Feroz Shah Mosque	Nabi Karim
10.	Kunwari Begam Ka Burj	Qadam Sharif Nabi Karim
11.	Enclosures/walls Qila Qadam Sharif	Qadam Sharif Nabi Karim
12.	Tomb	Tail Mill Road, Ram Nagar

13.	Hari Masjid	Chuna Mandi Paharganj
14.	Mosque	Chitra Gupta Road Paharganj
15.	Chitra Gupta Temple	Paharganj
16.	Haveli	Opp. Hare Kishan Guest House Paharganj
17.	Mosque	116, Main Bazar Road, Paharganj
18.	Municipal Corporation Primary School	Main Bazar Road, Paharganj
19.	Residence	110, Gali Krishna Paharganj
20.	Residence	104, Gali Krishna Paharganj
21.	Tomb	Qutab Road
22.	Mosque/Imambara	Qutab Road
23.	Shivalaya	New Delhi Railway Station
24.	Mosque	New Delhi Railway Station
25.	Police Station	Sadar Bazar
26.	Balika Chaman	New Delhi Railway Station
27.	Northern Railway Rest House	Connaught Place
28.	Sarhindi Masjid	Lahori Gate
29.	Gular Wali Masjid	Fatehpuri
30.	Ghazi-ud-Din's Mosque	Fatehpuri
31.	Muthasib's Mosque	Fatehpuri
32.	Gateway	Tilak Bazar, Fatehpuri
33.	Masjid Ramzan Shah	Fatehpuri
34.	Haveli	Bazar Naya Bans, Fatehpuri
35.	Durga Mandir Shivalaya	Fatehpuri
36.	Hauzwali Masjid	Naya Bans, Fatehpuri
37.	Tahawwu Khan's Mosque	Naya Bans, Fatehpuri
38.	Residnce	306, Kuncha Sanjogiram, Naya Bans, Fatehpuri
39.	Fatehpuri Masjid	Chandni Chowk
40.	St. Stephens Church	Chandni Chowk
41.	Bhowai Shankar Ki Kacheri	Fatehpuri, Chandni Chowk
42.	Dharamshala Rai Sahib Lala Laxmi Narayan	Church Mission Road, Fatehpuri
43.	Bhairav Mandir	Chandni Chowk

44.	Municipal Corporation Primary Girls School	Kucha Ghasiram, Chandni Chowk
45.	Gateway	322, Kucha Ghasiram, Chandni Chowk
46.	Gateway	154, Kucha Ghasiram, Chandni Chowk
47.	Namak Haram Ki Haveli	Kucha Ghansiram, Chandni Chowk
48.	Namak Haram Ki Haveli	316, Kucha Ghasiram Chandni Chowk
49.	Gateway	759, Katra Neel, Chandni Chowk
50.	Shivalaya Kunniji Maharaj	793, Katra Neel, Chandni Chowk
51.	Shivalaya	515, Katra Neel, Chandni Chowk
52.	Mankchanda & Visvesvaranath's Shivalaya	577 Katra Neel, Chandni Chowk
53.	Bada Shivalya	701, Katra Neel, Chandni Chowk
54.	Residence	574, Katra Neel, Chandni Chowk
55.	Shivalya Ghanteshwar Mahadev	598, Katra Neel, Chandni Chowk
56.	Residence	575, Katra Neel, Chandni Chowk
57.	Residence	596, Katra Neel, Chandni Chowk
58.	Dhuminal's Shivalaya	602, Ghanteshwara Mahadev Katra Neel, Chandni Chowk
59.	Residence	649, Katra Neel, Chandni Chowk
60.	Pandit Hari Ram Ji ka Shivalya	689, Katra Neel, Chandni Chowk
61.	Dharamshala	Bagh Diwar, Fatehpuri
62.	Temple School	Bagh Diwar, Fatehpuri
63.	Residence	508, Haveli Haider Quli, Chandni Chowk
64.	Haveli	507, Haveli Haider Quli, Chandni Chowk
65.	Residence	509, Haveli Haider Quli, Chandni Chowk

66.	Residence	499, Haveli Haider Quli, Chandni Chowk
67.	ANZ Grindlays Building	534, Chandni Chowk
68.	Union Bank of India Builing	628, Chandni Chowk
69.	Oriental Bank of Commerce Building	681, Chandni Chowk
70.	Gateway to Katra Neel	Katra Neel Chandni Chowk
71.	Lala Chuna Mal's Haveli	Katra Neel Chandni Chowk
72.	Mirza Galib's House	2298, Gali Qasim Jan, Billimaran, Chandni Chowk.
73.	Mirza Galib's in-law's House	Billimaran.
74.	Mahadev Mandir	S.P. Mukherjee Marg
75.	Old Delhi Railway Station	S.P. Mukherjee Marg
76.	Police Station	Chandni Chowk
77.	Punjab National Bank Building	458, Katra Mohan, Chandni Chowk
78.	MCD Office	Kucha Bagh, Chandni Chowk
79.	Hakim Mihar Ali Shah's Mosque	Gali Kucha Bagh, Chandni Chowk
80.	Sunehri Masjid	Chandni Chowk
81.	North Brook Fountain	Chandni Chowk
82.	Gurudwara Sis Ganj	Chandni Chowk
83.	Central Baptist Church	Chandni Chowk
84.	Gujrati Temple	1739, Dariba Kalan
85.	Hardayal Municipal Public Library	Gandhi Ground, Chandni Chowk
86.	Gateway	2255, Kaudiya Pul, Chandni Chowk
87.	Bhagirath Place	Chandni Chowk
88.	Fort View Hotel	Chandni Chowk
89.	St. Mary's Church	S.P. Mukherjee Marg
90.	Gateway of Zeenat Mahal	Lal Kuan
91.	Office Block	Bazar Lal Kuan
92.	Gateway	Bazar Lal Kuan
93.	Gateway	Farash Khana Off Bazar Lal Kuan
94.	Yogmaya Mandir	Kuncha Sanjogiram Bazar, Naya Bazar,
95.	MCD Dispensary	Lal Kuan
96.	Residence	Mohalla Roadgran, Lal Kuan

97.	Graves enclosure of Nawan Iradtmand Khan & Nawab Masayar Khan	Mohalla Roadgran, Lal Kuan
98.	Gateway	Bazar Sikriwalan, Fatehpuri
99.	Sikriwala Mosque	Bazar Sikriwalan, Hauz Quazi
100.	Masjid Mubarak Begam	Bazar Sikriwalan, Hauz Quazi
101.	Houz Qazi Mosque	Hauz Quazi Chowk, Fatehpuri
102.	Gateway	Gali Qasim Jan, Fatehpuri
103.	Residence	2168, Gali Qasim Jan, Billimaran, Chandni Chowk
104.	Haveli	2160, Ahata Kale Saheb, Billimaran, Chandni Chowk
105.	Hindustani Dawakhana	Billimaran, Chandni Chowk
106.	Gateway	3639, Chawari Bazar
107.	Shri Digambar Jain Naya Mandir	Fatehpuri
108.	Anand Aushdhlaya	Billimaran, Chandni Chowk
109.	Shri Agarwal Digambar Jain Panchayati Mandir	Fatehpuri
110.	Residence	2293, Dharampura, Fatehpuri
111.	Residence	2218, Dharampura, Fatehpuri
112.	Shri Digambar Jain Maru Mandir	Fatehpuri
113.	Prakash Nursery School	Dharampura, Fatehpuri
114.	Commercial-cum-Residential Building	Fatehpuri
115.	Residence	2942, Katra Kushal Rai, Kinari Bazar, Chandni Chowk
116.	Residence	1961, Katra Kushal Rai, Kinari Bazar, Chandni Chowk
117.	Ram Nath Inder Devi trust	Kinari Bazar, Chandni Chowk
118.	Jain Temple	Kinari Bazar, Chandni Chowk
119.	Naugharana	Kinari Bazar, Chandni Chowk
120.	Residence	West end of Kinari Bazar, Chandni Chowk

121.	Nawab Shahib's Mosque	Kinari Bazar, Chandni Chowk
122.	Gateway	Near Panchayati Jain Mandir
123.	Residence	Dariba Kalan, Chandni Chowk
124.	Jain Temple	1541, Dariba Kalan, Chandni Chowk
125.	Jain Temple	1513, Dariba Kalan, Chandni Chowk
126.	Gate to Kucha-I-Ustad Hamid	Kishan Gali Jama Masjid
127.	Indraprastha Hindu Girls Senior Secondary School	Jama Masjid
128.	Lal Mandir	Chandni Chowk
129.	Kasturba Janana Hospital	Daryaganj
130.	Chatta Agha Jan Masjid	Daryaganj
131.	Bridge Near Lahori Gate, Red Fort	Red Fort
132.	Baoli	158, Red Fort
133.	Army Barracks	Red Fort
134.	Mosque of Gaziuddin Khan	Ajmeri Gate
135.	Anglo-Arbic Public School	Ajmeri Gate
136.	Rehmani Masjid	Ajmeri Gate
137.	Commercial Building	Ajmeri Gate
138.	Residence	4642-4649, Ajmeri Gate
139.	MCD Primary Boys School	290-295, Ajmeri Gate
140.	Residence	4110-4141, Gali Shah Tara, Ajmeri Gate
141.	Guler Wali Masjid	Kucha-I-Shah Tara, Ajmeri Gate
142.	Unchi Masjid	Kucha-I-Shah Tara, Ajmeri Gate
143.	Masjid	Kucha-I-Shah Tara, Ajmeri Gate
144.	Residence	4346, Kucha-I Pandit, Ajmeri Gate
145.	Residence	504, Kucha Pati Ram, Ram Bazar Sitaram
146.	Nav Jyoti Public School	939, Kucha Pati Ram, Bazar Sitaram
147.	Jain Mandir	908, Kucha Pati Ram, Near Hauz Qazi

148.	Residence	901, Kucha Pati Ram, Bazar Sitaram
149.	Residence	908, Kucha Pati Ram, Near Hauz Qazi
150.	Residence	834, Mohalla Imli, Bazar Sitaram
151.	Holy Trinity Church	Turkman Gate
152.	Badi Masjid	Turkman Gate
153.	Telion ka Phatak	Turkman Gate
154.	Kalan Masjid	Turkman Gate
155.	Lal Darwaja	Bazar Sita Ram
156.	L. Madan Mashal Lal Ayurvedic Charitable Dispensary	Bazar Sita Ram
157.	Haveli	2549, Churiwalan, Bazar Sita Ram
158.	Municipal Corporation Ayurvedic Dispensary	1424, Bazar Sita Ram
159.	Haksar Haveli	Bazar Sita Ram
160.	Bhartiya Bal Sadan Society	Bazar Sita Ram
161.	Dharamshala Lala Pyare Lal Madho Ram	Bazar Sita Ram
162.	Amrudwali Mosque	Bazar Sita Ram
163.	Residence	2837, Rehman Building, Bazar Sita Ram
164.	Anjuman Masjid Chandni Chowk	Bazar Sita Ram,
165.	Tomb of Shah Turkman Turkman Gate	Mohalla Qabristan,
166.	Tomb Raziya Sultan	Bulbuli Khana, Turkman Gate
167.	Mosque	Bazar Matmatya Mahal, Near Jama Masjid
168.	Mosque Shah Gulam Ali	Kuncha Mir Hashim, Turkman Gate
169.	Dargah Shah Gulam Ali	Kuncha Mir Hashim, Turkman Gate
170.	Residence	3460, Netaji Subhash Marg Daryaganj
171.	Sunehri Masjid	West of Netaji Subhash Marg Daryaganj
172.	Shri Digambar Jain Mandir	Delhi Gate
173.	Masjid Saiwali	Kuncha Chetan, Daryaganj
174.	Jain Temple & School	Daryaganj

175.	Hotel Moti Mahal	Netaji Subhash Marg, Daryaganj
176.	Residence and Commercial Building	4,Netaji Subhash Marg, Daryaganj
177.	Commercial Street	8-14, Netaji Subhash Marg, Daryaganj
178.	Residence and Commercial	15-16, Netaji Subhash Marg, Daryaganj
179.	Commercial Street	19-23, Netaji Subhash Marg, Daryaganj
180.	Street with 14 buildings	26-40, Netaji Subhash Marg, Daryaganj
181.	Dargah Shah Shabir Baksh	5051, Netaji Subhash Marg, Daryaganj
182.	Masjid Beriwali	5052, Netaji Subhash Marg, Daryaganj
183.	Police Station	Daryaganj
184.	Residence, DCP Central	Daryaganj
185.	H.M. D.A.V. Middle School	Daryaganj
186.	Shroff Eye Hospital	Daryaganj
187.	Hindi Park Housing Area	Hindi Park, Daryaganj
188.	Mosque	Hindi Park, Daryaganj
189.	City Wall South Darya Ganj	Daryaganj
190.	Mortello Tower	Daryaganj
191.	Residence	Ansari Road, Daryaganj
192.	Residence, Dr. Ansari House	Ansari Road, Daryaganj
193.	Pathak Habsh Khan	Tilak Bazar, Fatehpuri
194.	Gateway	Billimaran, Fatehpuri
195.	Allahabad Bank Building	Chandni Chowk
196.	Town Hall	Chandni Chowk
197.	Company Bagh	North of Town Hall
198.	Gateway to Katra Nawab	Chandni Chowk
199.	State Bank of India	Chandni Chowk
200.	Residence	1222, Chandni Chowk
201.	Mahabir Jain Bhawan	1417, Chandni Chowk
202.	Haveli of Ahsanullah Khan	Bazar Sikriwalan, Off Lal Kuan
203.	Residence	5012, Pathak Bans, Lal Kuan
204.	Residence	5051, Bazar Sikriwalan
205.	Lal Kuan	Bazar Lal Kuan
206.	Residence	962, Kuncha Pati Ram, Bazar Sita Ram

207.	Residence	505, Kuncha Pati Ram, Bazar Sita Ram

Zone - B, Karol Bagh

S.No.	*Buildings*	*Location*
1.	Shikargah	Jonti village, Kanjhaola
2.	Haveli	Jonti village, Kanjhaola
3.	Well	Jonti village, Kanjhaola
4.	Temple	Jonti village, Kanjhaola
5.	Mukhal Tank	Kanjhaola
6.	Shivalaya	Jonti village, Kanjhaola
7.	Milestone/Memorial	Tirki Border, Rohtak Road
8.	Ramjas S.S. School	Anand Parbat
9.	Tibbia College	New Rohtak Road
10.	Residence	New Rohtak Road, Opp. Tibbia College
11.	Lal Masjid	Northern end of Faiz Road, Karol Bagh
12.	Bari Masjid	Bara Hindu Rao
13.	MCD Co-ed School	Rani Jhansi Road, Bara Hindu Rao
14.	MCD Dispensary	Bara Hindu Rao
15.	Shidion Ki Masjid	Karol Bagh

Zone - C, Civil Lines

S.No.	*Buildings*	*Location*
1.	Tank	Kuraini Village, Narela
2.	Wall Mosque	Kuraini Village, Narela
3.	Memorial	Azadpur Market, G. T. Road
4.	Coronation Memorial	Kingsway Camp
5.	Coronation Bank	Kingsway Camp
6.	Embankment	Majnu Ka Tila
7.	Ammunition Store	Mall Road, Civil Lines
8.	Ammunition Store	Mall Road, Civil Lines
9.	Ammunition Store	Brig. S. K. Majumdar Marg, Mall Road, Civil Lines
10.	Colonial Building, Majumdar Marg	Engineers Office, Brig. S. K. Mall Road, Civil Lines
11.	Pathan ki Masjid	Mall Road, Civil Lines
12.	Mosque	G. T. Road, opp. State Bank Colony, Delhi - 7.

13.	Gateway of Mahaldhar Khan's Garden	G. T. Road
14.	Gateway	G. T. Road
15.	Faculty of Arts	Delhi University
16.	Delhi University Office	Delhi University
17.	Gwyer Hall	Delhi University
18.	St. Stephen's College	Delhi University
19.	Chopal	St. Stephen College
20.	Principal's Residence	St. Stephen College
21.	Guard House	Hindu College
22.	Old Secretariat	Civil Lines
23.	I. P. College for Woman	Civil Lines
24.	Defence Science Centre	Ring Road, Vidhan Sabha
25.	National Institute of Communicable Diseases	Civil Lines
26.	Meena Devi Jindal Medical Institute and research Centre	Civil Lines
27.	Sant Parmanand Hospital	Civil Lines
28.	Mosque of Shah Wajid	Roshanara Garden
29.	MCD Primary School	Roshanara Garden
30.	Residential Building	Roshanara Garden
31.	Dharamshala	Sabzi Mandi
32.	MCD Primary School	Roshanara Road
33.	Hindu Rao Hospital	Civil Lines
34.	Methodic Church	Tis Hazari
35.	Queen Mary's School	Tis Hazari
36.	Principal's Residence	Tis Hazari
37.	Mosque	Tis Hazari
38.	St. Stephen's Hospital	Tis Hazari
39.	St. Stephen's Hospital Chapel	Tis Hazari
40.	Residence	10, Under Hill Road, Civil Lines
41.	Residence	8, Under Hill Road, Civil Lines
42.	Teachers Hostel	Rajniwas Marg, Civil Lines
43.	B. M. Ganga Girls School	Rajniwas Marg, Civil Lines
44.	Residence	19, Rajniwas Marg, Civil Lines
45.	Chapel	19, Rajniwas Marg, Civil Lines
46.	Delhi United Christian Sr. Sec. School	Civil Lines
47.	Paulas Sadan	Civil Lines

48.	St. Xavier's School	Civil Lines
49.	Buter Memorial Girls School	Boulevard Road
50.	Residence	Boulevard Road
51.	Residence	North East of Stephens Hospital, Boulevard Road
52.	St. Stephen's Community Centre	Rajpur Road
53.	St. Anne's School	Rajpur Road
54.	Residence	Court Road, Rajpur Road
55.	Cambridge Brotherhood	Court Lane, Civil Lines
56.	Hotel Oberoi Meridian	Civil Lines
57.	Exchange Store	Civil Lines
58.	Residence	17, Sham Nath Marg
59.	Canal Rest House	Qudsia Bagh
60.	Maharaja Agrasen Park	Boulevard Road
61.	Shia Masjid	Mori Gate
62.	Suiwali Masjid	Mori Gate
63.	Gulam Nabi's Mosque	Mori Gate
64.	Burhya's Mosque	Mori Gate
65.	Gulerwali Masjid	Ram Bazar.
66.	Hamilton Road School	Mori Gate
67.	James Skinner's House	Kashmere Gate
68.	Dargah Panja Sharif	Kashmere Gate
69.	Badrudin's Grave	Kashmere Gate
70.	Residence	Chotta Bazar, Kashmere Gate
71.	Bengali Club	Kashmere Gate
72.	Kashmere Gate Market	Kashmere Gate
73.	NCC Office	Kashmere Gate
74.	Residence	Lal Sultan Singh Estate, Kashmere Gate
75.	School	Kashmere Gate
76.	Lal Masjid	Kashmere Gate
77.	Colonnaded Building	MCD Office, Kashmere Gate
78.	Circular Baradari	MCD Office, Kashmere Gate
79.	Madarsaa Amina Islam Arbad	Bara Bazar, Kashmere Gate
80.	Ayurvedic Dispensary	Kashmere Gate
81.	Office of the Election Commission	Kashmere Gate
82.	Hamid Ali Khan's Mosque	Kashmere Gate
83.	Kucheri Court for Traffic Offences	Kashmere Gate
84.	Water Bastion	ISBT, Kashmere Gate
85.	NCC Office	Traffic Court, Kashmere Gate

86.	Gallows Bastion	Kashmere Gate
87.	Office of Northern Railways	Kashmere Gate
88.	St. James Church	Kashmere Gate
89.	St. James Annexe	Kashmere Gate
90.	Skinner Family's Cemetery	Kashmere Gate
91.	Delhi College of Engineering	Kashmere Gate
92.	Archaeological Museum	Kashmere Gate
93.	Delhi Institute of Technology	Kashmere Gate
94.	Commemorative Column	Lothian Road, Near Post Office
95.	Post Office	Kashmere Gate
96.	Nigam Bodh Ghat	Kashmere Gate
97.	Northern Railway Officers Rest House	Mukherjee Road
98.	Lothian Bridge	Mukherjee Road
99.	Nili Chhatri Temple	Yamuna Bazar
100.	Jail	Salimgarh Fort
101.	Museum	Salimgarh Fort
102.	Ammunition Rooms	Salimgarh Fort
103.	Market	Club Road off Boulevard Road

Zone - D, New Delhi

S. No.	*Buildings*	*Location*
1.	Lok Nayak Jai Prakash Narayan Hospital	Jawaharlal Nehru Marg
2.	Lok Nayak Hospital Administrative Block	Jawaharlal Nehru Marg
3.	Mosque Mehndiyan	Near Maulana Azad Medical College
4.	Nursery Mosque	North Maulana Azad Medical College
5.	Chaunsath Khamba	West of Maulana Azad Medical College
6.	Dargah	West of Maulana Azad Medical College
7.	Enclosure	West of Maulana Azad Medical College
8.	Memorial	Maulana Azad Medical College
9.	Jamait Ulama Hind Masjid	Bahadur Shah Zafar Marg

10.	Tomb of Shiekh Muhammad Sahib	South of Vikas Marg
11.	Mosque	South of Vikas Marg (DDA)
12.	Matka Pir	Mathura Road South West Corner of Pragati Maidan
13.	Hammam	Purana Quila, Mathura Road
14.	Tomb	Delhi Zoo, Mathura Road
15.	Azimganj Sarai	National Zoological Park, Sunder Nagar
16.	Mosque	Lal Bahadur Shastri Marg
17.	Do Sariya Gumbad	Nizamuddin
18.	Tomb	Nizamuddin
19.	Gateway	West of Nizamuddin Village
20.	Gateway	Nizamuddin
21.	Khan-E-Dauran Khan's Mosque	Nizamuddin
22.	Tomb	Nizamuddin
23.	Northern Gateway of Dargah Complex	Nizamuddin
24.	Tomb	North West Corner of Nizamuddin
25.	Chini Ka Burj	Nizamuddin
26.	Tomb of Bai Kodaldai	Nizamuddin
27.	Arcade Building	Nizamuddin
28.	Gateway to Inner Enclosure of Dargah	Nizamuddin
29.	Dalan of Itgah Khan	Nizamuddin
30.	Enclosure of Nawab Mustafa Khan	Nizamuddin
31.	Majlis Khans	Nizamuddin
32.	Jamaat Khana Mosque	Nizamuddin
33.	Tomb	Dargah Complex, Nizamuddin
34.	Dalan of Mirdha Ikran	Dargah Complex, Nizamuddin
35.	Langar Khana	Dargah Complex, Nizamuddin
36.	Eastern Gateway of Dargah	Dargah Complex, Nizamuddin
37.	Gateway of the House of Mirza Jahangir	Dargah Complex, Nizamuddin
38.	Residential	Nizamuddin
39.	Gateway of Leading to the tomb of Atgan Khan	Nizamuddin
40.	Dalans	Atgah Khan's Tomb Complex

41.	Bari ka Gumbad	East of Atgah Khan's Tomb Complex
42.	Gateway	On the Main Entry from Mathura Road, Nizamuddin
43.	Well	East of Chaunsath Khamba, Nizamuddin
44.	Gateway	North West Chaunsath Khamba
45.	Mirza Galib's Tomb	Nizamuddin
46.	Kali Masjid	Nizamuddin
47.	Gateway of Inner Kot	Nizamuddin
48.	Bastion of Inner Kot	Nizamuddin
49.	Tomb of Khan-I-Jahan Tilagani	Nizamuddin
50.	Wall of Inner Kot	Nizamuddin
51.	Shiv Mandir	G-Block, Nizamuddin West
52.	Chakarwali Masjid	At the Inter Section of Lodi Road and Mathura Road
53.	Tomb	South of DPS Mathura Road
54.	Wall Mosque	South of DPS Mathura Road
55.	Well	Humayun's Tomb Complex
56.	Well	Sunder Nursery, Nizamuddin
57.	Mosque	Sunder Nursery, Nizamuddin
58.	Tomb	Northern side of Humayun's Tomb
59.	Grave Platform	North side of Humayun's Tomb
60.	Chilla Nizamuddin	North side of Humayun's Tomb
61.	Tomb of Sayyid Yasin	Mathura Road, Nizamuddin
62.	Gateway	Nizamuddin East, Mathura Road
63.	Western Gateway	Kotla Mubarakpur, South Ext.
64.	Residence	Kotla Mubarakpur, South Ext.
65.	Baoli & Well	North of Mubarak Shah Tomb Kotla Mubarakpur, South Ext.
66.	South Gate of Kotla Mubarakpur	Mubarak Shah Tomb Kotla
67.	Gumti	South of Chaupal, Village Kotla Mubarakpur
68.	Bridge	North West Edge of Kotla Mubarakpur
69.	St. Paul Cathedral	Hospital Marg, Bhogal
70.	Mosque	Masjid Marg, Bhogal

71.	MCE Office	Jal Vihar, Shiv Mandir Marg, Lajpat Nagar
72.	Shivalaya	Jal Vihar, Shiv Mandir Marg, Lajpat Nagar
73.	Gateway of Temple	Kilokari Village
74.	Domed Building	Kilokari Village
75.	Tomb of Kale Khan	Sarai Kale Khan
76.	Gumti of Sheikh Ali	Defence Colony
77.	Gateway	Defence Colony
78.	Tomb of Basti	Defence Colony
79.	Mosque of Basti	Defence Colony

Zone - F, South Delhi

S.No.	*Buildings*	*Location*
1.	Temple	NH-8, Naval Area, Rao Tula Ram Marg
2.	Two Temples	Rao Tula Ram Marg
3.	Tomb	Rao Tula Ram Marg
4.	Gateway	CAMS Complex, Cantonment
5.	Qasai Wala Gumbad	Vasant Vihar
6.	Mosque	Vasant Vihar
7.	Tomb	Vasant Vihar
8.	Baoli	Vasant Vihar
9.	Bara Lao ka Gumbad	Vasant Vihar
10.	Tomb Known as Baradari	Vasant Vihar
11.	Mosque	Basant Lok Market, Vasant Vihar
12.	Garden Wall	Vasant Vihar
13.	Mosque	DTC Depot, Vasant Vihar
14.	Wall Mosque	Sec-5, R. K. Puram
15.	Wall Mosque	Sec-5, R. K. Puram
16.	Mosque	Sec-5, R. K. Puram
17.	Residence	214, Village Munirka
18.	Malik Munirka Mosque	117, Village Munirka
19.	Mosque	Between Sec-3 & 4, R. K. Puram
20.	Mosque of Haji Langa	Sec-3, R. K. Puram
21.	Haji Langa Gumbad	Munirka
22.	Gateway	Sec-3, R. K. Puram
23.	Tomb	Sec-3, R. K. Puram
24.	Tomb	Mohammadpur Village
25.	Chaupal	Mohammadpur Village
26.	Tomb	Mohammadpur Village
27.	Mosque	Mohammadpur Village

28.	Domed Building	Mohammadpur Village
29.	Well	Humayunpur Village
30.	Maluk Chand ka Gumbad	Humayunpur Village
31.	Dalan	Humayunpur Village
32.	Gumti	Humayunpur Village
33.	Hauz Khas Tank	Dist. Park, Safdurjung Encl.
34.	Munda Gumbad	Dist. Park, Safdurjung Encl.
35.	Idgah	Hauz Khas Village
36.	Turrent	Hauz Khas Village
37.	Plinth	Deer Park, Hauz Khas Village
38.	Mosque	Deer Park, Hauz Khas Village
39.	Kali Gumti	Deer Park, Hauz Khas Village
40.	Wall Mosque	Deer Park, Hauz Khas Village
41.	Tufewala Gumbad	Deer Park, Hauz Khas Village
42.	Well	F-Block, Green Park
43.	Barah Khamba	Green Park
44.	Structure Unknown	Green Park
45.	Enclosure Wall of Kharera Village	Green Park
46.	Mosque	Kharera Village
47.	Mosque of Darwesh	Gulmohar Park
48.	Bridge	Sirifort Residential Complex
49.	Bulbulki	Sirifort Residential Complex
50.	Baradari	Shahpur Jat Village
51.	Building	Masjid Moth, South Extn - II
52.	Gateway	Masjid Moth
53.	Tomb	Gautam Nagar
54.	Tomb	Near L.S.R. College
55.	Gateway	Lala Lajpat Rai Marg
56.	Tomb	Zamroodpur Village
57.	Tomb	Zamroodpur Village
58.	Tomb	Zamroodpur Village
59.	Tomb	Near House no. 88, Zamroodpur Village
60.	Tomb	Lane 62, Zamroodpur Village
61.	Mahavir Library	N Block, G. K. Part-I
62.	Gateway	Kalkaji Mandir
63.	Kalka Mandir	Kalkaji
64.	Dharamshala	Kalkaji Mandir, Kalkaji
65.	Bund	Mahipalpur Village
66.	Mahal	Mahipalpur Village
67.	Ruins	Mahipalpur Village

68.	Ruins	Sec-C, Pkt-9, Vasant Kunj
69.	Enclosure Wall	Vasant Kunj
70.	Ruins	Vasant Kunj
71.	Tomb	Katwaria Sarai Village
72.	Dalan	Katwaria Sarai Village
73.	Khangah	Sarvpriya Vihar
74.	Mosque	Kalu Sarai Village
75.	Chaupal	Kalu Sarai Village
76.	Gateway of Mosque	Adchini Village
77.	Mosque	Adchini Village
78.	Gateway	Adchini Village
79.	Wall Mosque	Malviya Nagar
80.	Wall Mosque	Malviya Nagar
81.	Wall Mosque	Lal Gumbad Complex
82.	Wall Mosque	Malviya Nagar
83.	Wall Mosque	Malviya Nagar
84.	Mahal	Malviya Nagar
85.	Mosque	Malviya Nagar
86.	Enclosure	Malviya Nagar
87.	Enclosure	Shiekh Sarai, Phase-I
88.	Dukh Bhajan Gurudwara	Shiekh Sarai, Phase-I
89.	Kharbuze ka Gumbad	Shiekh Sarai, Phase-I
90.	Tomb of Shiekh Allauddin	Shiekh Sarai, Phase-I
91.	Tomb	Shiekh Sarai, Phase-I
92.	Tomb	Shiekh Sarai, Phase-I
93.	Tomb of Shiekh Salauddin	Shiekh Sarai, Phase-I
94.	Mosque	Shiekh Sarai, Phase-I
95.	Mosque	Shiekh Sarai, Phase-I
96.	Tomb	Shiekh Sarai, Phase-I
97.	Tomb	Shiekh Sarai, Phase-I
98.	Majlis Khana	Shiekh Sarai, Phase-I
99.	Mosque	Khirki Village
100.	Mosque	Khirki Village
101.	Tomb of Sheikh Usman Saiyan	Khirki Village
102.	Lal Gumbad II	Panchsheel Enclave
103.	Madarsa Zeenatul	Panchsheel Enclave
104.	Northern Gateway, walls of Chiragh Delhi	Chiragh Delhi
105.	Circular Bastion and Chattri	Chiragh Delhi
106.	Eastern Gateway of Chirag Delhi	Chiragh Delhi

107.	Southern Gateway and Walls of Chiragh Delhi	Chiragh Delhi
108.	Western Gateway and Walls of Chiragh Delhi	Chiragh Delhi
109.	Eastern Gateway of Inner Enclosure	Chiragh Delhi
110.	Tomb of Roshan Chiragh Delhi	Chiragh Delhi
111.	Mosque of Faruksiyar	Chiragh Delhi
112.	Tomb	Chiragh Delhi
113.	Tomb of Shiekh Zainuddin	Chiragh Delhi
114.	Tomb of the Grand Daughter of Shiekh Farid Shakarganj	Chiragh Delhi
115.	Mosque	Chiragh Delhi
116.	Mehfil Khana	Chiragh Delhi
117.	Tomb	Chiragh Delhi
118.	An Enclosure	Chiragh Delhi
119.	Tomb	Chiragh Delhi
120.	Majlis Khana	Chiragh Delhi
121.	Grave Enclosure	Chiragh Delhi
122.	Gateway	Chiragh Delhi
123.	Pahar	Chiragh Delhi
124.	Gateway	Near House no. 344, Chiragh Delhi
125.	Tomb	Chiragh Delhi
126.	Tomb of Haji Khanam	Near House no. 344, Chiragh Delhi
127.	Turret	Near House no. 344, Chiragh Delhi
128.	Jain Temple	Near House no. 344, Chiragh Delhi
129.	Hanuman Temple	Chiragh Delhi
130.	Kos Minar	Mathura Road
131.	Tomb	M. B. Road, Lado Sarai
132.	Tomb	Ladho Sarai
133.	Mosque	Ladho Sarai
134.	Tomb of Sheikh Haidar	M. B. Road
135.	Residence	Saidulajab Village
136.	Plinth of Mosque	Saidulajab Village
137.	Roof	Press Enclave
138.	Tomb - Kala Gumbad	Tughlaqabad Institutional Area
139.	Well	Tughlaqabad Institutional Area
140.	Plinth and Well	Tughlaqabad Fort

141.	Embankment	Tughlaqabad Fort
142.	Kos Minar	Badarpur Sarai
143.	Northern Gateway	Badarpur Sarai
144.	Central Gateway	Badarpur Sarai
145.	Shahi Masjid	Badarpur Sarai
146.	Southern Gateway	Badarpur Sarai
147.	Kos Minar	Mathura Road
148.	Qutab Guest House	Mehrauli
149.	The Form house restaurant	Mehrauli
150.	Metcalfe's Folly 1,2	Mehrauli
151.	Colonial Buildings	Mehrauli
152.	Mosque	Mehrauli
153.	Chaumukha Darwaza	Mehrauli
154.	Anangtal	Lalkot Excavation
155.	Residence	Ward-I, Mehrauli
156.	Mosque of Wafab Shah	Mehrauli
157.	Mehrauli Public Library	Mehrauli
158.	Haveli	Ward-I, Mehrauli
159.	Residence	Ward-I, Mehrauli
160.	Temple of Jogmaya	Ward-I, Mehrauli
161.	Priest's Residence	Ward-I, Mehrauli
162.	Residence	10/6, Ward-1, Mehrauli
163.	Baradari at Jogmaya Temple	10/4, Ward-I, Mehrauli
164.	Primary School	Ward-I, Mehrauli
165.	Residence	6653, Ward-I, Mehrauli
166.	Residence	10/8, Mehrauli
167.	Prachin Sidh Shri Hanuman Mandir	Mehrauli
168.	St. John Church Complex	Mehrauli
169.	Mosque of Quazian	Near Mehrauli
170.	Primary Health Centre	Mehrauli
171.	MCD House Tax Office & Vocational Training Centre	Ward-I, Mehrauli
172.	Wall Mosque	Ward-I, Mehrauli
173.	Gateway	1081, Ward-I, Mehrauli
174.	Residence	1018, Ward-I, Mehrauli
175.	Original Gateway of Dargah Sharif	Ward-I, Mehrauli
176.	Residence	994, Ward-7, Mehrauli
177.	Noorie Masjid	965, Ward-7, Mehrauli
178.	Dilkusha Mosque	Mehrauli
179.	Residence,	324, Ward-4, Mehrauli

180.	Residence,	299, Ward-4, Mehrauli
181.	Residence,	300, Ward-4, Mehrauli
182.	Residence,	294, Ward-4, Mehrauli
183.	Well	324, Ward-4, Mehrauli
184.	Residence	445, Ward-3, Mehrauli
185.	Residential Street	431-436, Ward-3, Mehrauli
186.	Residence	260, Ward-2, Mehrauli
187.	Residence Gateway of Mohalla	450, Ward-3, Mehrauli
188.	Residence	341, Ward-4, Mehrauli
189.	Residence	341, Ward-4, Mehrauli
190.	Residence	254, Ward-4, Mehrauli
191.	Residence	359, Ward-4, Mehrauli
192.	Residence	535, Ward-5, Mehrauli
193.	Chowk	Ward-5, Mehrauli
194.	Residence	554, Ward-5, Mehrauli
195.	Residence	646, Ward-5, Mehrauli
196.	Residence	667, Ward-5, Mehrauli
197.	Residence	515, Ward-5, Mehrauli
198.	Shop cum Residence	494, Ward-6, Mehrauli
199.	Chaupal	Ward-6, Mehrauli
200.	Sarai Wall Masjd	Ward-7, Mehrauli
201.	Shop cum Residence	796, Ward-6, Mehrauli
202.	Gateway Leading of Residential Cluster	802, Ward-6, Mehrauli
203.	Gateway	936, Ward-7, Mehrauli
204.	Residence	813, Ward-6, Mehrauli
205.	Residence	435, Ward-6, Mehrauli
206.	Commercial Cum Residence Street	Ward-6, Mehrauli
207.	Hazi Jamal-ud-din building	877, Ward-6, Mehrauli
208.	Residence	Behind 877, Ward-7, Mehrauli
209.	Gateway	Ward-6, Mehrauli
210.	Hijron ka Khangah	Ward-6, Mehrauli
211.	Shop cum Residence	848, Ward-8, Mehrauli
212.	Veterinary Clinic	882, Ward-6, Mehrauli
213.	Kali Chand Building	895, Ward-8, Mehrauli
214.	Mosque	Ward-6, Mehrauli
215.	Tomb	Mehrauli
216.	Dargah of Hazrat Sheikh Abdul Haq Muhadis Dahalvi	Mehrauli

217.	Dalan Adjacent to Grave of Sayyid Niyaz Muhammad	Mehrauli
218.	Naalnandon-ki-masjid	Mehrauli
219.	Godown	Ward-6, Mehrauli
220.	Sarai of Sheikh Inayatullah	893, Ward-8, Mehrauli
221.	Tomb	892, Ward-8, Mehrauli
222.	Hauzi-I-Shamsi	Ward-8, Mehrauli
223.	Mosque	Ward-8, Mehrauli
224.	Tomb	Ward-8, Mehrauli
225.	Auilya Masjid	Ward-8, Mehrauli
226.	Jharna	Ward-8, Mehrauli
227.	Pankhe Wale Mosque	Mehrauli
228.	Mosque of Mulana Jamil	Ward-8, Mehrauli
229.	Mosque of Tomb	Ward-8, Mehrauli
230.	Mosque	Ward-8, Mehrauli
231.	Mosque	Ward-8, Mehrauli
232.	Tomb & Mosque of Makhdam Samauddin	Ward-8, Mehrauli
233.	Gateway/Tomb	Mehrauli
234.	Northern Gateway of Dargah of Qutab Sahib	Mehrauli
235.	Dargah and Mazar of Saika Baba	Mehrauli
236.	Gateway of Maulana Fakhruddin	Mehrauli
237.	Residence	Dargah of Qutab Shah, Mehrauli
238.	Mosque	Dargah of Qutab Shah, Mehrauli
239.	Grave & Mosque Motamad Khan	Dargah of Qutab Shah, Mehrauli
240.	Tomb of Maulana Fakhruddin Dargah of Qutab Shah,	Mehrauli
241.	First Gateway of Farrukh-siyar	Dargah of Qutab Shah, Mehrauli
242.	Inner Gateway of Farrukh-siyar	Dargah of Qutab Shah
243.	Dargah of Khawaja Qutu-ubuddin Bakhtiyar Kaki	Dargah of Qutab Shah
244.	Tomb of Khwaja Abdul Aziz Bastami	Dargah of Qutab Shah
245.	Mazar of Hazrat Qazi Hammeduddin Nagauri	Dargah of Qutab Shah
246.	Mosque & Grave of Zabita Khan	Dargah of Qutab Shah

247. Mosque of Qutab Sahib	Dargah of Qutab Shah
248. Baoli of Qutab Sahib	Dargah of Qutab Shah
249. Majlis Khana	Dargah of Qutab Shah
250. Graveyard	Dargah of Qutab Shah
251. Gateway	Dargah of Qutab Shah
252. Grave of Murad Bakht	Dargah of Qutab Shah
253. Tomb	Dargah of Qutab Shah
254. Entrance Gateway	Dargah of Qutab Shah
255. Gultashi Wali Masjid	Dargah of Qutab Shah
256. Gateway	Dargah of Qutab Shah
257. House of Mirza Babar	Ward-8, Mehrauli
258. Walled Garden	Ward-8, Mehrauli
259. Tomb Enclosure	Ward-7, Mehrauli
260. Tomb	Ward-7, Mehrauli
261. Tomb of Sheikh Suleman	Ward-7, Mehrauli
262. Tomb	Ward-7, Mehrauli
263. Gateway	Ward-7, Mehrauli
264. Gateway	1003, Ward-7, Mehrauli
265. Metcalf's Boathouse	DDA Park, Mehrauli
266. Gatepost	DDA Park, Mehrauli
267. Well	DDA Park, Mehrauli
268. Well	DDA Park, Mehrauli
269. Tomb	DDA Park, Mehrauli
270. Tomb	DDA Park, Mehrauli
271. Mosque	DDA Park, Mehrauli
272. Mosque	DDA Park, Mehrauli
273. Walled Enclosure	DDA Park, Mehrauli
274. Two Arched Dalans	DDA Park, Mehrauli
275. Collonade	DDA Park, Mehrauli
276. Mosque	DDA Park, Mehrauli
277. Mosque & Tomb	DDA Park, Mehrauli
278. Mosque	DDA Park, Mehrauli
279. Mosque	DDA Park, Mehrauli
280. Mosque	DDA Park, Mehrauli
281. Enclosure	DDA Park, Mehrauli
282. Arched Dalans	DDA Park, Mehrauli
283. Walled Mosque	DDA Park, Mehrauli
284. Canopy	DDA Park, Mehrauli
285. Walled Mosque	DDA Park, Mehrauli
286. Ruins Balban's Tomb	Mehrauli
287. Tomb	DDA Park, Mehrauli
288. Dalan	DDA Park, Mehrauli

289.	Tomb	DDA Park, Mehrauli
290.	Wall	DDA Park, Mehrauli
291.	Tomb Enclosure	DDA Park, Mehrauli
292.	Tomb of Khan Sahib	DDA Park, Mehrauli
293.	Stables	DDA Park, Mehrauli
294.	Mosque	DDA Park, Mehrauli
295.	Arched Dalans	DDA Park, Mehrauli
296.	Tomb	DDA Park, Mehrauli
297.	Tomb	DDA Park, Mehrauli
298.	Mosque of Maulana Majduddin	DDA Park, Mehrauli
299.	Guard House	DDA Park, Mehrauli
300.	Domed Building	DDA Park, Mehrauli
301.	Ashoka Mission	DDA Park, Mehrauli
302.	Bhagichi ka Masjid	DDA Park, Mehrauli
303.	Mosque	Lado Sarai, Mehrauli
304.	Plinth of Wall Mosque	DDA Park, Mehrauli
305.	Takya of Kamli Shah	Lado Sarai, Mehrauli
306.	Gateway	Mehrauli
307.	Mosque and Domed Building	Mehrauli
308.	Mosque	Word-8, Mehrauli
309.	Mosque	DDA Park, Mehrauli
310.	Chihaitan Chihalman	DDA Park, Mehrauli
311.	Mosque	DDA Park, Mehrauli
312.	Enclosure	DDA Park, Mehrauli
313.	Sohan Burj	DDA Park, Mehrauli
314.	Mosque & Domed Gateway	DDA Park, Mehrauli
315.	Plinth of Mosque	DDA Park, Mehrauli
316.	Mosque	DDA Park, Mehrauli
317.	Idgah	Mehrauli
318.	Tomb	Near Idgah, Mehrauli
319.	Tomb of Sheikh Shihabuddin	Near Idgah, Mehrauli
320.	Platform	Mehrauli
321.	Chillagah	Mehrauli
322.	Mosque	Badarpur Road, Mehrauli
323.	Metcalfe's Folly	Mahipalpur Road, Mehrauli
324.	Baoli	Mahipalpur Road, Mehrauli
325.	Dadabari Jain Mandir	Mehrauli
326.	Ruins of Arch	Andheria More, Mehrauli
327.	Saubate Tomb	Kishangarh, Mehrauli
328.	Enclosure Walls	Kishangarh Pahari, Mehrauli
329.	Mosque	Kishangarh Pahari, Mehrauli

330.	Gateway	Kishangarh Pahari, Mehrauli
331.	Enclosure	Kishangarh Pahari, Mehrauli
332.	Wall Mosque	Kishangarh Pahari, Mehrauli
333.	Ruins	Kishangarh Pahari, Mehrauli
334.	Embankment	Sultanpur
335.	Baoli	Sultanpur
336.	Unnamed	Ward-8, Mehrauli
337.	Unknown Structure	DDA Park, Mehrauli
338.	Building Unknown	DDA Park, Mehrauli

Zone - G, West Delhi

S.No.	*Buildings*	*Location*
1.	Delhi Gate, Najafgarh	Najafgarh
2.	Jami Mosque	Najafgarh
3.	Residential-cum-Commercial	Najafgarh Main Street
4.	Residential-cum-Commercial	Najafgarh
5.	Dharamshala	Near Temple Chowk, Najafgarh
6.	Residence	Najafgarh, Adjacent to Arya Samaj Mandir
7.	Well	Police Station, Najafgarh
8.	Mosque	Police Station Compound, Najafgarh
9.	Haveli	Mitraon Village, West of Najafgarh
10.	Domed Chattri	Mitraon Village, West of Najafgarh
11.	Samadhi of Mitra Sen	Mitraon Village, West of Najafgarh
12.	Temple	Mitraon Village, West of Najafgarh
13.	Haveli	Mitraon Village, West of Najafgarh
14.	Ruins of Haveli	Mitraon Village, West of Najafgarh
15.	Dalan	Main Highway, Mitraon Village
16.	Tomb of Rana Sahib	East of Najafgarh
17.	Minar	Hasthsal Village, West of Vikaspuri
18.	Hathi Khana	Hasthsal Village
19.	Dalans	Hasthsal Village
20.	Residence	Pehladpur Village, Palam Road, Near Air Force Museum

21.	Residence	Pehladpur Village, Palam Road
22.	Residence	Pehladpur Village, Palam Road
23.	Tomb of Sohel	Adjacent to Indira Gandhi International Airport
24.	Gateway	Mehram Nagar, Opp. Indira Gandhi International Airport
25.	Mosque	Mehram Nagar, Opp. Indira Gandhi International Airport
26.	Eastern Gateway	Mehram Nagar, Domestic Airport
27.	Enclosure Walls	Sarai Mehram Nagar
28.	Katra	North Mehram Nagar
29.	Garden of Mehram Khan	North Mehram Nagar

Zone - H, North Delhi

S.No.	*Buildings*	*Location*
1.	Well	District Park, Adjacent to Police Station, Shalimar Bagh
2.	Well	Swami Narain Road, Shastri Nagar
3.	Police New Clothing Depot	Shahzada Bagh, Old Rohtak Road
4.	Ruins	Ring Road, Shakurpur

Bibliography

Ahmad, Nazir, *The Bride's Mirror*, Permanent Black, New Delhi, 2007.

Andrews, C.F., *Zaka Ullah of Delhi*, W. Heffer, Cambridge, 1929.

Ara, Matsuo. *Delhi: Architectural Remains of the Delhi Sultanate Period*. 3 Vols. University of Tokyo, Tokyo, 1970.

Ara, Matsuo. *Dargahs of Medieval India*. University of Tokyo, Tokyo, 1977.

Asher, Catherine B., 'Mapping Hindu-Muslim Identities through the Architecture of Shahjahanabad and Jaipur' in *Beyond Turk and Hindu*. Ed. Gilmartin, David and Bruce B. Lawrence, India Research Press, New Delhi, 2003, pp. 121–148.

Bernier, Francois, *Travels in the Mogul Empire 1656–1668*. Translated by Archibald Constable. Asian Education Services, New Delhi, 1996.

Blake, Stephen P., *Shahjahanabad; The Sovereign City in Mughal India 1639–1739*. Foundation Books, New Delhi, 1993.

Bullock, Humphery, *The Fifteen Cities of Delhi*. The Roxy Press, New Delhi, 1949.

Butler A.S.G., The Architecture of Sir Edwin Lutyens, 3 Vol., London/ New York, 1950.

Byron Robert, Asian Educational Services, New Delhi, 1997.

Carr Stephen, *The Archaeology and Monumental Remains of Delhi*, Aryan, New Delhi, 2002. (Reprint of 1876 edition)

Chandra, Satish, *History of Architecture and Ancient Building Materials in India,* Tech Books International, New Delhi, 2003.

Codell, Julie F, *Power and Restraint*–The Delhi Coronation Durbars, Alkazi Collection of Photography, Mapin Publishing, Ahmedabad, 2012

Dayal, Maheshwar. *Rediscovering Delhi.* S. Chand & Co., New Delhi, 1975.

Dalrymple, William. *City of Djinns.* Flamingo, London, 1994.

Delhi Development Authority, Master Plan for Delhi–2021, MOUD, New Delhi.

Delhi Improvement Trust, Annual Reports, 1937–50, Delhi.

Desai, Madhavi, Miki Desai and Jon Lang, The Bungalow in Twentieth Century India, Ashgate, Surrey, UK, 2012

Dube D.N. and Promodini Verma, *Delhi and its Monuments.* Spantech Publications, New Delhi, 1987.

Dupont Veronique, Emma Tarlo and Denis Vidal, *Delhi, Urban Space and Human Destines.* Manohar, New Delhi, 2000.

Eicher Delhi City Map, Eicher Goodearth, New Delhi, 2001.

Ehlers, Eckart and Thomas Kraft, *Shahjahanabad: Old Delhi: Tradition and Colonial Change.* Manohar, New Delhi, 2003.

Franklin, William, 'An Account of the Present State of Delhi' in *Asiatic Researches* 4 (1795).

Frykenberg, R. E. ed., *Delhi Through the Ages: Essays in Urban History, Culture and Society,* OUP, Delhi, 1986.

Gavin Hambley. *Cities of Mughal India,* G.P. Putnam, New York, 1968.

Ganyor Barten and Laurraine Malone. *Old Delhi-10 Easy Walks,* Rupa, New Delhi, 1988.

G.H.R. Tilotson, *Architectural Guide for Travellers: Mughal India* Viking, 1990.

G.H.R. Gibbs. *Selection of The Travals of Ibn Batuta, London,* 1929.

Goodfriend, D.E., *The Delhi Master Plan* (1962), *A Critical Reappraisal,* SPA Journal, July 1980, New Delhi.

Government of India, *The Historical Record of the Imperial Visit to India, 1911,* Published for Government of India by John Murray, Albemarle St. London, W. 1914.

Greenburg A., Lutyons' Architecture Restudied, in Perspecta 12, 1969, Connecticut.

G.R. Hearn. *The Seven Cities of Delhi,* London, 1902.

Gupta Narayani. *Delhi, Between Two Empires,* 1803–1931, OUP, New Delhi, 1981.

Hardinge, Lord, *My Indian Years–1910–16: The Reminiscences of Lord Hardings of Penshurst*, London—John Murray, Albemarle St. First Edition, 1948.

Havell, E.B., *Ancient and Medieval Architecture of India;* London, 1915.

H. Shar, *Delhi—Its Story and Buildings*, Delhi, 1921.

Hodges, William, *Select Views in India Drawn on the Spot*, London, 1786.

INTACH and Conservation Society Delhi. *Mehrauli Heritage Maps.* INTACH, New Delhi, 1993.

INTACH, *Delhi : The Built Heritage* (2 vols), New Delhi - 1999.

Irving Robert Grant, *Indian Summer*, New York, 1981.

Irene Gajjar, *Ancient Indian Art and the West*, Tarporewala, Bombay, 1971.

I.H. Qureshi, *The Muslim Community in the Indo-Pakistan Sub Continent*, The Hague, 1963.

Jackson, Peter. *The Delhi Sultanate a Political and Military History*, Cambridge University Press, Cambridge, 1999.

Jain, A.K., *The Cities of Delhi.* Management Publishing Co., New Delhi, 1994.

Jain A.K., *Delhi Under Hammer*, Rupa Publications, New Delhi, 2010.

Jain A.K., *Low Carbon City – Policies, Planning and Practice* (2009), Discovery Publishers, New Delhi.

Jain A.K., *Urban Housing and Slums*, Readworthy Publishers, New Delhi, 2009.

Jain A.K., A *Sustainable Vision for Urban India,* Kalpaz Publishers, Delhi, 2008.

Jain, A.K., *Inclusive Planning and Social Infrastructure*, (2010), Bookwell, New Delhi

Jain, A.K. *Urban Planning and Governance* — A New Paradigm (2009), Bookwell, New Delhi.

Jain, A.K., *Ecology and Natural Resource Management,* 2001, Management Publishing Co. Delhi.

Jain, A.K., *River Pollution: Regeneration and Cleaning* (2009), Aashish Publishing, New Delhi.

Jain, A.K., *Indian Megacity and Economic Reforms* (1996), Management Publishing, Delhi.

Jain, A.K., *The Making of a Metropolis: The Planning and Growth of Delhi*, NBO, New Delhi.

Jain, A.K., *Lutyens Delhi*, Bookwell, New Delhi, 2010.

Jagmohan, *Rebuilding Shahjahanabad*, Vikas, 1975.

Jagmohan Mahajan, *The Raj Landscape*, Spantech, New Delhi, 1988.

Jhabvala CSH, Delhi Phoenix City, Penguin, 2012.

Jodidio, Philip, The Aga Khan Historic Cities Programme–Strategies for Urban Regeneration, Prestel, Munich/London/New York, 2011.

Joseph Rykwert, *The Idea of a Town*, Faber & Faber London, 1976.

J. Baillie Fraser. *Military Memoir of Lieut, Col. James Skinner*, C.B. 2 Vols. London, 1851.

K.P. Acharya. *Architecture of the Mansara,* London & Bombay 1933.

Kaul H.K, *Historic Delhi—An Anthology*. Oxford University Press, Delhi, 1985.

Kaye, M.M. ed., *The Golden Calm*. Viking Press, New York, 1980.

Keene M.G., *Handbook for Visitiors to Delhi,* Rewritten by E.A. Duncan, Calcutta, 1904.

Khushwant Singh, *Delhi—A Portrai*t, Oxford, 1983.

King, A. Colonial Urban Development, London, Routledge Keegan Paul, 1976.

Koch, Ebba. *Mughal Art and Imperial Ideology*. OUP, New Delhi, 2001.

Krishen, Pradip, *Trees of Delhi,* INTACH, Delhi Tourism and DK Publishers, New Delhi, 2006.

Lall, John. *Begum Samru*. Roli Books, New Delhi, 1997.

Lang, Jon, Madhavi Desai and Mikki Desai: *Architecture and Independence.* Oxford Indian Paperbacks, New Delhi, 2000.

Lang, Jon. *A Concise History of Modern Architecture in India,* Permanent Black, 2002.

Lewis. Charles and Karoli Lewis, *Mehrauli*, Harper Collins, New Delhi, 2002.

Legg. Stephen(2007) Beyond the European Province, Faucault and Geography Aldershor, Ashgatt, R.

Legg, Stephen, Spaces of Colonialism, Delhi's Urban Govern mentalities Blackwell, UK, 2008

Lawrence Lockhart., *Nadir Shah* Londaon, 1935.

Losty, JP (editor), Salman Khurshid, Ratish Nanda & Malvika Singh, Delhi: *Red Fort to Raisna*, Lustre Roli Books, New Delhi, 2012.

Martin Hurlimann, *Delhi, Agra and Fatehpur Sikri, T & H* London, 1965.

Masselos, Jim and Narayani Gupta. *Beato's Delhi 1857*, Ravi Dayal, New Delhi, 2000.

Menon, AGK, Swapna Liddle and Annabel Lopez (Eds.), Delhi-A Living Heritage, INTACH and IGNCA, New Delhi, 2010.

Metcalf, Thomas R., *An Imperial Vision. Indian Architecture and Britain's Raj.* Oxford Indian Paperbacks, New Delhi, 2002.

Muhammad Nazim., *The Life and Times of Sultan Mahmud of Ghazana*, Cambridge, 1931.

Mirza Muhammad Rusva, *Umrao Jan Ada*, Translated by K. Singh and M.A. Husaini, Calcutta, 1961.

Mukherji, Anisha Shekhar, *The Red Fort of Shahjahanabad*, OUP, New Delhi, 2003.

Nanda, Ratish. *Delhi–the Built Heritage: A Listing, New Delhi,* DDA and, INTACH, 2000.

Nath, Aman, *Dome over India. Rashtrapati Bhawan,* India Book House, New Delhi, 2002.

Nath, R., *History of Sultanate Architecture,* Abhinav Publications, New Delhi, 1978.

Patwant Singh., *The Ninth Delhi,* Journal of the Royal Society of Arts, London, 1917.

Patwant Singh and Ram Dhamija., Delhi—*The Deepening Crisis, Sterling,* New Delhi, 1989.

Percival Spear., *1991, Twilight of the Mughals: Studies in Late Mughal Delhi,* Cambridge, Reprinted by Munshiram Manohar Lal, New Delhi.

Percival Spear., *Delhi, A Historical Sketch,* Oxford, London, 1937.

Peck,. Lucy, Delhi—A Thousand Years of Building, Roli Books, New Delhi, 2005

Peter Hardy., *Historians of Medieval India,* London, 1960.

Philip Davies., *Splendours of the Raj,* Dass Media, New Delhi & John Muray London, 1985.

Punjab Government, *A Gazetteer of Delhi 1883–4,* Vipin Jain, Gurgaon, 1988.

Raman, Sunil and Rohit Agarwal, Delhi Durbar 1911, the Complete Story, Lotus-Roli, New Delhi, 2012.

Riberio E.F.N & Jain A.K. (Eds.). *The Future of New Delhi,* Delhi Development Authority, New Delhi, 1984.

Romila Thapar and Percival Spear. *A History of India, 2 Vols. London, 1965–66.*

R Nath., *Monuments of Delhi,* Ambika 1979, New Delhi.

Russell, Ralph., *The Oxford India Ghalib: Life, Letters and Ghazals.* OUP, New Delhi, 2003.

Satish Chandra., *Parties and Politics at the Mughal Court, 1707–1740, Aligarh.*

Sarkar, Sir Jadunath, *Fall of Mughal Empire,* Calcutta, 1932–50

Sharma, Y.D., *Delhi and its Neighbourhood*. Archaeological Survey of India, New Delhi, 1964 and 1990.

Sharp, Henry., *Delhi, Its Story and Buildings.* Humphere Milfort, OUP, Bombay, 1928.

Saksena, Banarsi Prasad., *History of Shahjahan of Delhi,* Central Book Depot, 1973.

Singh, Dhirendra and Mohan Joseph, Sentinels, of Raisina Hill, Timeless Books, New Delhi, 2011.

Singh, Malvika., New Delhi, *Making of a Capital,* Lustre Press, Roli Books, 2009.

Sinha, R., *Lal Kot to Lodi Gardens.* Rupa, Calcutta, 1996.

Skinner, Captain Thomas, *Excursions in India.* London, 1832.

Smith, R.V. *Lesser-known Monuments of Delhi,* Journalists' Literary Circle, New Delhi, 1999.

Soundara Rajan., Islam Builds in India, Agam Kala Prakashan, New Delhi, 1983.

S. Nilsson, *European Archtecture in India,* Faber and Faber, London, 1968.

Stuart Piggot, *Some Ancient Cities of India,* Oxford 1945, London.

Toy, Sidney, *The Fortified Cities of India,* Heinemann, London, 1965.

Volwahsen, Andreas, *Imperial Delhi.* Prestel Verlag, Munich, 2002.

Zafar Hasan., *Monuments of Delhi, 3 vols.* Aryan Books International, New Delhi, 1997.